INFORMATION
SECURITY EVALUATION

MANAGEMENT OF TECHNOLOGY SERIES

INFORMATION SECURITY EVALUATION
A HOLISTIC APPROACH

Igli Tashi and Solange Ghernaouti-Hélie

EPFL Press

A Swiss academic publisher distributed by CRC Press

CRC Press
Taylor & Francis Group

Taylor and Francis Group, LLC
6000 Broken Sound Parkway, NW, Suite 300,
Boca Raton, FL 33487

Distribution and Customer Service
orders@crcpress.com

www.crcpress.com

Library of Congress Cataloging-in-Publication Data
A catalog record for this book is available from the Library of Congress.

This book is published under the editorial direction of
Professor Philippe Wieser (EPFL).

Previously published in the *Management of Technology Series*:
The Office Process Redesign Language
J.-L. Chappelet, M. Sherwood-Smith

Essentials of Logistics and Management
F.-L. Perret et. al., editors

EPFL Press

is an imprint owned by Presses polytechniques et universitaires romandes, a Swiss
academic publishing company whose main purpose is to publish the teaching and
research works of the Ecole polytechnique fédérale de Lausanne (EPFL) and other
universities and institutions of higher learning.

Presses polytechniques et universitaires romandes
EPFL – Rolex Learning Center
Post office box 119
CH-1015 Lausanne, Switzerland
E-mail: ppur@epfl.ch
Phone: 021/693 21 30
Fax: 021/693 40 27

www.epflpress.org

© 2011, First edition, EPFL Press, Lausanne (Switzerland)
ISBN 978-2-940222-53-7 (EPFL Press)
ISBN 978-1-4398-7915-3 (CRC Press)

Printed in Italy

To Emi, Helena and Hana,
To Solange for all those years of working together and
shared adventures.

Igli Tashi

I hope that this book will contribute to an increased
mastery of information security for all those who need to
address these issues, and to a digital society that supports
durable development.

Solange Ghernaouti-Hélie

Acknowledgement

The authors wish to signal their gratitude to their friend and colleague David Simms, researcher at the University of Lausanne (SeDgE research unit) a native English speaker who possesses long experience in the field of IT audit, for his assistance in rereading the drafts of this work and offering technical and practical advice.

Preface

Evaluating the information security posture within an organization is becoming a very complex task. Currently, the evaluation and assessment of information security are often carried out using frameworks, methodologies and standards that consider the various aspects of security independently. Unfortunately this is ineffective because it does not take into consideration the necessity of having a global and systemic multidimensional approach to the evaluation of information security. At the same time the overall security level is globally considered to be only as strong as its weakest link. This book proposes a model called the *Information Security Assurance Assessment Model* (ISAAM) that aims to assess holistically all dimensions of security in order to minimize the likelihood that a given threat will exploit the weakest link. A formalized structure taking into account all security elements is presented; this is based on a methodological evaluation framework in which information security is evaluated from a global perspective.

The information security evaluation model proposed in this book is based on and combines different information-security best practices, standards, methodologies and research expertise in order to define a reliable categorization of information security. After the definition of terms and requirements, an evaluation process should be performed in order to assess whether or not the information security within the organization is being adequately managed. The most useful elements of these sources of information have been integrated into the proposed model, with the goal of providing a generic model able to be implemented in all kinds of organizations.

The value added by this evaluation model is that it is easy to implement and operate, and that it addresses concrete needs in terms of reliance upon an efficient and dynamic evaluation tool through a coherent system of evaluation. On this basis, the model could be implemented internally within organizations, allowing them to govern better their information security.

In order to produce a book that is timeless and generic and that is not obviously dependent on particular situations or technologies, we deliberately do not include any examples or case studies, whether hypothetical or drawn from the real world.

Our policy has been to address the global approach, the philosophy, the methodological constants and the means of assessing, in a holistic manner, the level of information security within organisations, regardless of their information technology environment and of the nature of their activities. This book has been designed to give security professionals the means to adopt the ISAAM assessment approach and to apply it in their specific environment, with the intent to develop a generic approach that will allow managers to prepare for and react to new situations. We have thus avoided documenting the application of the ISAAM model to specific examples. Indeed, as a consequence of the diversity of organization's objectives and the evolution and development of environments and situations, any context built around case studies would become rapidly outdated or too limited. Independent of any specific technologies, information systems configurations, risks or threats, the ISAAM approach will help managers and their organizations to develop adequate know-how to be able to confront in a secure manner the emergence of threats, to identify existing security gaps, and to take advantage of the rapid evolution of new information system architectures, technologies or security measures.

Book presentation and structure

In the first Chapter of this book, we focus on the definition of *information security*; this concept is then used as a reference point for the evaluation model. The inherent concepts of the contents of a holistic and baseline information-security program are defined. Based on this, the most common bases of trust in information security are identified.

Chapter 2 focuses on an analysis of the difference and the relationship between the concepts of information risk and security management. Comparing these two concepts allows us to identify the most relevant elements to be included within our evaluation model. Clearly situating these two notions within a defined framework is of the utmost importance for the results that will be obtained from the evaluation process.

The evaluation model, our Information Security Assurance Assessment Model (ISAAM), is described in Chapter 3, where we will see how in depth how it addresses issues relating to the evaluation of information security. Within this chapter the underlying concepts of assurance and trust are discussed. Based on these two concepts, the structure of the model is developed, in order to provide an assurance-related platform, as are the three evaluation attributes: *assurance structure*, *quality issues*, and *requirements achievement*. Issues relating to each of these evaluation attributes are analysed with reference to sources such as methodologies, standards and published research papers. We then discuss the actual operation of the model. Assurance levels, quality levels and maturity levels are defined in order to perform the evaluation.

Chapters 4 to 7 are related to the implementation of ISAAM according to the information-security domains. This is where the evaluation model is put into a well-defined context with respect to the four pre-defined information security dimensions: the *organizational dimension* (Chap. 4), *functional dimension* (Chap. 5), *human dimension* (Chap. 6), and *legal dimension* (Chap. 7). For each dimension, a two-phase evaluation path is followed.

The first phase concerns the identification of the elements that will constitute the basis of the evaluation. This implies the identification of the key elements within the dimension, as well as its *focus areas* (i.e., the identifiable security issues) and *specific factors* (the security measures or controls to address the security issues).

The second phase concerns the evaluation of each information-security dimension by the implementation of the evaluation model, based on the elements identified for each dimension within the first phase, by identifying the security tasks, processes, procedures, and actions that should be performed by the organization to reach the desired level of protection. The maturity model for each dimension, as a basis for reliance on security, is then established.

For each dimension we propose a generic maturity model that could be used by every organization in order to define its own security requirements. Our final conclusions and remarks can be found in Chapter 8.

The construction of the ISAAM model is the result of many years of research and analysis. It is our hope that this book, with its emphasis on the holistic approach, will allow organizations to reconsider, re-organize and substantially improve the mastery of information security, for their own benefit as well as for the benefit of our evolving digital society.

Igli Tashi
Solange Ghernaouti-Hélie
Lausanne, Switzerland
March, 2011

Contents

Chapter 1

What is Information Security?

This chapter discusses the concept of information security as commonly used in organizations in order to identify the different facets of the information security evaluation methodology proposed in this book.

1.1 Information security stakes and challenges in a competitive world

The technological explosion is nowadays forcing organizations[1] to change their structures and ways of operating. The use of Information and Communication Technologies (ICT), their role and importance are increasing daily. Technology is becoming the main factor for productivity growth and the competitiveness of organizations, and it often also allows effective cost reductions.

An organization's communication center and information systems have thus become increasingly important as they are increasingly depended upon. A malfunction of the ICT infrastructure can paralyse the whole organization and might have disastrous consequences for the company at many levels (financial, reputational, etc.). The risk of paralysis could be even more critical for companies whose principal asset and added value is information. A typical highly vulnerable sector for such risks is, for example, the services sector. Security issues within an organization must therefore be treated as a priority at top managerial level.

On the other hand, and based on new ways of operating businesses, modern organizations collaborate increasingly with other organizations, their costumers, and other stakeholders by technological means. This emphasises the need for a reliable and secure ICT infrastructure. The organization, and more specifically its information systems, will operate within an open and hostile environment. The organization thus has to deal with two contradictory objectives that have opposite impacts on information security.

- The first is the need to remain competitive, which obliges the organization to adopt a structure based on extensive communication.

---

[1]   The word *organization* is used to designate any kind of ordered structure responding to a given set of objectives to be achieved, independently of their commercial character or not. Within the notion of *organization* are included *business establishments*, *governmental bodies* and *non-profit organizations*.

- The second is the trust the organization has to inspire in its stakeholders, which requires a more restrictive environment, the environment associated with extensive communications not being fully compatible with the security instinct.

At first sight it seems that there is a contradiction between these two objectives and so a prioritization analysis should be performed in order to obtain the best compromise. Operating within an open environment introduces new risks that are less significant than those introduced in a restrictive environment; in our view it is preferable to accept, and make appropriate efforts to mitigate, the ICT risks ensuing from the extensive communication structure.

In order to remain secure, the organization has to choose between the different techniques of controlling risk, such as preventive, deterrent and reactive means. Often all these means are interrelated and should be performed together in order to provide a reasonable level of security. The use of the term "reasonable level," in a context where a "definitive level" would not be realistic, brings with it the necessity for the consideration of

- a frame of reference for determining the meaning of the "level"; and
- measures of effectiveness and efficiency related to the "reasonable" property of the level.

A security evaluation (or assessment) framework should be developed in order to manage and maintain such a "reasonable level." The way of evaluating or assessing will be strongly related to two main features:

- The purpose of the evaluation (i.e. compliance, risk, certification, technical requirements, management issues etc.);
- The entity in charge of the evaluation and its finality (external evaluation, internal evaluation).

The top level of management must deal with information security management by considering it as a key part of their duties in running the organization, and one that increases the complexity of decision-making. Multiple strategic decisions concerning information security have to be taken at top management level in order to assess how many resources one has to allocate, which are the risks that the organization is ready and prepared to accept, which are the security needs of the organization, and so on. At the same time it is difficult to assess and evaluate the effectiveness of organizations' security installations. For that purpose, a governance approach in general, and more specifically the use of metrics to evaluate the effectiveness and efficiency of information security measures, are of the utmost importance for the organizations' management.

Before presenting the evaluation structure and process, we will briefly summarise, in the following chapter, some fundamental principles related to information security and to risk and security management.

1.2 A governance perspective on information security

Information and Communication Technologies (ICT) security considers the security of information from a technological perspective, while information security is a wider concept that considers all aspects of information, independently of the medium, as well as the handling of information. The concept of information security includes all the disciplines related to ICT security, such as network security, application security, physical security and logical security, as well as the business view. To improve the quality of the protection of the information infrastructure, these two concepts are covered within this book under the general label of *information security*.

1.2.1 From definition to interpretation

The European Network and Information Security Agency (ENISA) considers information security to be the means of providing the basis for operating in today's increasingly interconnected and technologically complex world.[2] In ENISA's definition, the purpose of information security is defined by its focus on the way it operates within businesses. This way of considering information security fully corresponds with the idea, frequently noted in the academic literature, that nowadays information security is more often a proactive activity driven by business leadership than a technology-driven function. From this perspective, the activities of the information security function should be the result of a group of requirements that are defined by the highest levels of the organization, since these levels are responsible for the continued existence of the organization. Information security is increasingly considered as a critical business function that keeps an organization and its critical assets secure in times of rapid expansion.

Information security management is used to protect assets and mitigate risks by applying and combining security technology and management practices. Information Security countermeasures are the direct response to the risks an organization probably could face.

1.2.2 The perspective of the standards

From a review of well-recognized and widely shared international standards, several different perspectives are taken into account in defining the concept of Information Security.

ISO/IEC 13335-1:2004[3] defines information security as being the preservation of the confidentiality, integrity and availability of information; these are also seen as the security objectives.

Information security appears to be, in this context, an operational function related to some well-defined and specific objectives such as those mentioned above. At the same time, standards related to risk management[4] consider information security to be the means of

---

2   ENISA, "A Users' Guide: How to Raise Information Security Awareness," *European Network and Information Security Agency*, Heraklion, Greece 2006. Available at:
     http://www.enisa.europa.eu/doc/pdf/deliverables/enisa_a_users_guide_how_to_raise_IS_awareness.pdf
3   ISO/IEC 13335-1, Information technology – Security techniques – Management of information and communications technology security – Part 1: Concepts and models for information and communications technology security management, International Organization for Standardization (ISO), Switzerland, 2004.
4   Such as the following two:
     ISO/IEC 15408-1:2009, Information technology – Security techniques – Evaluation criteria for IT security – Part 1: Introduction and general model, International Organization for Standardization (ISO), Switzerland, 2009.
     ITGI, Information Security Governance: Guidance for boards of Directors and Executive Management, *2nd Edition IT Governance Institute*, 2006. Available at:
     http://www.itgi.org/template_ITGI.cfm?template=/ContentManagement/ContentDisplay.cfm&ContentID=24384

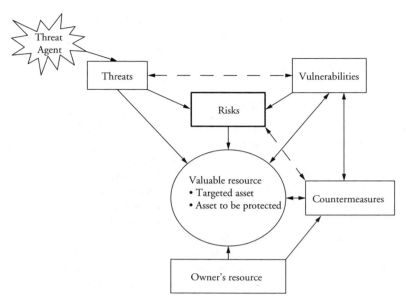

Fig. 1.1 Information security actors and relationships.

protecting information assets against the risk of loss, operational discontinuity, misuse, unauthorized disclosure, inaccessibility, damage and civil or legal liability, as shown in Figure 1.1.

ISO/IEC 27002:2005[5] defines information security as a process for protecting information from a wide range of threats in order to ensure business continuity, minimize business damage, and maximize return on investment and business opportunities by preserving the confidentiality, integrity and availability of information. As in the ENISA definition, the focus of the information security function still remains "business prosperity," modelled by the three above-mentioned security objectives. Loss of productivity, of revenue, or of reputation, or legal penalties, could result from ICT related risks.

The information security function becomes a business function akin to the other, traditional, business functions, meaning that supplementary added value could be provided if the information security function is operated in an "adequate manner". The Return on Investment (RoI), as well as the adequacy of the information security function, brings into focus the necessity of managing such domains as business functions.

The management process in its general sense addresses short-term issues related to the availability of budgets and resources or, more generally, creates conditions allowing activities to be performed as smoothly as planned. This means that all the ongoing processes, including the security measures, practices, procedures and activities, require the efficient use of the resources provided. In this sense, information security should provide the expected results based on the requirements that were derived from an in-depth analysis performed by the organization's senior management. In addition to effectiveness, the information security function should ensure the efficiency of its activities, considering them from an economic

---

[5] ISO/IEC 27002:2005, Information technology – Security techniques – Code of practice for information security management, International Organization for Standardization (ISO), Switzerland, 2005.

perspective. In order to do this, an approach based on management and control is needed, in order to ensure that the security requirements are addressed and excepted results are achieved; this is the main concern of a security governance function. Handling information security as a corporate governance issue can be seen as a natural evolution of the way that institutions manage ICT related threats and risks. In addition to the technical, managerial and regulatory compliance issues, information security is nowadays a strategic issue with which executives have to deal.

1.2.3 A business and organizational perspective

As time passes and organizations mature, the closer information security moves to the business functions and the more the effectiveness of information security depends on the way that this function is managed and controlled. Based on this, and given also the fact that in these circumstances technological knowledge and expertise in the provision of security solutions will have reached a high level, the remaining issues do not concern the level of technology but rather the way that technological opportunities are utilized in order to meet security objectives. In other words, the main concern regarding the level of protection of the organizational assets is the way that security is managed and how that could contribute to fostering trust in ICT environments. *Trust* is directly related to the level of information security and its effectiveness.

Information security life cycle

Information security can be broken down into three kinds of components:
- Information security requirements, representing the security goals;
- Information security policy, representing the steps to be undertaken in order to ensure an adequate level of security protection;
- Information security mechanism, representing the tools (technical, operational and managerial) to be used in order to enforce policy.

These components, grouped in a managerial framework, should contribute to mastering the information security lifecycle, to handling crisis recovery situations, and to protecting the information systems and making them operate as expected. Information security has become a necessary condition to ensure that everything goes as smoothly as planned in respect of Information Technology-related activities. As a result, the information security function is itself entrusted with another responsibility alongside the objective of moving organizational values out of danger: that of responsibility for the quality of the end result. This is the main reason why security increasingly tends to be a business process and why it is important to stress the importance of the management and governance processes of security with respect to the overall organization.

Information management framework and processes

Security management is a framework composed of a number of processes concerned with planning and managing a defined level of security. It has become the cornerstone of the effectiveness of the security program because the security focus itself has changed from a technical one (based on technical risks) to a governance approach.

Three sub-activities of the information security management can be distinguished:
- The implementation of the operational security measures;
- The information security plan, which covers the specific Service Level Agreements (SLAs) for information security representing the security goals to be achieved based on the security needs;
- The information security controls which consider information security as a process and address issues such as responsibility and policy statements.

Very often the drivers of internal information security are security incidents, relevant laws and regulations, and specific client requirements. This promotes a reactive approach to information security that is mostly focused on problem solving rather than on proactive activities. A proactive attitude would emphasise the efficiency and effectiveness of security measures by taking into account first the specific security needs that are derived from the various security constraints, both technical and economic. It should not be forgotten that technology still impacts Information security in three ways, by:
- Introducing new vulnerabilities;
- Changing the way the business is done;
- Changing the way the workplace is organized.

Furthermore, mastery of the technological issues has reached a high level, especially through the availability of relevant information, so that security breaches are often directly linked to the implementation and understanding of systems. This statement reinforces the idea that information security effectiveness relies mainly on the quality of controls in place, their implementation and management. Information security is a *managerial issue* rather than a technical one.

1.3 Information security program/system components

Based on the previous considerations, and specifically on the difference between the potential stages of information security and on the differences between an information security program and an information security system, the enterprise's attention should be increasingly focused on information security management; this has the ultimate goal of designing and implementing security strategies in an effective and efficient way. In addition, security is based on controls and security controls are processes designed to ensure that an organization meets its objectives of confidentiality, integrity and availability. Information security can thus be viewed as the efficient control of the uncertainty arising from malicious acts. When we talk about security effectiveness we mean that the object of the evaluation is the effectiveness of existing security controls. The purpose of the evaluation is to provide assurance over the quality of the controls and, more generally, over the level of information security within the organization.

Considering the level of maturity of the controls applied over the information security functions, an organization can differentiate three different stages where information security might be classified. These three stages are: information security function stage; information security program stage; and the information security system stage. If we take each one of these maturity stages, in other words, the de facto state of information security, we can argue that:

- The information security function will characterize certain information security activities performed within the organization that are focused on enabling activities (mostly, but not exclusively, technologically driven) for which the main targets remain the security events resulting from a malevolent action. An organization containing an information security function possesses[6] and uses some "classical" and baseline technological resources in order to prevent well-known security attacks. In this case common security technologies or common security practices are implemented without any specific and previously-analyzed objectives. A potential risk assessment process would have been followed, but without any formal methodology or strictness.
- The widespread use of information technologies and the increased focus on business benefits make it necessary for information security to cover a broader range of issues than merely ad-hoc technical security tasks.

An information security function can be transformed into an *information security program* if the security countermeasures used in the first stage are integrated into a managed program. A program represents an ensemble of planned series of activities or sequence of operations, according to the Oxford Dictionary.[7] It means that the security countermeasures to be implemented will be integrated into a structured framework corresponding to some clear objectives in terms of outputs. What is important to outline here is the fact that those objectives will not necessarily correspond to the same objective, but to a specific objective related to each different activity. Nevertheless, being part of the same program, each activity (or countermeasure or even control) should respond to a formal plan in terms of milestones or of time. Each one of the activities will be granted its own resources in order to provide the expected result. Evidence of an information security program, running inside a given organization, shows that information security is considered as a *proactive activity* driven by business leadership.

The third conceptual maturity level for organizational information security is the stage of being a system. A system is an ensemble of some organized elements interacting in a complex way. Two elements can be emphasised in order to define a system, namely the interactions between the elements of the system, and the purpose of the system. Based on this definition, the information security system has to be considered as a whole, composed of different elements, each one of them contributing to the same purpose, which is the protection of the organizational values. During the program stage of information security, the different activities performed corresponded to some specific objectives related to their specific purpose. An information security system incorporates all these activities into the same structure, whereas the latter responds to a single high-level objective, safety. The distinguishing feature between an information security program and an information security system is that the Information security system corresponds to governance logic and is directed in a centralized manner, but can be managed in a "local" manner. It should be underlined that an information security system, apart from the notions of effectiveness and efficiency, also addresses the coherence and relative importance of the program's elements dedicated to a single objective. A system,

---

[6] *Possessing* in this context means that the organization is able to provide evidence of the existence of the discussed subject, in our case the information security activities.

[7] *Oxford English Dictionary Online*, October 2008. Available at http://dictionary.oed.com/

by definition, is a complex construction and consequently it should be operated and directed by a centralized steering decision-making body.

Based on the functional analysis performed above, which explains the different stages of information security, the information security system stems from the different functions of the information security program where each information security program activity is composed of different security measures and controls.[8] In a more general way, when analysing information security architecture, four principal dimensions regarding information security can be identified, namely: the technical and operational dimension, the political and organizational dimension, the human dimension, and the regulatory and legal dimension. From a top-down perspective, this categorization of information security is used to define the information security dimensions of the evaluation model, each one corresponding to a precise objective in terms of information security. Each one of these dimensions will incorporate some activities in order to achieve the objective, and each one of these activities will be the result of the information security measures and controls operating inside the activity.

Security needs to cover the generic issues such as: value or asset identification; risk evaluation and analysis; technical and procedural dimension, organizational and human dimension, standards, laws and regulations; compliance and legal aspects. As described in the international guidelines for managing risks of information and communications statement, after the risk analysis step, six major activities related to the information security can often be identified:

- Development of policies;
- Assignment of roles and responsibilities;
- Design of the security framework through controls, standards, measures and procedures;
- Implementation;
- Monitoring;
- Awareness, training and education.

The components that an information security program should include are listed within the well-known standards, ISO/IEC 13355 and ISO/IEC 27002:2005[9]. Historically these standards drew a great deal of their inspiration from the universal principles presented within

---

8   A distinction is made between the two notions of *information security measure* and *information security control*. The notion of *measure* incorporates the *operational* aspect of the actions to be taken to achieve a particular purpose, while by information security *control* should be understood any activity related to the *verification* and the *direction* of such an action.

9   References:
ISO/IEC TR 13335-1, Information Technology – Guidelines for the management of IT Security – Concepts and models for IT Security, International Organization for Standardization (ISO), Switzerland, 1996.
ISO/IEC TR 13335-2, Information Technology – Guidelines for the management of IT Security – Managing and planning IT Security, International Organization for Standardization (ISO), Switzerland, 1996.
ISO/IEC TR 13335-4, Information Technology – Guidelines for the management of IT Security – Selection of safeguards, International Organization for Standardization (ISO), Switzerland, 1996.
ISO/IEC TR 13335-3, Information Technology – Guidelines for the management of IT Security – Techniques for the management of IT Security, International Organization for Standardization (ISO), Switzerland, 1996.
ISO/IEC 27002:2005, Information Technology – Security techniques – Code of practice for information security management, International Organization for Standardization (ISO), Switzerland, 2005.

the OECD's "Guidelines for the Security of Information Systems and Networks"[10] empha-sizing the promotion of the culture of security by requiring:

- Effective leadership and extensive participation;
- A security management framework;
- The understanding of the need for security.

The principles included in the OECD's guidelines concern issues such as awareness, responsibility, responses, ethics, democracy, risk assessment, security design and implementa-tion, and security management and reassessment.

Based on these principles, another well-known international non-profit organization, the Information Systems Security Association (ISSA), has published the "Generally Accepted Information Security Principles."[11] This publication attempts to document common prac-tices within the information security domain and describes three kinds of principles regard-ing information security, namely:

- Pervasive principles, multidisciplinary principles addressing areas such as propor-tionality, integration, timeliness, assessment and equity. These rarely change and are focused on the governance facet of information security;
- Broad functional principles, which are more detailed than the pervasive ones and address generally accepted elements of information security programs;
- Detailed principles that address methods to achieve compliance with the broad func-tional principles and concern the security mechanisms to be implemented based on a continuous evolution.

All of the above mentioned general principles reinforce the idea that information secu-rity is a question of *multitasking* activities within a *multidimensional structure* and one that should be managed in the same way as any other complex and multidimensional task within the enterprise. A well-structured information security program should thus include the fol-lowing areas, in order to allow evaluators to judge the level of assurance:

- Information security policy – to support standards, baselines, procedures;
- Education and awareness – to communicate the security policy to all personnel;
- Accountability – to hold parties accountable for information access and use;
- Information management – to catalogue and value information assets;
- Environmental management – to consider and compensate for internal and external environments;
- Personnel qualifications – to establish and verify the necessary qualifications related to the integrity, need-to-know and technical competencies of personnel;
- Incident management – to provide the capability to respond to and resolve informa-tion security incidents;
- Information system life-cycle – to ensure that security is addressed at all stages of the system lifecycle;

---

10   "OECD Guidelines for the Security of Information Systems and Networks ; towards a culture of security,"
     Organization for Economic Co-operation and Development, Paris 2002. Available at
     http://www.oecd.org/document/42/0,3343,en_21571361_36139259_15582250_1_1_1_1,00.html
11   ISSA, "Generally Accepted Information Security Principles V3.0," Information Systems Security Association
     USA 2003. Available at http://all.net/books/standards/GAISP-v30.pdf

- Access control – to establish appropriate controls to balance access to information;
- Operational continuity and contingency planning – to plan and operate appropriately to ensure continuity;
- Information risk management – to ensure that information security measures are appropriate to the value of the assets;
- Network and infrastructure security – to consider the potential impact of the shared global infrastructure;
- Legal, regulatory, and contractual requirements – to take steps to be aware of and address all legal, regulatory, and contractual requirements;
- Ethical practices – to respect the rights and the dignity of individuals.

Based on these factors, an information security plan should be developed that would constitute the basis for defining the operational security requirements and then specifying the security measures to be implemented. The evaluation model would be based on the structure presented in the list above, which constitutes the raw material of the information security program. Each of the exhaustive points in the list will serve as a *focus area* (information security issue) that the model aims to evaluate.

1.4 A holistic view of information security

The holistic concept, according to E. Freeman, in his article "Holistic information security: ISO 27001 and due care,"[12] comes from a medical philosophy encompassing therapies attempting to treat the patient as a whole. Addressing information security in such a holistic manner requires the inclusion of technology, personnel, organizational measures and legal dimensions. The holistic approach advocates a bottom-up approach to security that takes into account all of these security dimensions.

In order to manage security for a whole organization, the competing needs and pressures created by legal, operational, technical, cultural, and behavioural forces should be balanced and addressed (Figure 1.2).

To achieve this high-level objective, a governance approach is necessary. Information security governance requires formal reporting tools and mechanisms to provide top management with an easily understandable overview of ICT risks and how they are managed. Three kinds of information security controls exist. These are: computer-centric, concerning physical security measures; ICT-centric, concerning technical security measures; and information-centric, concerning all operational controls including policies, procedures and standards. The unifying factor of all these security countermeasures, measures and controls is that they will have been derived from the security requirements defined during the previous stages of risk management. Information security, from this perspective, follows a bottom-up approach involving all organizational levels, in which the information security countermeasures, measures and controls are designed on the basis of the value and utility of the assets being protected, which in this general case are information and all related subjects.

---

[12]   *Information Systems Security*, vol. 16 (5), pp. 291-294, 2007.

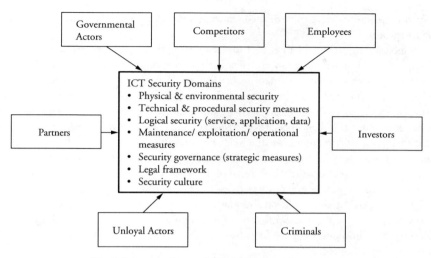

Fig. 1.2 Some parameters influencing information security.

Security measures cannot be relied upon to protect ICT infrastructures without transparency over their operation and verification of their effectiveness. The underlying idea is that nowadays the effectiveness of the information security measures will mostly depend on the capability an organization has to manage and govern (with the meaning of *direct and control*) its *technical and operational information security measures.* In its strategic document "Global Cybersecurity Agenda – Global Strategic Report,"[13] the International Telecommunication Union defines cybersecurity as being a system consisting of five pillars, three of which (Legal, Technical & Procedural, and Organizational) run parallel to each other, and two of which (Capacity Building and International Cooperation) focus on the human interactions within the topic of security to transversely become embedded in the three parallel pillars.

As a general principle, technical information security measures depend on the organizational controls to function, and the organizational controls depend on the human-focused controls to function well.

Considering information security holistically means, first of all, considering equally all significant information security topics, regardless of their classification. In the proposed evaluation framework, all these elements are dealt with under the denomination of "constitutive elements" on the basis that each one could contribute to increasing the security level and consequently to improving the protection level. It clearly emerges from this consideration that holistic information security should not, and must not, be exclusively technologically driven.

Holistic information security is minimally composed of four meta-dimensions representing the four facets of information security; these are the *organizational,* the *technical and operational,* the *human* and the *legal dimensions.* Each one of these dimensions is composed of relevant information security constitutive elements. There is no single, unique solution to the majority of challenges existing within information security, which is why the notion of

---

13   "ITU Global Cybersecurity Agenda (GCA) – High Level Experts Group (HLEG) – Global Strategic report,"
       International Telecommunication Union (ITU), Geneva, Switzerland 2008. Available at
       http://www.itu.int/osg/csd/cybersecurity/gca/global_strategic_report/index.html

security dimension (or meta-dimensions) working together to reach the same objective comes to the foreground.

Understanding the problem equals understanding the existing protection capacities of an organization. Understanding an organization's protection capacities means understanding the constituent elements of information security, the way they react, their key success factors, and so on. The most important aspect, however, is the coherence among the different constitutive elements or information security dimensions. The information security dimensions are interrelated and in order to be coherent they have to correspond to each of the other dimensions within their own lifecycle. For example, within the technical dimension of information security, a dimension such as the organizational one should be considered in order to be able to choose the best technology or procedures to be operated as stated by the organizational requirements or objectives. In addition, the human dimension should be considered by ensuring that sufficient human capacities do indeed exist within the organization to understand, support and implement a given technology or methodology. Last, but not least, each technology, or any other action to be undertaken, should conform to the legal rules or regulations in force.

To summarize, holistic information security is a program or a system, which is composed of a certain number of elements interacting in a coherent manner. The holistic attribute of information security should necessarily incorporate the notion that humans implement all the technological, procedural, organizational activities and that consequently the ultimate objective in information security terms should be the creation of a *security culture framework*. The information security culture in this context means that the security reflex should be inherent and thus should be present during everyday activities. This means that everyone within the organization should be concerned with security issues and should understand what concerns them and why.

The International Telecommunications Union, in its "Global Cybersecurity Agenda – Global Strategic Report" recognizes the importance of the culture of cybersecurity by considering it as "the best guarantee" of cybersecurity itself. According to the GCA Report, cybersecurity[14] depends upon the norms and behaviours that users follow voluntarily. Consequently the cybersecurity culture becomes the main aim to be established and assessed. We believe that there are two groups of elements that allow a reliable culture of cybersecurity to be attained. These two groups include:

- The constitutive elements enhancing the protection level of national strategic values;
- The "promotional" elements striving to familiarize participants with cybersecurity issues and their importance, so that they can inherently adhere to national cybersecurity efforts.

In respect of the constitutive elements of such a cybersecurity culture, international organizations such as UN, OCDE, and ITU have defined nine elements for the creation of a cybersecurity culture.

These nine elements can be placed into three principal groups:

- The first group is concerned with the weakest link of the security chain, which is human activities, and proposes activities such as raising awareness and the delineation

---

[14]   In our case and in more general terms it is about the information security program or system.

of responsibilities. These actions allow the active and effective participation of the human resources in cybersecurity tasks.

- The second group is mostly operation-centric, specifying baseline activities to be tackled in order to ensure that an appropriate protection level can be provided.
- The third group concerns conformity issues and is motivated by the evidence that national cybersecurity programs should be operated within acceptable limits driven by fundamental ethical and democratic values.

Schematically presented, achieving a cybersecurity culture means providing a holistic cybersecurity strategy that passes through certain stages and addresses certain topics, as presented in Figure 1.3.

Thus a reliable cybersecurity culture incorporates, and depends on, the effectiveness of two main processes, namely: the creation of a solid culture of cybersecurity and the promotion of cybersecurity to build confidence in the ICT environment. An information security culture should be considered as the end result that an information security program or system should achieve, as well as the principal variable to be assessed. It should be developed and promoted among all the organizational stakeholders, who should be able to:

- Share a common vision and common objectives regarding information security;
- Delineate roles and responsibilities;
- Act cooperatively.

From an assessment point of view, information security is a logical link associating a given security concern to an expected result represented as safety conditions and attainability of objectives. Holistically assessing the information security posture would mean having a clear, full picture of the information security issues, how to address them, and which responsibilities each participant should shoulder. Based on the positioning of the information security culture as the central aspect to be assessed from a high-level perspective, as well as considering the conceptual protection framework discussed in the previous section, the holistic

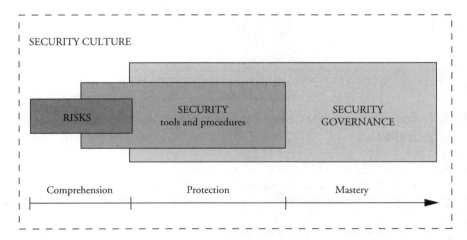

Fig. 1.3 Information security culture stages or maturity levels.

assessment methodology should look at triple assessment criteria (as presented in Figure 1.4) and these assessment criteria will consider information security from different perspectives.

Information security should be considered as a *structure* the completeness of which will be the main assessment criterion. By "completeness" is meant that the information security system in place, or the system to be designed, contains baseline components that interact with each other in a coherent manner. The absence of such elements is an important gap when considering the dependability of the cybersecurity system.

Cybersecurity has to be considered as a *valuable service* of which the effectiveness will be the main assessment criterion. In fact the effort to be undertaken, and the resources to be employed, within the information security program should necessarily correspond to some clearly identified goals resulting from an in-depth analysis of the security needs. Finally, information security has to be considered as an *ensemble of processes* for which excellence will be the main assessment criterion. By "excellence" should be understood the managerial capacities of the process owner to ensure a certain quality level regarding the process itself.

In practical terms an information security structure would be able to obviate misleading concepts, such as the view that maintaining that information security is exclusively an IT issue, or that it should be completely based on the experiences of previous years. Considering information security as a business concern provides a direct advantage in obtaining extra focus and attention from all the organizational levels. Consequently, the most important added value of the information security culture is in not considering the security as a financial cost, but as an added value for the quality and the health of the organization's business.

Fig. 1.4 The assessment criteria for a holistic information security program/system.

1.5 Information security baseline for evaluation purposes

In practice, organizations do not tend to manage security in a holistic way, even if this is recommended in the literature. It could be noted that the managerial dimension is embraced by a large percentage of the organizations as a result, in particular, of the regulatory[15] pressures

---

15   In this context regulatory means not only the legal and regulatory bills but also audits and the place these take within the managerial processes.

and the requirements for information security to conform to these regulations, at least minimally, and to provide some formal risk and security policies. While the risk and security
policies might exist in an organization, it is not necessarily the case that those policies are the
subject of strict implementation or update controls. Very often, even if policies exist, they
are derived from preformatted templates and not necessarily tailored to the specificities of
the organization itself. Information security activities are instinctively technologically driven.
After having reached a certain level of skill on the technological side, the organization organically moves into an efficiency-related rationale in order to make better use of the monetary
budget. But in spite of the potential weight of the budget, the common subordinate position
that the information security function holds within organizations often results in a poor
configuration that often neglects important components.

The evaluation model proposed within this book aims to holistically evaluate the security posture of a given organization based on a deep understanding of the features of information security, as well as the interactions which exist between them. As we have very often
underlined, information security must address the consistency of the different elements that
make it up. For that reason it is necessary that a baseline information security structure
should be identified which will serve as a starting point, either to build up a more elaborate
information security program/system, or to provide a minimum level of comfort.

The information security baseline infrastructure should present the same logical structure as a complete information security program. This means that the four dimensions previously mentioned, namely organizational, operational and technical, human, and legal, must
feature in this baseline structure. The holistic characteristics of information security should
also be reflected within the baseline structure. Given the fact that the technological-driven
controls will have to be organically implemented, particular effort should be made to pay
attention to the other information security aspects.

There are several literature sources defining baseline protection. The National Institute
of Standards and Technology (NIST), from the U.S. Department of Commerce, considers that activities such as contingency planning, incident response, information security
awareness, physical and environmental controls, as well as intrusion detection systems, are
minimally needed to provide a baseline protection, while stressing the fact that even that
may differ from one organization to another.[16] NIST considers that security baseline controls are the minimum-security controls recommended for an Information System that will
serve as a starting point to develop an information security program in order to provide a
good protection level against most known threats and under most circumstances. But, in
addition, within the NIST approach a clear distinction is made between common controls
related to the baseline information security controls, which should be centrally managed,
and the system-specific controls, which should be the responsibility of the information
system owner.

Based on this distinction, NIST identifies a list of information security baseline controls
according to the expected impact level (*low impact, moderate impact,* or *high impact)* of an

---

[16]   NIST, "Recommended Security Controls for Federal Information Systems and Organizations (SP 800-53,
       Revision 3)," U.S. Department of Commerce, National Institute of Standards and Technology, Computer
       Security Division 2009. Available at http://csrc.nist.gov/publications/nistpubs/800-53-Rev3/sp800-53-rev3-
       final.pdf

information system by defining four different priority levels for information security controls, namely[17]:

- (P1): Information security controls to be implemented first;
- (P2): Information security controls to be implemented after P1;
- (P3): Information security controls to be implemented after P1 and P2;
- (P0): Information security controls which are not selected as being baseline controls.

Nevertheless, there are eleven high-priority information security controls applicable to all kinds of organizations, independent of their information system impact level, which concern the program management supporting all the other common security controls. These are:

- Information security plan;
- Information security responsibility (Chief Information Security Officer – CISO);
- Information security resources;
- Information security action plan and milestones;
- Information systems inventory;
- Information security measures of performance;
- Enterprise architecture;
- Critical infrastructure plan;
- Risk management strategy;
- Security authorization process;
- Mission/business process definition.

These eleven high-priority information security controls will constitute the basis and the source of the evaluation within our evaluation model.

ISO/IEC 13335-4:2000[18] follows NIST by relating the structure of the information security baseline to the type of the information system and the fact that some baseline organizational safeguards should be applied for each IT system, including the following categories:

- Information security management and policies;
- Compliance checking;
- Incident handling;
- Personnel issues;
- Operational issues;
- Business continuity planning;
- Physical security.

The list proposed above contains general categories that still address information security from a high-level perspective and might include a great number of specific safeguards. Nevertheless, the categorization proposed by NIST regarding the priority of the safeguards might be a good reference in order to choose the information security controls of a primary issue. This logic brings us to the structure of ISO/IEC 27001:2005, which enumerates some 134 controls needed for an Information Security Management System (ISMS). Indeed,

---

[17] A detailed view of the information security baseline controls can be found at:
http://csrc.nist.gov/publications/nistpubs/800-53-Rev3/sp800-53-rev3-final.pdf

[18] ISO/IEC TR 13335-4, Information Technology – Guidelines for the management of IT Security – Part 4: Selection of safeguards, International Organization for Standardization (ISO), Switzerland, 2000.

ISO/IEC 27002:2005 might be considered as a security baseline by providing a package of essential security controls that provide a basic standard or level of security, thus establishing confidence in intra-company transactions. The information security baseline should include, for example:

- Information security policy;
- Organizational and responsibility issues;
- Personnel awareness and training;
- Monitoring, system administration, maintenance and incident reporting;
- Business continuity issues;
- Copyright issues;
- Backup issues;
- Compliance issues;
- etc.

In order to clarify the safeguards that should necessarily be included in the information security baseline, another aspect of information security, namely defence in depth, might be considered. This is considered as one of the most important security attributes and concerns the use of more than one countermeasure against threats. It comprises technologies ensuring protection, detection, and recovery mechanisms. This means that for each risky subject, different layers of security controls must be implemented in order to provide more assurance and trust.

To these information security baseline controls could be added a set of safeguards dedicated to the effectiveness of the security program through monitoring and security-related evaluation processes. There are several control activities considered as a baseline for an information security program:

- Risk assessment;
- The existence of documented policies and procedures;
- Security plan;
- Security awareness program;
- Periodic evaluation and assessment plans;
- Monitoring processes;
- Continuity and recovery processes.

The *information security policy* is the cornerstone of every information security program. It is inside this policy that will be found the baseline security measures. A minimal level of protection should include the following activities:

- Personnel security;
- Physical and environmental security;
- Communications and operations management;
- Physical and logical access control.

Very frequently the major security controls used within the respondent organizations are the classical[19] technical ones based on employee training and awareness and on the

---

[19] Antivirus; backup; password; access control; physical security; etc.

monitoring and auditing processes. In accordance with the standards discussed above, the most generally accepted elements to be considered as a baseline might be an information security policy; an information security awareness program; an asset inventory; a risk assessment process; the information security safeguards stemming from risk management; and at least a minimal reporting system.

These elements will constitute the minimum required, firstly to be able to claim that an information security program does exist and secondly to make it possible to evaluate this information security program meaningfully.

The analysis that has been performed to expound the notion of the information security baselines shows beyond doubt that there is no single information security baseline structure that could be applied to all kinds of organizations. For that reason we can only speak about an information security baseline *attitude*[20] rather than an information security baseline structure. Nevertheless, the information security baseline will constitute the starting point for the expansion of the latter into an information security program and/or system. As such the quality of the information security program itself will strongly depend on the attitude regarding the information security baseline.

1.6 Information security: general roots-of-trust

As discussed above, there is no universal information security baseline that can be adapted to all kind of organizations. Nevertheless, there are some information security elements, the absence of which will lead to an almost useless information security program or system, thus making the protection level uncertain. Those indispensable elements are identified within this book as being the roots-of-trust. The concept of roots-of-trust will include all the activities considered as a "sine qua non" condition of the achievement of the objectives of information security. These roots-of-trust concern all the evidence that could be gathered that demonstrates that the system in place is capable of offering not only an "adequate protection" but also a "trustable" one. They will carry the responsibility of resolving the risk and security issues. As such they will be observed within the lowest levels of the information security structure. Within our evaluation model the roots-of trust correspond to the "specific factors." While the information security baseline was mostly concerned with a holistic view of the program as a whole, the roots-of-trust concept concerns the necessary presence of some *essential safeguards*.

These safeguards should correspond to a double instinctive reaction, the first to put in place mechanisms providing the necessary time to understand a problem, the second to make it possible that security is considered early in the project. Obviously, an organization could not claim to adequately or reliably operate a security function if at least one dedicated fulltime information security position does not exist.

According to the BSI "IT Security Guidelines"[21] the essential security safeguards to ensure a systemic approach should be aggregated into the following categories:

---

[20]   *Attitude* and not "safeguards or countermeasures" because, as we have noticed, there is no *universal* information security baseline to be applied.

[21]   BSI, "IT Security Guidelines: IT Grundschutz in brief" Bundesamt für Sicherheit in der Informationstechnik (BSI), Bonn, Germany 2007. Available at https://www.bsi.bund.de/cae/servlet/contentblob/475854/publicationFile/28013/guidelines_pdf.pdf

- Setting up the risk and the security context in terms of value-related needs, frameworks to be applied, and the specification of the role of information security within the organization;
- Designing an appropriate operational framework for the information security through formal information security procedures, mechanisms, or any other implementation activities;
- Establishing an improvement environment by ensuring the accomplishment of activities related to the maintenance and monitoring of the information security program or system.

From an organizational point of view, the assessment of the information security requires a clear reference point and needs to be placed in a specific context. This point of reference might be the information security policy as well as related documents such as the information security strategic plan. The security policy itself will emerge from the risk analysis process, which includes the risk identification and the risk assessment processes. As such the risk management process should necessarily be performed recurrently. The strategic plan is a fundamental element and should include security objectives and goals, without which the security function would be judged as being managed in an informal manner; the strategic plan should thus take on the role of a roadmap to be followed in order to ensure an adequate security level for organizational assets. As mentioned above, the strategic plan should be based on requirements and set out within the security policy. The security policy must include different requirements concerning the essential control activities such as, for example, access controls, authentication and identification, responsibilities and ownership, monitoring, compliance, or physical security. Each of these control activities or security measures should be the target of a documented policy and/or a detailed procedure. Besides this, the organizational point of view should include and analyse four other interrelated requirements:

- To assign responsibilities in terms of information security;
- To segregate the duties in order that the assignment of the responsibilities makes sense;
- To create appropriate conditions allowing every organizational echelon to understand its information security role;
- To communicate the different information security concerns and duties.

The *operational framework*, which concerns the implementation of information security, should be based on a multiple viewpoint regarding the safeguards as well as the protection targets. The necessary mechanisms should be provided to deal with inherent threats (technological, environmental and internal threats). Among the safeguards, the following information security measures should be implemented:

- Technological security measures including virus protection, protection from most current environmental risk events (such as fire, flooding, electrical power), access controls and authentication issues, firewalls, backups, database security;
- Procedural measures corresponding to each of the technologies in use, including password management, data access possibilities and levels, problem management, redundancy management, recovery and emergency procedures;
- Human related measures including awareness and training.

At the same time all of these information security measures should be applied to the different layers of the infrastructure, such as the telecommunication infrastructure,[22] network infrastructure[23] and operating system infrastructure.

The last group of essential security safeguards concerns what we have called the improvement environment. This group embodies activities allowing the organization to fulfil one of the most important objectives aimed at by ISO/IEC 27001,[24] namely the continuous improvement of the information security management system. The essential safeguards to be included from this point of view are related to monitoring, to internal and external audits and to reviewing.

1.7 Chapter Summary

In this chapter the notion of information security has been discussed. This has been driven by the need to redefine information security and to decide the basis of what constitutes an information security program or system and the differences between these items. This is a very important aspect since it will constitute the basis of the evaluation and the assurance of the produced results will accordingly depend upon it. Based on the importance of the structure to be evaluated, we have focused our attention on the determination of the different aspects of an information security program. The components and the way they will be managed should reflect the specificities of each organization. Nevertheless, some high-level structures, based on the general principles and main best practices, should necessarily be in place within any given organization in order to be able to discuss assurance. For that reason we identify the elements of an information security program or system in order to then identify some baseline elements that determine the minimum effort that should be provided in order to demonstrate that information security is taken into consideration within the organization.

Our model foresees evaluating information security from a holistic perspective. For that reason one section has been dedicated to the question of the contents of a holistic information security program and the expected outputs of a holistic information program. We come to the conclusion that a holistic information security program or system should place human interactions at the centre of the program and that a governance approach should be adopted to administer the multidisciplinary character of the elements of the program. Based on this conception of the information security program, we have defined the general root-of-trust, which consists of the actions an organization must undertake in order to inspire trust in either its stakeholders or its evaluators. Complying with standards or regulations does not mean, however, that the organization has reached any measurable level of security. It only provides a common basis for considering security issues in developing, implementing and managing information security.

---

22   POTS, digital systems such as LANs, VANs, Internet, PBX, mobile communications, teleconferencing voice mail systems etc.
23   LANs, MANs, WANs, Internet gateways, VPNs, VANs.
24   Considered as being the reference framework for the security baseline.

Chapter 2

Risk Management versus Security Management

The objective of this chapter is to delimit two interrelated topics, namely risk management and security management.

2.1 Introduction

Information security, and security in general, includes all the actions to be undertaken preventatively in order to allow organizations to minimise risk. The outputs, however, are not necessarily identified immediately, or even at all. Very often it is a significant problem for corporate managers to justify security spending because of the absence of visible results. By security spending we mean all the cost of the security in an organizational concept, thus excluding the notion of national security, which is out of the scope of this book.

In practice, largely as a result of pressures in the financial sector, risk management is taking on an increasingly important role, since inherent risks need to be addressed immediately in order to obviate negative impacts. Moreover, international and national regulations increasingly specify risk management and related activities as mandatory tasks. The ultimate aim of risk management, together with security management processes, should be to define what constitutes "reasonable protection" for the organization's assets, characterized by certain best protection conditions that secure those assets in the context of specific identified risks. Setting up these two notions within a defined framework will be of the utmost importance for the results obtained from the evaluation efforts.

2.2 A definition of risk management

The concept of *management* is about defining and achieving goals while optimizing the use of resources.[1] Risk management is the process that allows business managers to balance the

---

[1] ISM3, "Information Security Management Maturity Model – Information Security Glossary," ISM3 Consortium, Madrid, Spain 2007. Available at
http://www.ism3.com/index.php?option=com_docman&task=cat_view&gid=1&Itemid=9

operational and economic costs of protective measures and to achieve gains in capability by protecting the business processes that support the business objectives or mission of the enterprise. The risk analysis is performed to show that "due diligence" has been performed. A risk management process can also be seen as a framework for determining and implementing acceptable security controls.

Risk management is a process whereby organizations methodically address the risks attached to their activities with the goal of achieving sustained benefit within each activity and across the portfolio of activities. This means that identification of the activities that provide an added value for the enterprise and their prioritization is very important within a cost-effective risk management approach. At a second stage, after having identified the important processes and activities, the risks concerning these activities are identified and prioritized.

Some sources combine both processes, security and risk management, under the larger concept of security risk management as being the practice of controlling and mitigating the amount of loss an organization will have to endure because of any adverse action or situation, whether intentionally or unintentionally initiated.

Many people within an enterprise are involved in risk management, such as:
- Staff designing and running business processes;
- Staff implementing and running applications;
- Staff in the security office setting policies;
- Staff in internal audit;
- IT operations staff.

Figure 2.1 sets out a common model for a risk management framework. There are four important attributes in respect of risk management: the terminology, the processes, the organization, and the objectives. Choosing as a starting point the output of the risk management process, the result of the risk analysis is the selection of information security controls.

As outlined, the risk management framework within this model proposes a countermeasures analysis based on their relevance with respect to the identified risks. The countermeasures are then selected, providing thus a piecemeal structure for the security processes

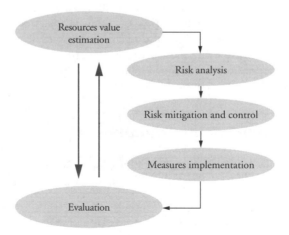

Fig. 2.1 Steps and constitutive elements of risk management process.

that follow. In our opinion, limiting the protection strategy to the identification of risks and the selection of countermeasures does not provide for efficient security. This model incorporates the notion of implementation, including the phases of test and of evaluation while maintaining a linear relationship between risk and security measures. The question that needs to be raised is whether information security should be strictly seen as a direct response to risks or as a business process with its own added value. Without risks there would be no need to implement security measures. But realistically a risk-free environment does not exist.

2.3 Presentation of the risk management process

2.3.1 Background

Threats and vulnerabilities are two main components relating to risk management irrespective of the application domain. They are the cornerstones of a risk management approach since risk is defined as the potential that a given threat will exploit vulnerabilities of an asset or group of assets to cause loss or damage.

A threat is a potential cause of an unwanted incident, which may result in harm for an organization. A vulnerability is a weakness, which is susceptible to being used by a threat. Vulnerabilities can be human failings, weakness or flaws in technology, or by extension anything else that does not conform to the expected state of operations. The threat – vulnerability pairs lead to unwanted events, the likelihood of which needs to be estimated or measured. This likelihood is the probability that a vulnerability will be exploited by a threat which leads to harm.

ISO/IEC TR 13335-1:1996 defines risk management as the entire process of identifying, controlling, and eliminating or minimizing uncertain events that may affect information technology systems.[2]

According to the ISO/IEC 27005[3] risk management is composed of six processes:
- The risk communication process;
- The system characterization or context establishment;
- The risk assessment process, which consists of two sub-processes: risk analysis and risk evaluation;
- The risk treatment process;
- The risk acceptance process;
- The risk management monitoring and review process.

Following the international standard ISO/IEC 27005 we consider that the risk management process contributes to identifying risks, assessing the consequences to the business and the likelihood of the occurrence, prioritizing the risk to be treated and identifying the

---

2   ISO/IEC 13335-1:2004, Information technology – Security techniques – Management of information and communications technology security – Part 1: Concepts and models for information and communications technology security management, International Organization for Standardization (ISO), Switzerland, 2004.

3   ISO/IEC 27005:2008, Information technology – Security techniques – Information Security Risk Management, International Organization for Standardization (ISO), Switzerland, 2008.
ISO 31000:2009, Risk Management – Principles and guidelines, International Organization for Standardization (ISO), Switzerland, 2009.

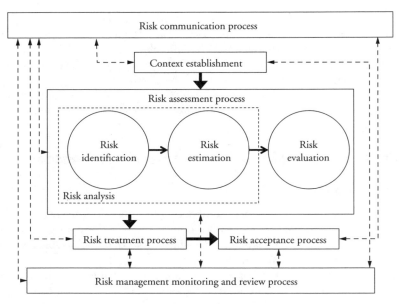

Fig. 2.2 A risk management process adapted from ISO/IEC 27005:2008.

risk reduction actions to be undertaken (Figure 2.2). For that reason, in the proposed model the risk management process is considered as an element of implemented security inside the whole information security program or process.

2.3.2 Communication process

A wide communication and consultation process including internal and external stakeholders is required. The consultation phase ensures that the organization's boundaries are discussed and relevant risks harming the organization are being taken into account. The communication phase ensures that interested parties have expressed their concerns based on their own risk perception.

2.3.3 The establishment of context

The establishment of context is about defining the scope and boundaries in terms of the organization's assets that require particular protection. This activity concerns the collection of information about the environment where informational assets are operated. It is also necessary at this stage to identify the basic criteria to be used in terms of evaluation, impact and acceptance. During this activity the basic metrics to assess and treat risks are defined and finally the responsibilities for the whole process have also to be defined. Each of these activities could utilise individual judgements of risk scenarios, formal models or risk checklists[4] corresponding to the relevant criticality and sensitivity.

---

4   See for example CIPS, "Risk Management Practice Guideline" Canadian Information Processing Society, Ontario, Canada 2007. Available at http://www.cips.ca/system/files/Risk_Management_May2007_5_1_0.pdf

2.4 Risk analysis and assessment process

2.4.1 Risk analysis

The risk assessment process concerns the identification, description and prioritization of risks harming organizational assets. The process consists of two main categories: risk analysis and risk evaluation. The risk analysis itself is made up of the *risk identification* and *the risk estimation*. This phase requires a deep knowledge of the organization and its environment, as well as a deep understanding of strategic and operational objectives. The identification and categorization of business objectives and information assets supporting the business objectives are thus required.

The risk identification consists of the identification of critical assets to be risk managed, relevant threats and vulnerabilities, in order to manage the consequences of the exploitation of a risk. One way of categorizing the business objectives is proposed in The ISF standard of Good Practice for Information Security,[5] where five categories of business objectives are set out: strategic; operational; financial; knowledge management and compliance. A general description or categorization of risks is then needed; this allows a comprehensive identification of risks and provides a means of determining risk issues with reference to the factors specific to the enterprise. This is a useful component of the process as a good risk management process is aligned with the strategic objectives.

The risk estimation consists of the assessment of consequences and likelihoods. The combination of consequences and likelihood provides *the risk level*.

To follow the Standard of Good Practice for information security (The Standard of Good Practices for Information Security (ISF)),[6] the risk analysis process should include the following steps:

- The potential level of business impact;
- Threat identification, both intentional and non-intentional;
- Vulnerabilities due to both control weakness and circumstances;

Performance of a risk analysis is considered evidence of appropriate diligence in overall risk management, which is an important objective for an enterprise's management. Figure 2.3 gives an example of the information that should be gathered and documented in order to provide a risk analysis process.

The risk analysis stage results in a clear *identification* of key risks, a *business impact* for each risk, and actions to *reduce* it. The major role of a risk analysis process is to identify appropriate security controls.

The NIST publication *Information security handbook: Guide for Managers*[7] requires an assessment of the state of existing security controls in order to estimate the real level of a given

---

5   AIRMIC, ALARM, and IRM, "A Risk Management Standard," The Institute of Risk Management, The National Forum for risk Management in the Public Sector, The Association of Insurance and Risk Managers, London, UK 2002. Available at http://www.theirm.org/publications/documents/Risk_Management_Standard_030820.pdf

6   *ISF-std. The standard of Good Practice for information security*, Information Security Forum, 2007.

7   P. Bowen, J. Hash, and M. Wilson; *Information security handbook: A Guide for managers (NIST Special Publications 800-100)* National Institute of Standards and Technology, 2006. Available at http://csrc.nist.gov/publications/nistpubs/800-100/SP800-100-Mar07-2007.pdf

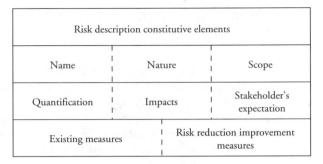

Risk description constitutive elements		
Name	Nature	Scope
Quantification	Impacts	Stakeholder's expectation
Existing measures		Risk reduction improvement measures

Fig. 2.3 Example of risk description.

risk to the risk-managed assets. For each risk, two parameters have to be determined using the evaluation criteria, as will be explained below: the probability and the impact.

Risk Evaluation

During the previous stages the most critical assets will have been identified and the risks related to these assets will have been identified and estimated. The risk evaluation phase consists of prioritizing the most probable and severe risks according to the evaluation criteria decided during the context establishment. The risks identified as important during this phase will be subject to specific measures.

Risk Treatment

Risk treatment[8], or *risk mitigation*[9] is the activity that aims to implement the different options to modify risks. There are four not mutually exclusive risk treatment options:
- Reduce through the selection of controls;
- Retain or accept without further actions;
- Avoid;
- Transfer to, or share with, another external party.

During this phase different options for addressing the risks are considered and the degree of residual risk is anticipated. Once the assessed risk is considered as acceptable, no additional actions are undertaken. If the risk based on the current assessment is considered to be unacceptable, some security controls will need to be chosen in order to reduce or mitigate the risk level. Of course, despite the implementation of security controls, a small part of the risk still remains; this is the residual risk. These activities make up the phase where the risk management process coincides with the information security domain. These two main domains are closely related and indeed the information security domain can, in a sense, be considered as an extension of the risk management process in that both processes share a common objective: a protected and safe informational infrastructure for the organization.

---

8   Term used in ISO 27005.
9   Term used in Information Security Handbook: Guide for managers (NIST publication).

The risk management process within the information security process

The risk environment is very dynamic and its attributes change continuously. As a consequence, the successful performance of the risk management process requires continuous reviewing and development. As given in the different definitions above, the risk management process has to be in concordance with strategic and operational objectives. As a result a methodical process should be undertaken.

The risk management process plays an ever-increasing role in security risk strategies; it is the first input to the second stage. BSI standard *Information security management systems*[10] and ISSEA *Systems security engineering capability maturity model*[11] consider risk management to be a part of information security management. ENISA[12] shares the same point of view, stating that *risk management and risk assessment* are major components of information security management (Figure 2.4).

A good risk analysis process should provide a good panoramic view of the implemented security controls. ISO/IEC 27001 *Information security management systems – Requirements,*[13] specifies that the controls implemented in an Information Security Management System (ISMS) scope shall be risk based. From that point of view, the risk management process could be considered as an input to the information security management process.

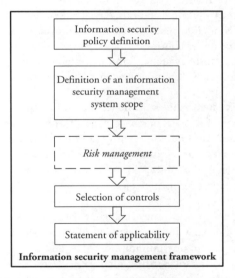

Fig. 2.4 Example of a risk management process within an information security management framework.

10   BSI-Std. 100-1, *Information Security Management Systems,* Bundesamt für Sicherheit in der Informationstechnik, Bonn, Germany, 2006.

11   *ISSEA. Systems Security Engineering Capability Maturity Model (SSE-CMM),* International Systems Security Engineering Association (ISSEA), 2003.

12   ENISA, "Risk Management: Implementation principles and Inventories for Risk Management/Risk Assessment method and tools," European Network and information security Agency – Technical Department Heraklion, Greece 2006. [Online] Available at http://www.enisa.europa.eu/rmra/files/D1_Inventory_of_Methods_Risk_Management_Final.pdf

13   ISO/IEC 27001:2005, Information technology – Security techniques – Information security management systems – Requirements, International Organization for Standardization (ISO), Switzerland, 2005.

2.5 Information security management definitions

According to ISO/IEC 27001[13], information security management is a system, part of the overall management system, that is based on a business risk approach and seeks to establish, implement, operate, monitor, review, maintain, and improve information security. This includes the establishment of an organizational structure and procedures, the definition of the information security policies and responsibilities with respect to information security in general and the policy itself, the elaboration of the planning activities, and the identification of the processes and resources needed to operate the information security program.

ISO/IEC TR 13335-1 defines security management as a process to achieve and maintain appropriate levels of confidentiality, integrity, availability, accountability, authenticity and reliability.[14] At the same time, the maturity model ISM^3 defines information security management as a system to prevent and mitigate the attacks, errors and accidents that can jeopardize the security of information systems and the organizational processes supported by them.[15]

Generally, information security is considered as a process aiming to implement the appropriate measures in order to eliminate the impact that various security-related threats and vulnerabilities might have on an organization. Nevertheless security is very often defined as freedom from danger or the condition of safety. The standard of good practice for information security (ISF) defines information security as a process for keeping the risk associated with information systems under control by means of clear direction from the top levels, the allocation of resources, security awareness, and the establishment of a secure environment. Top management's involvement provides evidence that security controls are implemented enterprise-wide.[16]

Information security management is the term used for planning and supervisory functions to ensure the meaningful development, practical feasibility and effectiveness[17] of information security measures. Information security concerns the protection of informational values. This purpose implies that there are two main categories of actions to be undertaken:

- The identification of the subjects for protection, for example against risks, losses;
- The definition of protection strategies.

Risk management as a process must be included in an information security program. From a pragmatic point of view information security management (ISM) allows management to ensure business continuity, minimize damage, and organize security activities in a cost effective manner. Information security management ensures that appropriate policies, procedures, standards, and guidelines are implemented to provide a proper balance of security controls and business objectives. Security management is the glue that ensures that the

---

14   ISO/IEC 13335-1, Information technology – Security techniques – Management of information and communications technology security – Part 1: Concepts and models for information and communications technology security management, International Organization for Standardization (ISO), Switzerland, 2004.

15   ISM^3, "Information Security Management Maturity Model," ISM3 Consortium, Madrid, Spain 2007. Available at http://www.ism3.com/index.php?option=com_docman&task=cat_view&gid=1&Itemid=9

16   ISF-std. The standard of Good Practice for information security information security Forum, 2007.

17   BSI-std. BSI 100-1, *Information Security Management Systems*, Bundesamt für Sicherheit in der Informationstechnik, Bonn, Germany, 2006.

risks are identified and an adequate control environment is established to mitigate those risks. Information security issues cover security policy, risk analysis, risk management, contingency planning and disaster recovery.

Based on the idea that risk management and information security are two processes within the same meta-structure that allow organizations to secure valuable assets, we propose in Figure 2.5 a complementary view of these two processes and the interactions between them.

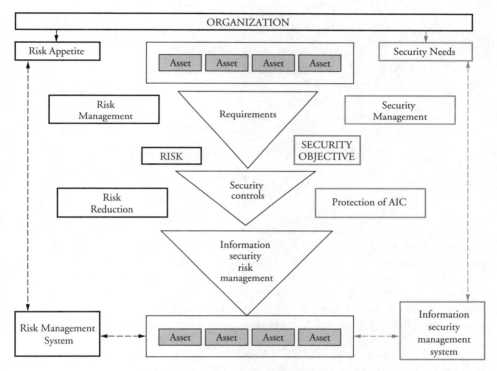

Fig. 2.5 Risk and security management interactions.

Managing security means planning, organizing, commanding, coordinating and controlling. Information security management is thus a system used to establish and maintain a secure environment by defining, achieving and maintaining the appropriate safeguards to counter the exploitation of risks. It should be a collaborative effort that utilizes a broad array of organizational capabilities in order to be successful. There is a consensus about the drivers requiring structured, formalized and managed information security management processes to be in place. The most important are technical and environmental complexity, as well as the increasing dependence on technology in doing business. Information security management is a process that is focused on the organization, while risk management contains variables that are outside the organization's boundaries.

Fig. 2.6 Example of information security management components.

As can be seen in Figure 2.6, the processes of risk management and security management are interdependent but interrelated. A process of risk management performed alone could be considered as a non-terminated process. In the same way, a security management approach that is not based in a prior risk assessment and analysis approach will not be a valid approach. Moreover, information security management starts once the risk management is completed; it starts with policies and describes "who should be allowed to do what." This statement emphasises a pure management perspective concerning the information security function.

Considering the elements described below, the information security management is concerned with controls and measures that are intended to minimize the risk impact on the valuable assets. More precisely, information security management is about planning, controlling and coordinating security activities in order to attain security goals. In general, information security management includes the following functions:

- Defining strategic actions in terms of objectives, policies, responsibilities;
- Performing the risk management process;
- Determining the implementation of operations and safeguards;
- Performing and supervising business continuity planning;
- Managing incident handling;
- Performing conformity activities in terms of audit and compliance.

Information security management is considered as a holistic activity in which different kinds of security, such as physical security, logical security, risk management, and business continuity management, converge.

2.6 Information security management components

Due to the importance of information security in public and private organizations, this topic is the subject of three international standards: ISO/IEC 13335, ISO/IEC 27002:2005 and ISO/IEC 27001:2005.[18]

- ISO/IEC 13335, entitled "Management of information and communications technology security" concerns the initiation and the implementation of information security processes.
- ISO/IEC 27002:2005 concerns the definition of a framework via a general basic conceptual structure in order to address a complex task such as information security.
- ISO/IEC 27001:2005 defines the controls to be put in place in order to satisfy the recommendations of ISO/IEC 27002:2005 is the only standard requiring a certification process.

Information technology security management is a process related to the security objectives such as availability, confidentiality and integrity, and includes the following functions:

- Determination of security objectives, strategies and policies;
- Determination of security requirements;
- Identification and analysis of risks;
- Specification and the implementation of safeguards;
- Monitoring and review of safeguards;
- Detection and reaction related to the incidents;
- Information Security awareness program.

The information security management methodology can be divided into six macroscopic phases:

- *Introductory phase:* consisting of the top-management's commitment and the consultation of information security best practices and standards.
- *Initial phase:* consisting of the appointment of a security manager and the definition of the security vision and strategy.
- *Analysis phase:* consisting of the security-related assignment of responsibilities and security related requirements.

---

18   ISO/IEC 13335-1:2004, Information technology – Security techniques – Management of information and communications technology security – Part 1: Concepts and models for information and communications technology security management.
ISO/IEC TR 13335-2:1997, Information technology – Guidelines for the management of IT Security – Part 2: Managing and planning IT Security (this part 2 was combined into the revised ISO/IEC 13335-1:2004).
ISO/IEC TR 13335-3:1998 Information technology – Guidelines for the management of IT Security – Part 3: Techniques for the management of IT Security (this part of the standard has been withdrawn and replaced by ISO/IEC 27005).
ISO/IEC TR 13335-4:2000 Information technology – Guidelines for the management of IT Security -- Part 4: Selection of safeguards (this part of the standard has also been withdrawn and replaced by ISO/IEC 27005).
ISO/IEC 27002:2005, Information Technology – Security techniques – Code of practice for information security management, International Organization for Standardization (ISO), Switzerland, 2005.
ISO/IEC 27001:2005, Information Technology – Security Techniques – Information Security Management Systems – Requirements, International Organization for Standardization (ISO), Switzerland, 2005.

- *Development phase:* consisting of the security structure definition in terms of policies, risk management procedures and security awareness.
- *Implementation phase:* consisting of the implementation of security controls.
- *Continuation phase:* consisting of the maintenance of the security program as well as monitoring, incident handling and audit.

Security controls, alternatively called safeguards or measures, are identified during the risk management process within the risk treatment phase, in order to mitigate impacts. Risk assessment, a sub-activity of the risk management process, is a source of security requirements beyond those arising from legal, regulatory, statutory, operational and business related requirements.

According to ISO/IEC 13335-1, "Guidelines for the management of IT security" there are eight processes attributed to information technology security management. The first is *configuration management*, requiring knowledge of changes that occurred within the system in order to evaluate if the safeguards in place are appropriate. The second is *change management*, which is the logical consequence of the first one, requiring the identification of new security requirements as a result of changes to the system. The third and the fourth concern *risk-related processes*, that is to say risk management and risk analysis. ISO/IEC 13335 considers risk management as the process for implementing the security strategy and security policy, where safeguards are selected and thus the level of residual risk is defined. By way of contrast, risk analysis concerns the identification of risks, that is to say the identification and the analysis of threats, vulnerabilities, and impacts. The fifth is *accountability*, dealing with the assignment and knowledge of responsibilities. These responsibilities include both responsibilities for identifying and valuing assets and those for the protection process itself. The sixth process is *security awareness*. This is a process involving personnel and their adherence to the information security program, practices and operations, since individuals are widely considered as being the weakest security link. Their adherence is specially related to the security objectives and security needs of the organization. This process consists of a number of distinct activities such as awareness materials, training, and educational activities. The seventh process is *information security monitoring*, focused on the appropriate functioning of safeguards. This activity is similar in concept to the risk monitoring but is focused on the safeguards rather than any changes in risk factors. The aim is to be sure that safeguards are functioning and are used in the expected manner. The last processes considered in ISO/IEC 13335-2 are *contingency planning* and *disaster recovery*. Because in reality zero risk does not exist, this is a fundamental part of information security management. This stage contains information about how to continue business operations in the event of an adverse occurrence and the unavailability of IT systems, as well as how to minimize unavoidable losses due to the event. Having an information security management system means that a given organization has a formal management framework where the security controls are implemented and documented and where records are maintained in order to allow the evaluation of the controls and of compliance with procedures and standards.

Focusing on structures, the Standard of Good Practices for information security (ISF)[19] identifies six main areas regarding information security management.

The first is high level direction, corresponding to the objective of the establishment of maintaining a positive security environment. This objective addresses the responsibility of

---

19   ISF-std. *The Standard of Good Practices for Information Security,* Information Security Forum, 2007.

top-level management to identify, classify and safeguard information assets. Top-level management has to ensure that security controls in place are proportionate to the risk acceptance criteria. They are responsible for the information security policy, which is the leading document for processes and Risk and information security management. As mentioned before, the human dimension of security is also a fundamentally important subject requiring particular attention from top-level management. Some formalized staff agreements need to be specified, comprising job descriptions and conditions of employment.

The second area concerns the security organization. A top-down management structure will implement structures in order to coordinate security activities. As mentioned previously, activities such as security awareness training have to be rolled out because security concerns have to be absorbed at all levels of the organization.

Security requirements is the third area of information security management. Requirements have to consider different aspects related to the effectiveness and efficiency of the Security function. This area starts with information classification, which is useful to define the protection level of information assets. Then certain documented requirements in terms of ownership and responsibilities, such as business requirements, Service Level Agreements and security reviews and/or audits, have to be defined.

Risk activities result from information security management. Finally a system to identify and interpret relevant laws has to be implemented, in order to ensure legal and regulatory compliance.

One of the principal objectives for information security is to ensure that valuable assets operate in a secure environment. Consequently a layered security architecture has to be built up, considering the following aspects:

- Organization Infrastructure;
- Policies, Standards and Procedures;
- Security Baseline and Risk Assessment;
- User Awareness and Training;
- Compliance.

An integrated framework such as the information security architecture is necessary because nowadays every element of an organization is concerned with the Information Technology systems and consequently each plays its own role in relation to the of security of assets. A secure environment includes other aspects such as *information privacy* and *identity and access management* corresponding to the objective of ensuring that information is used in an appropriate manner. These preventive controls have to be introduced alongside reactive controls such as those relating to *security incident management* and business *continuity planning*.

Malicious attacks have to be also considered within information security, constituting the fifth area of the process. This area takes into account third party access to the organization's assets and it is focused on both user behaviour and technological impact.

The standard of good practices for information security (ISF) also attributes specific topics to information security in order to provide secure conditions, namely cryptography, e-mail protection, remote working, third party access, electronic commerce and outsourcing.

The literature provides evidence that the risk assessment is an integral part of the information security management system. So we consider information security management as the main variable capable of sustaining trust within the evaluation methodology presented in this book.

2.7 The difference between risk management and information security management processes

Information security management can be considered as a business process focused on the protection of information technology assets, with an underlying objective that is the continuity of the organization as a whole. While the risk management process involved in risk identification and treatment is rather a technical task, information security is driven by policies and procedures. Unlike risk management, information security is based on a top-down approach. Consequently, in order to be effective, information security management has to be performed in an integrative manner.

The aim of a risk management process is generally to identify, evaluate and mitigate risks by choosing appropriate protective measures. The information security process goes beyond this by making sure that the information security measures in hand are correctly implemented, and they are not only effective but also efficient. In fact an effective information security process ensures that the protection measures are implemented in an appropriate and applicable way and that they are consistently applied. It also falls within the scope of the information security process to ensure that the impact of every organizational, technical and human change is considered and the process is updated regularly.

One specific process is *performance measurement*. During this process all information security fundamentals, such as objectives, strategies and policies, are reviewed in order to be up to date and provide a picture of the security situation as a whole. From this perspective information security management activities allow management to optimize "root actions" performed during the risk management phase.

Risk management focuses on the risks, while the security focuses on the organization. During the risk management phase risks are identified and during the security management phase the identified risks are placed in the context of the organization's environment. The risk treatment within a given organization changes over time due to many variables, such as time, current security level, and current exposure of the important assets.

NIST considers that risk management is an important component of a successful information security program.[20] Within the information technology security lifecycle, according to a Plan-Do-Check-Act (PDCA) approach, the *plan* phase matches exactly the risk management process. Activities such as the selection of the risk management method, risk classification, risk assessment and security control choice are imputed to the phase "Plan" of the PDCA process.

To summarize, risk management and information security management should not be considered as two distinct processes. It has been shown that they respond to the same objective, securing a valuable asset. In order to do that, both processes are necessary. Risk management will outline the appropriate security controls to be operated. Security management ensures that the security controls are operated in the most effective and efficient way. Different and complementary competencies are clearly required to perform each process.

---

[20]   P. Bowen, J. Hash, and M. Wilson, *Information Security Handbook: A Guide for Managers (NIST Special Publications 800-100)* National Institute of Standards and Technology, 2006. Available at http://csrc.nist.gov/publications/nistpubs/800-100/SP800-100-Mar07-2007.pdf

As shown in Figure 2.5, the two processes are driven by a different frame of reference; aiming to reach the same objective. Risk management aims to minimize the impact of the unwanted event, while security management focuses on the protection of asset's properties expressed through security objectives, generally but not limited to availability, integrity and confidentiality.

The information security process is driven by requirements, while risk management is driven by the importance of the impact and by acceptance criteria. This is because information security is policy-based responding to an efficiency-related objective. Risk management identifies a large range of events and chooses the appropriate controls to be implemented. Information security management, via policies, strategies, and requirements, prioritizes risk and related controls.

Another distinction could be made when considering the result of processes. For risk management, the result is the *selection of countermeasures* to mitigate risk impacts. For information security, the result is a security condition based on, but not restricted to, *security controls*.

An integrative concept is in use, security convergence, aligning physical and logical security risk mitigation controls to risk management. As a consequence of the level of reliance of businesses on Information Technologies, new topics managed by information security have emerged, such as compliance, and thus new risks such as non-compliance have been introduced. These could have same impacts as traditional risk in terms of financial losses, unavailability or reputational damage.

2.8 Information security evaluation issues

One of the major issues in the domain of the evaluation of information security is in finding a good way to proceed between two commonly used evaluation-related "extremes" such as checklists and audit (internal or external). Obviously these two means each possess their own advantages, which is not the subject of this book. Many methodologies and frameworks exist in order to perform both information security assessments based on both checklists and audits. The motivation for this book was to fill the gap between them and provide a means of assessment that goes into more depth than a simple checklist but does not demand as many important resources as the audit does.

In spite of their advantages, security checklists and information security audits remain a static way of evaluating the information security of an organization. Moreover, security checklists often arise directly from audit frameworks or methodologies as a simplified tool to show the degree of conformity with the audit framework's requirements. The output of such checklists will be an evaluation of the state of information security in comparison with the standard, but not necessarily in comparison with an organization's specific needs. On the other hand, by their nature security checklists do not necessarily lend themselves to justification and analysis from the moment that yes/no responses are requested. Therefore, the relationship between different control processes or security measures is difficult to detect.

Not enough attention is paid to the specificities of the each organization's security requirements or to the social nature of organizations. The perspective obtained from, and analysis performed on, audit activities is often very high level, even before considering the reality that security audits frequently do not have the explicit objective to assess and evaluate the security level of a given organization, but rather are part of a process to verify that the internal control system provides assurance about the reliability of organizational financial statements. In our opinion, a deep understanding of the methodology, rather than a deep understanding of the organization that is the subject of the audit, is preferable when considering audit activities. Based on the degree of granularity and the consequent audit effort necessary, it is often very difficult to plan and perform audits covering all relevant security concerns during a single period. Consequently, and under the pressure of being as exhaustive as possible, audits that concern different security domains are performed over different periods.

The mission of information security goes beyond this by providing assurance that a wide range of risks and their impacts are considered and addressed. This is not only in terms of information reliability but also in terms of availability and confidentiality and can be related to other security criteria.

Another gap introduced by the extensive use of the checklists or audits is that such reviews are often performed or updated periodically, often every six months or annually, which does not conform to the continuous nature of security. This is not to say that audits have no relevance to the security level of an organization, but that within audit activities, objectives of compliance and conformity tend to prevail over those relating to security optimization. The holistic view, which might be a good basis to inspire trust over the security system in place, is not achieved. Evaluation activities such as checklists and audits respond more to the "what" related issues rather than the "how" related issues.

Overall we can say that the assessment for certification according to a standard demonstrates similar weaknesses to the general audit approach, even if the assessment might concern some very specific and technical aspects of security. What is missing here is the holistic requirement regarding an information security program or system as a whole. It needs to be underlined that a fundamental distinction should be made between the "system" and "program" attributes, when considering information security. The distinction made between these two attributes is related to the maturity level of the information security function under evaluation. Indeed, an information security program will show the state of a given information security level in circumstances where a roadmap to perform security tasks does already exist and security functions within the organizations are in an initial phase, while an information security system is characterized by all the coordinated, managed and governed security activities in the case when the information security within the organization is fully implemented and efforts are being made to reach a standardized stage.

Even dedicated standards, such as ISO/IEC 27001:2005[21] for information security management, do not permit the evaluation of information security as a process, being limited only to the architectural characteristics. Behind each standard is hidden a procedure of conformity and compliance. Consequently the conclusion should be that the primary goal remains conformity with the standard. Based on the standard's structure it has to be underlined that those organizations that follow the standard's guidelines will still make efforts in terms of adjustments regarding their specific activities. Complying with security standards is important but not sufficient. Complying with a given standard presents the main problem that the measures in place have not necessarily been validated but have been driven by an appeal to common practices, and consequently are generic in scope.

---

[21] ISO/IEC 27001:2005, Information technology – Security techniques – Information security management systems – Requirements, International Organization for Standardization (ISO), Switzerland, 2005.

2.9 Questions raised with respect to the information security-related ISO/IEC standards

The requirement for information security to be effective and efficient demands a deep knowledge of the organization and its business objectives in order to build up not only a coherent information security system but also a coherent information security evaluation system. Based on a deep knowledge of the organization, the security objectives will naturally follow from the security needs of the organization and the information security system that will be put in place will fulfil a group of requirements rising from attainable objectives that make sense both individually and when taken together. This coherence becomes even more important when considering the fact that the adherence of employees is a condition of success for an effective information security approach.

We can take the example of a widely used best practices standard for information security, ISO/IEC 27002:2005[22] and ask the following questions:

- Does ISO/IEC 27002:2005 allow the organization to reach a certain security level and;
- Is this level the most efficacious one for the organization?

There is no doubt that being in conformity with dedicated international standards can be of great utility. But how do the requirements of the international standards correspond to those of a specific organization?

Information risk and the way to assess it are a matter of perception; having a good level of information security management will depend on this perception and on having a well-defined vision of both risk protection and safety conditions. In general, satisfying ISO/IEC 27002:2005 requirements shows compliance with the design of measures but does not provide comfort over their effectiveness. This standard is a checklist of procedures and controls

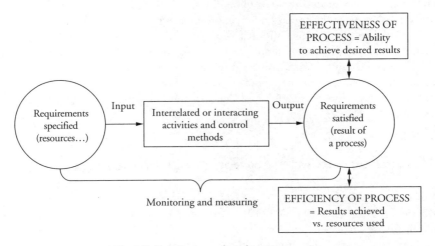

Fig. 2.7 Generic process for information security.

22   ISO/IEC 27002:2005, Information technology – Security techniques – Code of practice for information security management, International Organization for Standardization (ISO), Switzerland, 2005.

to be implemented that emphasise conformity but, as is shown in Figure 2.7, the required output of a process alongside conformity should be effectiveness and efficiency. Here we are confronted with an important gap introduced by the use of, and the importance imputed to, standards: they provide a baseline, generalised approach. Although standards and best practices provide an important input into security they should not be relied on blindly.

ISO/IEC 27001 provides a model for establishing, implementing and maintaining an information security management system. The question to be posed is: will a security management system that conforms to that given in ISO/IEC 27001 work in an optimal manner? Nowadays there are many companies that sell ISO conformity. There is frequently, however, an ambiguity about the "conformity" they sell; the tendency is to sell advice on building security policies or evaluating the organization's security processes in order to comply strictly with ISO security standards framework. Security issues are thus very often treated in a very generic way.

Security managers need to work to produce effective security, as following standards by themselves is not sufficient. ISO standards give directives but do not specify their effectiveness or how a security level can be achieved. A larger set of tools is needed in order to achieve the principal goal of a better security level. The information security driver is to build confidence in ICT infrastructures. Does being in conformity with a standard necessarily generate confidence in security? This is another question we have to answer when we consider an IT security management process. Expressing confidence through conformity is not sufficient; it must be linked to the quality of the system. Satisfying the requirements of ISO/IEC 27002 and ISO/IEC 27001 does not in itself show the way to build the management system at the moment, as complying with a standard does not necessarily mean going into depth. As we have seen, information security is an ongoing process undertaken in a dynamic environment while conformity (or certification when it exists) is only valid for a static state of a process or component. Conformity does not include the mandatory anticipation dimension of the security management process that is required by the evolving nature of IT risks. At present, the trend is to state that the organization is appropriately protected if it complies with specific regulations and standards. This is mostly a legal protection that does not produce IT security. Legal and regulatory constraints should be seen as key factors to oblige the organization to put in place an effective information security management framework. To do that international standards can help, but one should keep in mind that an organization's competitiveness depends on its security effectiveness and that it is not conformity that guarantees security effectiveness.

2.10 Evaluating information security management

Evidence that an information security management system has been and is established, maintained and reviewed gives a strong indication that a given organization is using a systematic approach for the management of information security risks. This statement demonstrates the importance the other dimensions of the information security gradually take with respect to the technical one. This statement implies a direct relationship between the level of the security provided within a given organization and its organizational and managerial capacities. In this light, the German information security standard and the German Standard (BSI)

100-1[23], state that information security organization and information security policy are tools that the management uses to implement its security strategy. In that way, evaluating the management system of the subject under review (in our case the information security) means evaluating the quality of the implementation of the security objectives.

Information security historically has been, and often in practice still is, considered as a technical discipline. For that reason information security processes predominantly focus on risk mitigation in respect of technical vulnerabilities. For example, threats such as viruses or unauthorized access to information are often, and wrongly, addressed by purely technical means such as antivirus software or firewalls. However, virus contamination or unauthorized access to information arises from a misuse of these technologies rather than from deficiencies in technical installations. In the case of viruses the origin of the breach is commonly the fact that a user or administrator has forgotten or aborted an automated procedure to update the software. A well-defined managerial process rather than the degree of skill typically rectifies such kinds of issues. The need for managerial quality ensues from the complexity of the information and communication technologies environment. This complex environment involves a multiple number of procedures, activities and controls. Furthermore responding to the increasing number of threats and vulnerabilities requires a great number of solutions for which, besides their effectiveness and efficiency, a manager has to evaluate their cost/benefit ratio. As we have already mentioned, this environment is interdependent and interoperable, hence there does exist a real and increased need to improve the managerial skills related to information security.

A main concern within the information security management area is that security managers have to deal with multiple subjects and fields of disciplines that require a good understanding of technical, economical, ethical, legal and managerial issues. Security issues are among those rare organizational ones that require the mobilization of all the organization's resources. Information security management needs to adopt a coherent and complementary approach based on:

- *Business functions* such as policies, standards, procedures involving many stakeholders such as policy teams, compliance department, human resources department, and the IT department;
- *Operational stages* which include tests and controls, physical and organizational safeguards, incident handling involving developers, system administrators response teams, and project teams;
- *Assurance processes* such as auditing, knowledge and awareness processes involving auditors, trainers, and experts.

Thus the information security architecture has to integrate a great number of components and fulfil many functions at many levels, absorbing a significant part of the organization's skills and resources. Taking into account these considerations, managing information security issues is a rather complex process. According to the standard ISO 9000:2005,[24] a

---

[23] BSI-Std. BSI 100-1, *Information Security Management Systems*, Bundesamt für Sicherheit in der Informationstechnik, Bonn, Germany, 2006.

[24] ISO 9000:2005, Quality Management Systems – Fundamentals and Vocabulary, International Organization for Standardization (ISO), Switzerland, 2005.

process is defined as a set of interrelated or interacting activities, which transform inputs into outputs as shown in Figure 2.7 above.

A key problem for information security is in addressing all these interrelated or interacting activities and processes while taking into consideration the constraint that an organization's security system is only as strong as its weakest link. Every process, component, tool, and activity has to be subject to the same scrutiny.

Managing the complex domain of information security requires a well-defined methodology and procedures. At the same time, as a result of the interoperability and interdependent variables the required methodology has to be shared by all relevant parties who need to share the same understanding of what an information security management framework should look like, which are the areas to be considered, and which are the most effective procedures for meeting the organization's security goals and requirements.

Ten information security functions can be identified, among which are: identification of the security targets, authentication, the privacy of sensitive data, traceability, auditing, imputability, authorization, access control, content protection, and information security management. Each one of these functions addresses a specific element within the security of the organizational assets, while information security management addresses the overseeing of all the other security functions and plays an integrator role.

This has led practitioners to develop guidelines and standards to better follow and unify the different practices encountered within the information security domain such as the ISO standards. The problem is that even after a potentially expensive process of certification or compliance, there is not necessarily any assurance over, or evidence of, the effectiveness or efficiency of the system in place; instead, there is assurance that the security processes are managed in a reasonable way, as the standard describes and requires.

2.11 Why choose to evaluate information security management in the context of trust?

Within this book, and according to the different definitions discussed above, the information security function is considered as the response to the concretisation of risk. It is the only variable an evaluator can measure, the risk being an independent one. Risk is a function of the likelihood that a threat could exploit a vulnerability and provoke a negative impact on a valuable asset. Variables such as threat and impact do not fully depend on the level of preparedness of the organization. The European Network and Information Security Agency, in its report "Risk management: implementation principles and inventories for risk management/risk assessment method and tools," states that: the maintenance and continuous update of an information security management system provide a strong indication that a company is using a systematic approach for the identification, assessment and management of security risks.[25]

---

25   ENISA, "Risk Management: Implementation Principles and Inventories for Risk Management/Risk Assessment method and tools," European Network and information security Agency – Technical Department Heraklion, Greece 2006. [Online] Available at
      http://www.enisa.europa.eu/rmra/files/D1_Inventory_of_Methods_Risk_Management_Final.pdf

Contrary to the popular belief that security is a technical issue, even the best efforts to buy software-based security solutions and build security into developed software and operational systems encounter "considerable resistance because the problem is mostly organizational and cultural, not technical". Technical security and security related products are not sufficient to protect an organization without two fundamental attributes: good management policy and good implementation. In order to build trust in the information security function within the enterprise, however, the concepts of good management and good implementation need to be defined and measured. For that, measurable and widely shared attributes related to the topic have to be identified and analyzed continuously. There are several aspects to be taken into account while evaluating the information security and the following four variables have a strong impact on the information security management process:

- IT competence of business line managers;
- Environmental uncertainty;
- Industry type;
- Organization's size.

The way to manage security processes within the enterprise is to use global elements to provide assurance. In fact, assurance can be provided only by some induced behaviour. As stated in contemporary studies, one of the most important objectives at a high managerial level is to ensure the continuity of the business, an issue widely called durability. This means that risks that could harm this aspect should be identified and treated in such a way that their impact becomes minimal.

Information security processes make sure that safeguards are correctly implemented and are effective and efficient. Doing this gives assurance about the level of protection. Evaluating information security means *evaluating the assurance level*, which is the most appropriate manner to evaluate trust. As argued above, information security management incorporates the activities performed during the risk management phase. That means that the evaluation of information security brings a more holistic view than a single evaluation focused on risk management activities. To summarize, focusing evaluation efforts exclusively on the way risks are managed will answer the question: what is being done? Including the elements that are encompassed within information security will answer another very important question: how is it being done?

2.12 Chapter summary

In performing a comparative analysis of risk management and security management processes, the challenge is to find the appropriate elements in order to be capable of responding to the question of *where risk management ends* and *where security management begins?* Do these fall under the same responsibility or not, and do these two processes demand different expertise? If this is the case, what kind of expertise is required? In spite of all these questions, we propose throughout this chapter the idea that it is not of great importance to make a clear distinction between these two processes; rather, we have here two processes that should necessarily be performed together in order to provide the expected result, which is the security of assets. The absence of one of these processes means that only half of the work is done and as such, half of the work, in security terms, would be an objective that simply has not been achieved.

Chapter 3

Information Security Assurance: an Assessment Model

The aim of this chapter is to present the Information Security Assurance Assessment Model (ISAAM), through its structure and evaluation attributes and to define the assurance levels, quality levels and maturity levels related to the model.

3.1 The need for a holistic approach to evaluating information security

The need to evaluate information security might arise from different sources. The source most directly concerned is the management of the organization that will be aware of the added value and costs that information security related activities bring to the organization in business terms. This means that their first objective will not be to provide the highest level of security, but rather to provide a security level that is not too restrictive and allows the business to reach its financial and operational objectives, fostering thus the competitive capabilities of the organization. This is why the managerial level must participate in information security efforts and indeed be the source of the risk management activities that determine the information security objectives and activities. The evaluation of information security will be a tool in managers' hands to administer information security, to determine whether information security objectives have been met and thus determine whether risk objectives have also been satisfied. This also allows managers to determine whether security activities are performed as designed. Generally speaking the security evaluation will help executive levels to govern security and consequently to govern risks. To do that, executives should rely on multidimensional evaluation tools that give a wide, multidimensional view of the security.

The security level of the organization also concerns external business partners. As has been stated above, nowadays business is performed in a networked and interrelated environment with massive use of ICT technologies. The security level of the organization must inspire trust and confidence in order to base the business relationship on solid foundations. The partners will not always have the right or the possibility of performing their own evaluation, but they will typically have a great interest in obtaining comfort that an appropriate level of security is in place.

Other external stakeholders are also interested in the topic, particularly those that are obliged to perform their own evaluation, such as governmental agencies, insurers or external auditors. We have already mentioned that the auditors often possess their own frameworks and methodologies for producing their results and we have discussed the gap that might be constituted when the evaluation is based only on audit objectives.

Other external partners might base their evaluation, of course, on the audit results or even require an evaluation based on the standards or the best practices. To be effective, this approach requires specific skills and experience in interpreting and understanding the potential subtleties and impacts of such detailed texts, skills that may not be readily available. In other cases the external partners may not be directly interested in a formal and specific evaluation, but are rather more interested in having an impression of where the organization is situated in security terms. This could be the case with insurers, for example, who would be interested in the security quality of the organization in order to evaluate the risks they might be taking on by insuring the organization. They are more concerned about on-going security activities and how these are performed in relation to specific risks, rather than the fact that the organization is certified by a standards body or that it can demonstrate compliance with a piece of legislation. We underline the fact that we are not saying here that certification, standardization, and compliance are of no value, but rather that each has a specific focus and scope and that no single certification will address all aspects of information security management.

3.2 The ISAAM model

3.2.1 Main expectations and assumptions

The aim of the proposed evaluation model is to fill the gap left by several of the evaluation methods that are commonly used for evaluating information security. This initiative is largely driven by the expected utility of such methods from the point of view of users such as internal stakeholders, external business partners and other external parties.

The objective is to produce a conceptual framework that permits the holistic evaluation of the information security system of an organization in order to allow a certain level of confidence and trust in the security practices operated within and around that system. The end product will be an assessment model, to be called the Information Security Assurance Assessment Model (ISAAM), which aspires to be less time consuming and labour intensive than less structured approaches.

Information security is a discipline that includes several dimensions and is measured by its weakest link. The weakest link might be located within any of the domains, so each must be evaluated and assessed using consistent methods.

The model is based on the assumption that the following aspects of security are true for the organization in question:

- Information security issues have been considered and identified;
- An information security management system or similar is in place;
- Security structures are in place and security policies and procedures have been established;
- Security dimensions (organizational, operational, human and compliance) have been established;

- Relevant security products have been installed, configured and maintained; and
- Some measurement of efforts and outputs is performed and reported.

It is essential for such a baseline level of security to exist within the organization because our evaluation model cannot be based on occasional or inconsistent security activities.

3.2.2 Different perspectives

In our conceptual evaluation model we consider information security from three different perspectives (Figure 3.1).

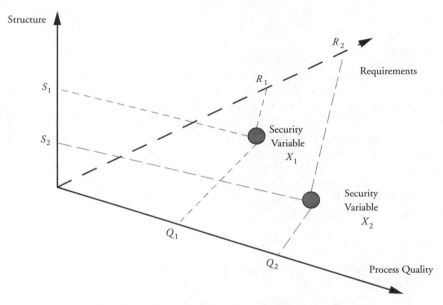

Fig. 3.1 Multidimensional view of information security level.

The first view is of *information security as a program,* characterized by its structure. The information security approach must include several sub-activities performed together in order to create a security posture that corresponds to business requirements. Indeed, the information security posture is the state of protection that results from measures, both general and specific, formal and informal, designed to ensure security objectives. The structure demonstrates three main characteristics:
- Completeness;
- Capability;
- Coherence.

The second view is of *information security as a process,* characterized by its quality. After having evaluated the architecture and the structure of the information security system, it can be confirmed that some baseline conditions for success do already exist within the organization. The challenge for this second view is to implement and operate the inputs of the first phase in the best possible way. This structure demonstrates three main characteristics:

- Effectiveness;
- Manageability;
- Testability.

The third view is of *information security as a business activity*, characterized by and based on its requirements or needs. Historically one of the major issues related to information security activities has been the way that they were often considered by executive levels to be a technical matter and, consequently, seen as a cost centre. Nowadays it is widely accepted that appropriate security activities provide a competitive advantage. This structure demonstrates three main characteristics:

- Measurement;
- Effectiveness;
- Optimization.

In this way each security variable under evaluation is positioned and analysed according to these three different attributes, namely the assurance structure, process quality, and the fulfilment of information security requirements. As can be seen in Figure 3.1 a holistic view of all the information security variables could be generated and consequently actions could be undertaken in order to improve these variables. In the diagram we take the example of two *information security variables*, X_1 and X_2. According to the analysis, it could be concluded that X_1 possesses a better assurance structure than X_2. But at the same time X_2, in spite of its incomplete assurance structure, demonstrates that the information security measures and controls that have been implemented are functioning properly and correspond to a specific need, and some specific objectives, of the organization.

3.2.3 The level of trust

The Evaluation of the information security program or system based on these three points of view aims to generate as a final product a "level of trust" in the information security system. This level of trust will be an overall and general index, based on the evaluator's perceptions and the analysis of the evidence gathered while reviewing the environment. As mentioned in previous chapters, the evaluator could be any interested party, external or internal, that is concerned by the security level of the organization.

3.2.4 Domains and dimensions

The model views the information security management system as separable into four principal domains that correspond to specific security concerns. These are:

- Organizational Dimension;
- Operational Dimension;
- Human Dimension;
- Legal Dimension.

Additionally, the information security domain can be divided into four information security dimensions that represent the nature of the information security activities that are included within the dimension. The dimension defines the *focus areas* that represent the main security issues within that given dimension. Then each focus area, that is to say each security issue, will be addressed by one or several *specific factors*.

At a high level, each domain corresponds to the same objectives as the risk impact mitigation, but uses different procedures or tools to satisfy it. The underlying idea is that the same risk could be linked to more than one weakness in the domain and exploit different breaches to cause harm. On the security side, each domain plays a role in meeting information security objectives or criteria – availability, integrity and confidentiality. The *risk-security association* is an "n-to-n" relationship, which does not allow evaluators to generate an exhaustive list of correlations. For that reason, in order to reduce the complexity of the evaluation model we have introduced this meta-structure that limits the capacity to respond to a given risky situation. The organization can choose to prioritize or not a particular information security dimension according to the capacities or resources available. As a result, instead of evaluating risk exposure the focus is on the level of preparedness to face risks. As an example, for an organization attention might be not exclusively focused on the likelihood that a flood may occur, but on the security mechanisms and the level of preparedness within the organization to mitigate such an eventuality.

3.2.5 The expected outputs from the assessment model

Each of the security dimensions is divided into different sub-categories identified as "sources of concern" in that dimension. Conceptually a security measure or control should correspond to every source of concern. As a result of the structure of the model, therefore, three specific outputs could be derived from the three dependent variables identified above (information security structure (*posture*), information security process quality, and information security effectiveness).

In respect of the *security structure*, the expected output is a trusted structure of security elements related to the key components for success. Formalizing the security structure allows organizations or evaluators to base their analysis on a solid evaluation framework that consists of baseline, standard elements. A second level of evaluation concerning process quality concerns will then be performed. From this analysis five attributes are identified that relate to the performance of the dimension. In respect of *information security as a process*, the expected output is the reliable performance of the processes related to the key success components within the dimensions.

In this stage we have a well-defined security framework that is made up of various components allowing the mitigation of the impact of risk. Naively, if we base our analysis on a cause and effect link, we could assume that the more security components we put into the system, the better the security level will be, and consequently the higher will be the level of assurance. Practically, however, organizations need to work under a number of constraints, one of which is limited resources. For that reason they have to identify their most significant security needs and reach a certain security level based on those. In order to do this they need to develop a security system that responds to these needs or try to apply an existing one.

Based on this analysis the third dependent variable of our evaluation model is introduced. This is information security effectiveness and is related to the fulfilment of information security needs and requirements. In respect of *information security effectiveness*, the expected output is the reliable accomplishment of the security requirements for the chosen security level.

Generally, the trust level of an information security program or system will be evaluated based on these interconnected variables (needs and requirements) as shown in Figure 3.2 and Figure 3.3: in other words, a structure introduced within a system bordered by the specific security needs.

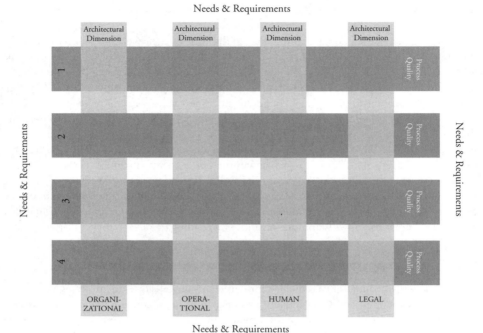

Fig. 3.2 A conceptual representation of the holistic approach.

The quality of the information security management system, appraising each relevant security dimension with respect to its "what" and "how," will be determined by its success in addressing the potential risks harming the organization while preserving the opportunities that these might offer.

Fig. 3.3 Prerequisites of trust regarding the information security system.

3.2.6 The main objective of the assessment model

The main objective is to define a methodological framework capable of evaluating the information security program or system based on a wide, holistic view of the structures in place. In order to design such a framework, we need to discuss existing assessment methodologies, identifying their strong points and recognising their weaknesses, particularly in respect of focusing too closely on specific issues and ignoring the bigger picture. In this section, therefore, we will consider the fundamental principles behind evaluating information security, starting with a definition of terms and discussion of some key concepts.

3.3 The concept of assurance within the domain of information security

Security assurance is a concept habitually related in some way to the concepts of trust and confidence; behind it is the idea of meeting certain specific security requirements regarding each component of a given system. The concepts of confidence and trust are very closely related. Trust can be defined as possessing sufficient credible evidence to believe that a given system will meet a set of given requirements. Assurance can be defined as a measure of confidence in the accuracy of a risk or security measurement. This means that assurance is derived from confidence, and confidence is built up by a structured, complex set of evidence.

According to Oxford English Dictionary[1] Online, confidence is the mental attitude of trusting in or relying on a person or thing. As such it is very closely related to the concepts of reliance and faith. Others[2] define confidence as being a feeling of trust, a feeling of certainty or even the quality of trusting. In an information security context, confidence can be related to the information security policy that creates the rules regarding which actions are or are not authorized within the system. Confidence is more a question of formal judgement, while trust depends on a feeling that will be based on positive, confident expectations. From the above, our working definition is that, independently of the evaluator's focus, based mostly on trust rather than on confidence or vice versa, providing assurance means being able to provide *evidence* of the achievement of security requirements.

As such we can state that trust in a given information security system will be reached based on confidence in the constituent elements of information security. A distinction needs to be made between information assurance and information security assurance.

3.3.1 Information assurance concept

Information assurance is the ability to access information and to preserve the quality and the security of the information. This concept is very often used as a synonym for security, allowing the migration from a preventive approach to information security to an enabling approach. This allows security functions to be aligned with local objectives and with corporate objectives and strategies. Information assurance is also defined as being the certainty that the information within an organization is reliable, secure and private, while information security assurance is considered as a discipline integrating several techniques that ensure the integrity and availability of stored data. Looking at these definitions, we can conclude that information assurance is possible only if a good level of security exists.

Information Assurance can be characterized by the following criteria:

- Reliability;
- Accuracy;
- Security;
- Availability.

1   *Oxford English Dictionary Online*; available at http://dictionary.oed.com/
2   For example, as found at http://wordnet.princeton.edu/

The information assurance objectives are information systems protection, attack detection, and the measures to respond to attacks, known as reaction measures. In this framework these measures are considered within the information security function itself. This is the reason why we have chosen to evaluate the information security function based on the information security controls and measures in place. The need for an information assurance process comes from two main catalysts, namely:

- New regulations;
- Constant risk; by "constant" is meant continuous, scalable and dynamic.

This is the case for most operational technological environments and is introduced in current organizational structures and business models.

Another concept, namely *reasonable assurance*, has been advanced by the Sarbanes-Oxley Act.[3] The idea is to closely monitor the usage of digital assets internally as a result of two requirements: one resulting from Section 404 requiring a system of documented internal controls, and the other resulting from Section 302, requiring legal and direct responsibility of the Chief Executive Officer (CEO) and Chief Financial Officer (CFO) for internal control weaknesses.

3.3.2 Information security assurance concept

Insecurity is the norm, according to Bruce Schneier in his book *Schneier on Security*.[4] As such, the assurance question is the cornerstone of discussions of security, which do not specifically relate to the absolute strength of the information security system/program in place but are rather based on a panorama of the security issues based on a certain level of confidence. In this way all the activities that have been performed or will be undertaken are based on a sound knowledge of the potential scope of problems.

Schneier puts forward the idea that assurance is about confidence building activities, demonstrating that:

- The internal policies are consistent and reflect the requirements;
- There exist sufficient information security functions supporting the policy;
- The information security functions meet a desired set of properties;
- The information security functions are correctly implemented;
- Assurance can be obtained through the manufacturing, delivery and life cycle of the system.

Information security assurance is closely related to the concept of confidence that depends on security related properties and functionalities as well as on operational and administrative procedures. In the same way, there is a relationship between the assurance concept and confidence, specifying that assurance is a measure of confidence in the accuracy of a risk or security measurement. In this way we can derive the argument that a high assurance level equals a high security level and/or a low risk level. Considering that assurance is closely related to confidence and this is a difficult element to measure, we can conclude that testing and measuring the security level means already having reached a high level of assurance.

As we have previously specified, *security assurance* is defined as the harmonization of the components of information security. In fact, in order to support assurance, the information

---

3   "Sarbanes and Oxley Act 2002," Congress of the USA, 2002.
4   Schneier, B., *Schneier on Security*, Wiley Publishing, Inc. 2008.

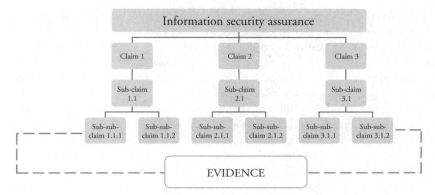

Fig. 3.4 Information security assurance nested structure.

security requirements should conform to the security needs, the information security policy should conform to the information security requirements, and information security functions should conform to the information security policy. Based on the arguments mentioned above, the cornerstone of the assurance concept from a security point of view is the set of security requirements or expected outputs. In order to provide evidence, requirements must include a set of claims related to each information security activity property according to a nested structure, as we propose in Figure 3.4. These claims are supported by evidence in the form of documentation.

This reasoning ensues from the logical relationship between trust (representing the finality of our evaluation model) and assurance, which is the path that leads to the trust. As mentioned above, the trust is the belief in the reliability or the ability of a subject to provide a given and expected result. The notion of the assurance encompasses the accuracy of the measurements to be taken in order to bring confidence in the subject. The confidence could then lead to trust in the subject, in our case information security. To summarize, the subject provides some expected results (which means that it inspires trust) when confidence is given that the subject's constituent elements are accurately evaluated (responding thus to an assurance level).

From a more microscopic perspective, each claim involves different subjects and predicates. A subject is categorized into: people, process, environment, technology and enterprise, while predicates are the characteristics of each subject. In other words, in order to gain assurance, which means that safeguards function as intended, the path below should be followed:

Assurance → Argument → Claim → Evidence.

3.3.3 Information security assurance principles

Usually security assurance is an engineering concept; as such it has to respond to an engineering structure (as described below), and at the same time has to be in accordance with engineering principles as acknowledged in most security-related international standards.[5]

---

5   ISO/IEC 15408-2:2008, Information technology – Security techniques – Evaluation criteria for IT security – Part 2: Security functional components International Organization for Standardization (ISO), Switzerland, 2008.
ISO/IEC 15408-3:2008, Information technology – Security techniques – Evaluation criteria for IT security – Part 3: Security assurance components, International Organization for Standardization (ISO), Switzerland, 2008.
ISO/IEC 15408-1:2009, Information technology – Security techniques – Evaluation criteria for IT security – Part 1: Introduction and general model, International Organization for Standardization (ISO), Switzerland, 2009.

In order to be believable and realistic, it has to be accepted that zero risk does not exist and consequently absolute security does not exist either. This is the *first principle*. Implementing safeguards means increasing resistance, and thus "buying some time" in order to stop an attack. In the same sense, another important principle, the *second principle* of security assurance, is that there should be a series of overlapping layers of information security controls and countermeasures that provide the assurance that the attack will be countered. This is known as the protection in depth principle and is illustrated in Figure 3.5. Information security controls and countermeasures should take into account all available means of ensuring protection and limiting damages and losses, such as prevention, detection and response safeguards, that are based on different layers offering the desired level of Information Assurance (IA). As stated above, information security assurance is closely related to the security requirements that allow evaluators to review the evidence and thus gain confidence and trust. *The third principle* states that information security depends on two types of requirements: functional and assurance. This means doing the right things in the right way. *The fourth principle* delimits the information security scope, which is the protection of availability, confidentiality and integrity.

A multidimensional structure concerning the concept of assurance itself allows the categorization of information security assurance in three groups of dimensions:

- *Direct dimensions* representing a level of confidence in the target of assurance itself;
- *Indirect dimensions* representing the way to examine evidence about the direct dimension;
- *Discrete dimensions* representing elements helping to organize evidence into logical groups.

To take an example to illustrate this multidimensional structure, we can consider the *organizational dimension* of information security. Based on our model:

- The direct dimension could be the *information security governance*;
- The indirect dimension could be the *assignment of responsibilities*;
- The discrete dimension could be the *information security control measures* in terms of technical or operational measures, human related measures, and the associated metrics.

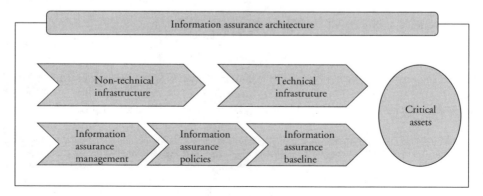

Fig. 3.5 A defence in depth approach.

Three views to be taken into account in order to understand a complex system and claim its trustworthy character can also be proposed:

- The *structural view* that concerns the interrelated elements of the system and the way they fit together;
- The *piecewise view* that concerns the identification of the smallest relevant part of a problem;
- The *synoptic view* considering the system as a whole.

ISAAM evaluation model, presented in 3.12, takes into consideration this point of view through the proposed assurance structure that divides information security into dimensions according to their nature, *focus areas* according to the security issues, and *specific factors* according to the element addressing the issue.

3.3.4 Trust as an assurance related concept

It is very important to analyze the trust concept in the domain of information security since trust is considered as crucial wherever risk, uncertainty or interdependence exists. Three concepts are closely related with trust; these are attitude, belief and behaviour. In order to evaluate or even assess the security level of a given organization there are three elements capable of holistically indicating a high-level security view.

- The first is the *trusting stance* – the general assumption that a better outcome is achieved by dealing with people as though they are well meaning and reliable;
- The second is the *structural assurance* – success is likely because guaranties, contracts, regulations, promises, legal recourse, process or procedures are in place;
- The third is *trusting belief predictability* – if somebody believes that the other's actions are consistent enough, he can forecast them in a given situation.

The question one has to answer while evaluating a subject such as information security systems is how to demonstrate (in order to gain confidence) that all these requirements for the existence of process and procedures, their reliability and predictability, really exist. Trust could be gained based on the ability to effectively understand and communicate the security goals, where these goals encompass the intentions, aims, tasks, deadlines, purposes and objectives. In order to build confidence in the information security system in place, one should possess some clear security requirements specifications and adopt a clear planned and controllable attitude. Evidence should not be provided without some clearly defined objectives. Within the TCSEC standard[6] it is stated that there should necessarily exist a statement of requirements in order to consider a computer system as being secure. The underlying idea is that there are components making up the system that are likely to meet a defined and communicated purpose.

When discussing information security issues a distinction has to be made between trusted and trustworthy. A system could be considered as trusted when it provides predictable and reliable behaviour, whereas the trustworthy concept considers the cases where the information security policy is not enforced. A system is judged as being trustworthy when it meets the security requirements set out in the security policies. Both concepts of trusted

---

6   Department of Defense (USA). *Department of Defense Trusted Computer System Evaluation Criteria* (TCSEC), Washington, USA, 1985.

and trustworthy will depend in the end on the roots-of-trust. As a result of this, in order to gain confidence in an information security system the first action to be taken is to identify the roots-of-trust of every information security related dimension, and then to evaluate every element following the formal structure of the defence in depth schema.

The trust model incorporates security (only technical issues are considered), privacy, safety, usability, reliability and availability, which are all integral components and objectives of an information security system as defined in this book. The *paradigm* of trusted computed systems holds that trust is a property of a system that could be assessed according to a given set of standards with respect to some domain of action. If this is true, trust can be formally modelled, specified and verified. This could be achieved by a formal method of evaluation of the information security assurance, as will be demonstrated below.

To summarize, it is impossible to state that a confidence structure will allow a system to be trusted. For that an assurance structure should be devised. Building a system based on assurance properties provides important benefits for the organization, which are focused on three main categories:

- *Operational benefits* rising from resilient business processes, improved costumer service, better information usage, improved responsiveness;
- *Tactical benefits* rising from easier compliance, better control, better understanding of the opportunities, and the commitment of business partners and customers;
- *Strategic benefits* rising from better governance, cheaper equity, lower costs, etc.

3.4 Information security assurance for a culture of security

On July 2002 the Organization for Economic Co-operation and Development (OECD) published guidelines for the security of information systems and networks[7]. Within this publication, information security is considered in a holistic way as part of a very large framework where many elements are enumerated. This means that under the assumption that the security level will be as strong as its weakest link, the idea of evaluating all security components (both technical non-technical) contributes to minimizing the likelihood of the existence of a breach causing harm or to minimizing the impact of the harm itself. Through this section we attempt to apply the logic path (assurance → argument → claim → evidence) to a high level document such as the OECD Principles of Security Culture. The document sets out eight security principles as a framework for considering security issues regrouped into three main categories, namely:

1. *Foundation principles*
   - Awareness
   - Responsibility
   - Response
2. *Social principles*
   - Ethics
   - Democracy

---

7   OECD, "OECD Guidelines for the Security of Information Systems and Networks: towards a culture of security". Organization for Economic Co-operation and Development, Paris 2002. Available at: http://www.oecd.org/document/42/0,3343,en_21571361_36139259_15582250_1_1_1_1,00.html

3. Security lifecycle principles
- Risk assessment
- Security design and implementation
- Security management
- Reassessment.

OECD guidelines give a macroscopic view of the principal information security concerns and treat information security in a holistic way. Using the assurance model presented in the Systems Security Engineering Capability Maturity Model (SSE-CMM)[8], OCDE security principles could be conceptualized in the following manner:

Argument: AWARENESS
Claim 1: *Personnel issues*
Evidence 1:
- Top-down leadership
- Recruitment importance related to information security
- Training
Claim 2: *Security awareness and education*
Evidence 2:
- Mandatory security training with appropriate frequency
- Taking into consideration external stakeholders

Argument: RESPONSIBILITY
Claim 1: *Management involvement*
Evidence 1:
- The existence of different security related functions at different levels
- The existence of processes and mechanisms to evaluate security
Claim 2: *Security policy*
Evidence 2:
- Information security holistically considered
- Dedicated personnel to develop and maintain the security policy
- A procedural and documented security policy

Argument: RESPONSE
Claim 1: *Incident handling and response*
Evidence 1:
- Responsibilities and procedures for a fast and effective response
- Reporting procedures
- Incident handling training for employees
Claim 2: *Cooperation and data sharing*
Evidence 2:
- Sharing through designated employees and procedures
- Data anonymization

---

8   ISSEA, *Systems Security Engineering Capability Maturity Model (SSE-CMM)*, International Systems Security Engineering Association (ISSEA), 2003.

Claim 3: *Business continuity and disaster recovery*
Evidence 3:
- BCP/DRP existence
- BCP/DRP tests and updates

Argument: ETHICS and DEMOCRACY
Claim 1: *Ethics*
Evidence 1:
- Compliance with relevant security best practices, legal and regulatory obligations.
- Acceptable policies and practices

Claim 2: *Democracy*
Evidence 2:
- Policies, practices and procedures are compatible with values
- Internal monitoring
- Openness and transparency in order to convey trust.

Argument: RISK and RISK ASSESSMENT
Claim 1: *Risk mitigation*
Evidence 1:
- Identification, prioritization, and action plans periodically reviewed
- Multilevel risk analysis

Argument: SECURITY DESIGN and IMPLEMENTATION
Claim 1: *Designed-in Security*
Evidence 1:
- Integrate security in a product or system development process
- Pre-established security requirements

Claim 2: *Solutions implementation*
Evidence 2:
- Security products related to the organization's needs
- Well designed security planning

Claim 3: *Use of Best Practices and Standards*
Evidence 3:
- Compliance with commonly accepted industry best practices
- Third party evaluation

Argument: SECURITY MANAGEMENT
Claim 1: *Roles and responsibilities*
Evidence 1:
- Accordance between responsibilities and job role
- Segregation of duties
- Updates related to job responsibilities and privileges
- Co-operation between different functions

Claim 2: *Information classification*
Evidence 2:
- Information inventory and classification
- Protection in accordance with information sensitivity

Argument: REASSESSMENT
Claim 1: *Continued effectiveness*
Evidence 1:
* Third party scrutiny
* Regular reviews and assessment

3.5 Lessons learned from the current methodologies related to the information security assurance structure

3.5.1 The Information System Security Assurance Architecture (ISSAA) standard

The Information System Security Assurance Architecture (ISSAA) standard[9] is a risk management process framework for determining and implementing acceptable security controls based on a set or family of risk-management functional components. A System Under Review (SUR) is defined and its boundaries are determined. For the functional components specified within the ISSAA standard see Figure 3.6. The proposed IEEE Information System Security Assurance Architecture (ISSAA) standard specifies the architecture of a systematic approach for managing the health/state of the security controls of an information system without describing the functional characteristics of each component.

Fig. 3.6 A risk management framework example adapted from IEEE-Std. 1700.

---

9   IEEE-Std. 1700, IEEE P 1700: Information System Security Assurance Architecture (ISSAA) Standard, IEEE, USA 2008.

The ISSAA standard recommends the existence of a Master Control Catalogue (MCC) composed of some families regrouping the specific controls. The standard recommends that every organization should possess its own MCC. Every specific security control specifies what function the control is intended to perform. A control is defined as being policies, procedures, practices and organizational structures that allow business objectives to be achieved (Figure 3.7).

The ISSAA standard is focused on a given element (the "functional component") that is subject to the evaluation. This security assurance-related standard fulfils the fundamental requirement to consider the ongoing properties of a system, such as information security. The standard considers all changes occurring within the information system that impact security, environmental factors, the passing of time, and the control's efficiency. The standard fully complies with the PDCA model recommended by the widespread standard ISO/IEC 27001:2005[10] for information security management systems.

As shown in Figure 3.6, the first step of the ISSAA standard,[11] is the *security categorization*. This step concerns a security-focused categorization in order to prioritize the most valuable assets and their protection. This component corresponds to the idea of asset inventory required by many other regulations.

After that, the second step is the *security control selection component*. In this stage we go through an asset categorization characterized by security objectives (availability, integrity, confidentiality)[12] to a security control categorization regrouping all the assets corresponding to the same security objective.[13] This stage could be considered as the first moment when the

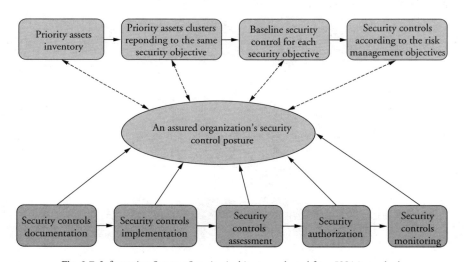

Fig. 3.7 Information Systems Security Architecture adapted from ISSAA standard.

---

10   ISO/IEC 27001:2005, Information technology – Security techniques – Information security management systems – Requirements, International Organization for Standardization (ISO), Switzerland, 2005.
11   For more information see Annex 2.
12   Also called Security Categorization Triple (SCT); Source:
      IEEE-Std. 1700, IEEE P 1700: Information System Security Assurance Architecture (ISSAA) Standard, IEEE, USA 2008.
13   Also called Single Security Category Value (SSCV); Ibid.

evaluation begins to be formalized. During the security control selection component a set of baseline security controls are selected corresponding to the first set of assurance requirements.

This stage allows the procedure to go to the next stage, named *security control supplement component,* that aims to perform a risk assessment process. In this stage security controls become more specific. During this stage a target set of security controls to be implemented are identified and variables such as threats, vulnerabilities and residual risk are assessed.

At this point a security controls structure and posture has been defined. This leads to the other component of the ISSAA, which is the *security control documentation component.* The objective is the development of an information systems security plan entailing the security requirements, security controls (that have been planned or are in place), the key security documents,[14] and responsibilities.

The *security control implementation* is the other component of an assured Information Security, which will be based on the security plan defined during the previous steps. This component ensures that formal implementation documents are provided, leading thus to obtaining results and evidence from tests that verify that assurance requirements are met.

The next component is the *security authorization component* implying the assessment of the risk level after the implementation of the security measures in order to take the decision to operate or not. The decision to operate will mean that the risk level, after the application of all security measures, is considered as acceptable.

The last component is the *security control monitoring component* providing continuous monitoring in an improvement scope. Monitoring could be performed by using different techniques such as security reviews, self-assessment, security testing and evaluation.

3.5.2 Common Criteria (CC) and its predecessors' approach to assurance issues

Other sets of standards for evaluating the level of security exist within the literature. The evaluation is performed by considering security mechanisms from a technical point of view in terms of strength, accuracy and other criteria. The evaluation consists of formal methods based on a number of evaluation criteria in order to show that a security mechanism fulfils all the requirements according to the predefined assurance level. Historically individual countries or groups of countries had their own evaluation criteria and requirements, a situation that resulted in different stages of assurance levels. That was the case with the European Community and USA and their local standards.[15] The need to harmonize the evaluation criteria and related procedures to obtain the assurance level has led to a widespread certification procedure, called Common Criteria (CC). The CC has led to the three following international standards:

- ISO/IEC 15408-2:2008, Information technology – Security techniques – Evaluation criteria for IT security – Part 2: Security functional components International Organization for Standardization (ISO), Switzerland, 2008.

---

14   Such as operations, security policies and regulations, disaster planning, contingency planning etc. Ibid.

15   Department of Defense (USA). Department of Defense Trusted Computer System Evaluation Criteria (TCSEC), Washington, USA, 1985.
    Office for Official Publications of the European Communities. Information Technology Security Evaluation Criteria (ITSEC), Luxembourg, 1991.

- ISO/IEC 15408-3:2008, Information technology – Security techniques – Evaluation criteria for IT security – Part 3: Security assurance components, International Organization for Standardization (ISO), Switzerland, 2008.
- ISO/IEC 15408-1:2009, Information technology – Security techniques – Evaluation criteria for IT security – Part 1: Introduction and general model, International Organization for Standardization (ISO), Switzerland, 2009.

In order to ensure the delivery of a secure and reliable service, a security tool has to fulfil all the security requirements relating to the security target. ITSEC,[16] for example, identifies three security attributes:

- *Security objective* that represents the desired functionality the security mechanism is supposed to provide;
- *Security enforcement function* that represents the functionality the security mechanism must provide;
- The *security mechanism* representing how the functionality is provided.

The general idea within these different standards is that in order to provide assurance over a security feature, procedure, or architecture (generally called a target of evaluation), the target has to be broken down into many other components representing given functionalities and expected behaviours. Functionalities and the expected behaviour should fulfil the security requirements. Assurance is reached when evidence is provided that the security feature, procedure or architecture meets the expectations.

Security expectations concern a range of goals passing from a generic or a high level scope, generally called *security objectives,* to a more concrete level, which are the *security requirements.* Evidence can be provided when two conditions are in place:

- The auditability, which means the possibility to verify the activity;
- The accountability, which means the possibility to hold individuals responsible.

ITSEC also considers security requirements based on policies, functionality, effectiveness, and strength. From a TCSEC point of view the source of the Security Requirements still remains the security policy. Nevertheless TCSEC emphasizes the subject to be protected and its requirements in terms of prioritization, access issues and accountability, which itself relies on audits, records and other relevant elements. Focusing the evaluation process on the requirement component underlines the idea that a previous analysis has been performed of the security feature, procedure or architecture under evaluation.

To sum up, assurance arguments should include the following components:

1. *Claims,* which is the particular property defining the subject of the evaluation and the functional requirements;
2. *Evidence* representing empirical data that will contribute to the believability;
3. *Reasoning,* which will link the evidence to the claims;
4. *Assumption zone,* which delimits the space where claims are accepted without evidence.

---

16 Office for Official Publications of the European Communities. Information Technology Security Evaluation Criteria (ITSEC), Luxembourg, 1991.

The system under evaluation is then split into logically related components and sub-components in order to provide a formal structure. The formal structure is required to assure that all relevant components are considered and are subject to the evaluation. Thus the security subject under evaluation is dissected into classes, families, components and elements (Figure 3.8) according to Common Criteria (CC), which provides assurance through active investigation.[17]

The underlying principle is that information security must be embraced from the beginning of the design of a security mechanism. For doing that the CC proposes two kinds of security requirements:

- Security functional requirements;
- Security assurance requirements.

Security Functional Requirements include the requirements for the security mechanism under evaluation, which will satisfy the security objectives for the IT environment where the mechanisms will operate. It maintains a semi-formal structure composed of classes, families and components.

A functional class describes a common approach to satisfy security objectives, while a family addresses a specific security problem that will be solved by the family's components.

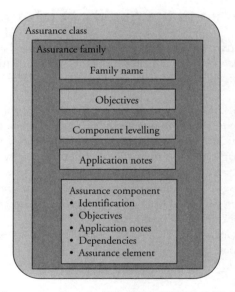

Fig. 3.8 Example of an assurance hierarchy adapted from ISO/IEC 15408-3:2008, Information technology – Security techniques – Evaluation criteria for IT security – Part 3: Security assurance components, International Organization for Standardization (ISO), Switzerland, 2008.

---

17   ISO/IEC 15408-2:2008, Information technology – Security techniques – Evaluation criteria for IT security – Part 2: Security functional components International Organization for Standardization (ISO), Switzerland, 2008. ISO/IEC 15408-3:2008, Information technology – Security techniques – Evaluation criteria for IT security – Part 3: Security assurance components, International Organization for Standardization (ISO), Switzerland, 2008. ISO/IEC 15408-1:2009, Information technology – Security techniques – Evaluation criteria for IT security – Part 1: Introduction and general model, International Organization for Standardization (ISO), Switzerland, 2009.

On the other hand, the Security Assurance Requirements aim to specify the security requirements that the security mechanism under evaluation must contain in order to be trusted.

According to CC, assurance objectives could be reached by using the following techniques:

- Mere existence of necessary and mandatory processes and procedures;
- Verification of the implementation of the processes and procedures;
- The conformity between the processes and procedures in place and the security objectives;
- The existence of tests in order to evaluate the security mechanism and the analysis of their results;
- A formalized documentation of all these activities;
- Elements of evidence concerning all these claims.

To summarize, classes are a group of families sharing the same focus, families are a group of components that share a similar goal but may differ in emphasis or rigour, while a component is the smallest selectable set of elements on which requirements are based and an element is an indivisible statement of security need.

3.6 Issues related to the quality of information security

Quality is a very important aspect of information security viewed as a service. Within this book we defend the idea that without quality properties, an information security system cannot be considered as dependable. As such the evaluation model should necessarily include the aspect of quality.

ISO 9000:2005 defines quality as the degree to which a set of inherent characteristics fulfils requirements (Figure 3.9).[18] In order to be successfully operated a process needs to be controlled in a systematic manner. At this stage, a process is defined as a set of interrelated or interacting activities that transforms inputs into outputs. A quality approach requires considering the stakeholders' requirements, the definition of the processes in order to fulfil those requirements, and the way to keep these processes under control. Transforming this perspective into an Information Security Quality (ISQ) oriented assessment means that there are three existing dimensions that must be assessed:

- Security requirements;
- Security processes;
- Security control.

Dealing with the quality concept from a "process approach" point of view, ISO 9001:2000[19] puts the accent on continual improvement for a quality management system via a PDCA-like model including:

- Management responsibility;

---

[18]   ISO 9000:2005, Quality Management Systems – Fundamentals and Vocabulary, International Organization for Standardization (ISO), Switzerland, 2005.

[19]   ISO 9001:2000, Quality Management Systems – Requirements, International Organization for Standardization (ISO), Switzerland, 2000.

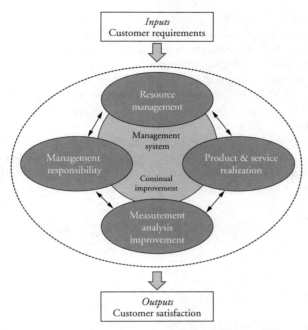

Fig. 3.9 Model of a process-based quality management system adapted from ISO 9000:2005, Quality Management Systems – Fundamentals and Vocabulary, International Organization for Standardization (ISO), Switzerland, 2005.

- Resource management;
- Product realization;
- Measurement analysis and improvement.

Quality is the act of meeting the objectives and standards in place. Quality can also be seen as a measure of meeting expectations and conforming to requirements. Evidence of quality is shown by the fact that the design is appropriate, the implementation is careful, and the subject under evaluation meets all the requirements. The quality evaluation of a subject (process, system, or procedure) involves performance measurements such as latency, reliability and availability.

In order to provide a quality management system according to ISO 9001:2000, an organization has to identify the processes constituting the system as well as the interactions that exist between them. After that it becomes mandatory to set up criteria for evaluation as well as to monitor, measure, analyze, and set up continual improving processes. After all, the general concept of ISO 9001 and ISO 9004 is to give the assurance that the needs (of customers) are met.

The Control Objectives for Information and related Technology (COBIT)[20] state that quality management, from an output point of view, is a process that impacts the effectiveness,

---

20   ISACA & ITGI, Control Objectives for Information and related Technology (COBIT) Information Systems Audit and Control Association and IT Governance Institute, 2007. Available at http://www.isaca.org/Template.cfm?Section=COBIT6&Template=/TaggedPage/TaggedPageDisplay.cfm&TPLID=55&ContentID=7981

efficiency, integrity, and availability of Information Systems. To do this, a prior business process analysis is needed, alongside a cartography of the services provided by each of the business processes, as well as the main requirements ensuing from the relevant Service Level Agreements (SLA). Broadly speaking, the quality of a service is about the ability to deliver the service, or it can simply be expressed as the availability of the service. A logical consequence of this statement is the fact that the security level of the service will be the degree of security with respect to the assurance. From this point of view the attribute of security becomes one of the quality attributes of the service.

Four different views of quality can be distinguished, when speaking about information quality, that is to say intrinsic, contextual, representational, and accessibility quality. Considering information security as the subject under evaluation and as a process, the intrinsic view seems to be the most appropriate view. In this direction, the intrinsic view should represent the following attributes:

- Accuracy;
- Completeness;
- Consistency;
- Reliability;
- Precision;
- Flexibility;
- Efficiency;
- Ease-of-use.

When considering information security as a system other attributes might still be considered. A quality management system is a set of rules or principles permitting the *continual improvement of performance.* Quality performance includes quality planning, contract review, design, purchasing, training and servicing. Six quality factors can be identified when handling the information security policy issue from a quality point of view:

- Functionality – existence of the functions required to perform;
- Maintainability – ease to maintain the system;
- Portability – ability to be transferred from one environment to another;
- Efficiency – amount of resources to perform the required functions;
- Reliability – capability to maintain performance;
- Usability – time and resources required to effectively use the subject.

Based on the ISO definition of quality assurance,[21] the quality is based on its specifications including its particular and essential character, the inherent features, the degree of excellence, the superiority in kind, and its distinguishing attributes. This is why it is very important to add the quality dimension when evaluating the information security posture. It is a high level evaluation that distinguishes organizations with an intrinsic need for integration security behaviour from those that perform information security activities as a patch only to ensure compliance with mandatory regulations or laws. The first type of organization should be considered as one that has a security attitude, the second as an organization that does not. The quality assurance comprises all the planned and systematic actions necessary to provide adequate confidence that a structure, system or component will perform satisfactorily

---

[21]   The totality of the features and characteristics of a product or service that bears on its ability to satisfy needs.

in service.[22] Moreover, another dependent variable can be introduced, the *service quality*, which holds the following attributes:

- Assurance;
- Empathy;
- Responsiveness.

Quality assurance involves the commitment of the executive level managers, the establishment of a managerial culture, which means that stakeholders could report the conditions of the risk. In the same way the main objective of a quality service or process is how to manage instances of non-conformity regarding a given objective and how to control the safeguards that are supposed to prevent the non-conforming event from happening. In other words, quality is also about documentation, inspection and testing, incident management, and crisis management. For doing that, a system of measurement ensuring a continuous improvement is needed. In terms of quality related to the safety concept, that quality is attained by improving the process continually.

When considering quality issues related to information security, attention can be focussed on the implementation attribute and here we propose a ten level model based on the ISO/IEC 27001 PDCA model. Within the process implementation model,[23] the quality of information security is mainly expressed from an organizational and managerial point of view. When evaluating the quality of an audit process four dimension of quality can be taken into account. These are:

- The management, related to the place of the identification of roles and responsibilities within the process under evaluation;
- The planning, related to forward planning conforming with a standard or a set of rules;
- The execution, related to the conformity of the process to a standard or a set of rules;
- The improvement, related to the continuous review and control.

3.6.1 The PDCA Model

The Plan-Do-Check-Act (PDCA) model is an integral part of quality management, considered as a continuous feedback loop to identify and reduce variations. The main idea of the PDCA model is to ensure a continual improvement of the process. The PDCA model (Figure 3.10) is the result of four actions, namely:[24]

- *Plan:* the establishment of the objectives in terms of contexts, policies and approaches.

---

22   U.S. NRC, "Quality Assurance Criteria for Nuclear Power Plants and Fuel Reprocessing Plants," in RC Regulations Title 10, Code of Federal Regulations: Requirements binding on all persons and organizations who receive a license from NRC to use nuclear materials or operate nuclear facilities, United States Nuclear Regulatory Commission, Ed.

23   More information about the model can be found in B. Barafort, J.-P. Humbert, and S. Poggi, "Information Security Management and ISO/IEC 15504: The link opportunity between Security and Quality," in Proceedings of the Sixth International Software Process Improvement and Capability Determination (SPICE) Conference, Luxembourg, 2006.

24   ISO/IEC 27001:2005, Information Technology – Security Techniques – Information Security Management Systems – Requirements, International Organization for Standardization (ISO), Switzerland, 2005.

- *Do:* the implementation of the process on the basis of a documented plan of action, the identification of selected controls. The Do stage makes it possible to establish the basis for measuring the effectiveness of the security program in place.
- *Check:* the use of monitoring and measurement processes to detect errors, identify possible security breaches, and to identify acceptable levels of risk. The Check stage makes it possible to measure the effectiveness of the security program in place.
- *Act:* the process of taking actions to continually improve the process.

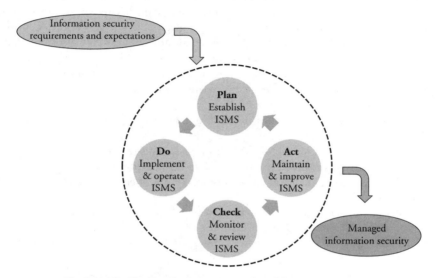

Fig. 3.10 The Plan-Do-Check-Act process adapted from ISO/IEC 27001.

There are four system areas to consider when looking at aspects of quality:
- Management activity: covering the existence of management commitment via policies, objectives, and planning. This requirement could be captured by the attribute number one of our model.
- Process approach management: covering the measurement approach to every process, which implicitly could be proved by the attribute number three of our model. Documenting a process gives the possibility to measure its performance under the assumption that the first attribute is (concerning policies and objectives) performed.
- Customer satisfaction: in our case, the customers will be all the end-users of the organization's Information Systems. For that a monitored and audited system, based on the objectives, could ensure that the requirements are fulfilled.
- Continual improvement: the PDCA model itself.

3.6.2 Security quality issues within the good practices for information security (ISF)

Quality attributes such as top management commitment, allocation of appropriate resources, and system design meeting the requirements, are also analyzed within the standard of good practices for information security (ISF),[25] particularly within the security management and systems development aspects. The choice of these two dimensions amongst the others existing within the ISF is determined by taking into account the two main requirements of the quality attributes mentioned in the paragraph below. Firstly, the security management aspect of security treated within the ISF tests the top management's commitment across the enterprise, as well as the allocation of the appropriate resources. The top management commitment assumes a double function: (1) allowing the information security function to take an important place in the centre of the organization and among all the operational levels; (2) enabling the information security function to increase its quality level. The system development aspect covers the coherent development as whole, ensuring that given criteria (in our case information security) are addressed at each stage of the cycle. This results in a robust system on which the organization can depend.

The ISF defines quality assurance as the process that provides assurance that the security requirements are defined, agreed, developed and met by the system under evaluation. Another requirement to be taken into account is the co-ordination of security activities and thus the assignment of responsibilities. Indeed, every system considered as being robust should have individual responsibilities defined. This is in order to ensure that security activities are carried out in a timely and accurate manner. After that, a thorough and regular security audit should be performed in order to enhance the quality level of the information security function. This activity will assess the status of the activity and ensure that security controls are designed effectively. By effectiveness is meant the ability of the system to provide the required output.

3.6.3 Assessing and evaluating the quality of the information security system

After having analyzed all these aspects related to the concept of quality with respect to a system or a process we can state that quality is determined by the following two points:
- An assurance-like structure regarding the information security function;
- Continuous improvement based on measurement against objectives.

Continuous improvement recalls the PDCA approach set out in ISO/IEC 27001:2005. The improvement process is the underpinning of *total quality management*. The idea of process improvement according to ISO 9000:2005 assimilates in itself the ability of the process to achieve overall success.

Considering all these aspects and in order to provide a quality system, the information security program of a given organization should consider the following attributes:
- The existence within the information security policy of the information security dimension issues for each family and class → claiming the availability attribute of a quality process = value 1.[26]

---

25   ISF-std. *The Standard of Good Practice for Information Security*, Information Security Forum, 2007.

26   There is a clear correlation between the security quality and the existence of the security controls within the security policy, according to the survey proposed by W. Baker and L. Wallace, "Is Information Security Under Control? Investigating Quality in Information Security Management," *IEEE Security & Privacy* vol. 5 (1), pp. 36-44, 2007.

- A designated person responsible for each focus area → claiming the responsibility attribute of a quality process = value 2.
- A documented information security for each group of specific factors → claiming the implementation attribute of a quality process = value 3.
- A monitored and audited component for each group of specific factors → claiming the effectiveness attribute of a quality process = value 4.

It should be noticed that the evidence values go from a high level perspective (evidence level 1, considering the dimensions) to more specific ones (such as the evidence value 4, considering the specific factors). As such, a quality average weighting level for each dimension (QL_N) could be determined, based on the observation of the evidence:

$$QL_N \in \{1 \rightarrow 4\}$$

Then, if needed, an overall information security system quality index (ISQ_i) could be calculated in order to measure the improvement level, or even to determine the current state of the quality related properties, where QL_N will represent the quality index of each dimension with 16 as the maximum value which can be attained, that is to say an evidence value equal to 4 for all the four classes.

$$ISQ_i = \left(\sum_{\text{Dimension } 1}^{4} QL_N \right) \div 16$$

It emerges from this formula that subsequent values for evidence cannot be reached if the previous one is not fully satisfied. This is because our model considers information security from a holistic point of view, thus prioritizing transversal values rather than a silo approach. This is based on the idea that the information security is a whole process rather than the sum of the different components.

3.7 Information security requirements based on maturity models

3.7.1 State of the art with respect to information security maturity levels

Before the construction of our model, the authors performed a literature search on *maturity models* already in use in order to leverage the existing know-how in this field. The maturity models that were chosen for review were selected on the basis of their use of the three main axes of evaluation, namely the *information security structure*, the *information security system* quality and the *information security requirements*.

There are many maturity models dedicated to the information security domain, but our analysis was focused on five of them, namely the CobiT maturity model,[27] Information

---

[27]   ISACA & ITGI, Control Objectives for Information and related Technology (COBIT) Information Systems Audit and Control Association and IT Governance Institute, 2007. Available at http://www.isaca.org/Template.cfm?Section=COBIT6&Template=/TaggedPage/TaggedPageDisplay.cfm&TPLID=55&ContentID=7981

Security Management Maturity Model (ISM3),[28] the Common Criteria Assurance Levels (CCAL),[29] the Systems Security Engineering Capability and Maturity Model (CMM)[30] and the Maturity Model for IT operations (MITO).[31]

For the structural and organizational part, the relevant maturity models used within this chapter are CobiT and ISM3. Both of these are focused on the management and governance dimension of information security. The first concerns the internal control system, while ISM3 concerns the operation of the key processes of the information security management system that are aligned with business objectives. CobiT's maturity model contains six levels and the ISM3 five levels. Considering the fact that a "non-existent" level is not eligible for our evaluation model, the first level of CobiT was not retained (see the next section). Despite the similar focus of these two maturity models on governance and security management, their point of view on security differs. CobiT is mostly focused on the way the internal controls are constructed and managed while ISM3 focuses on the existence or not of process metrics and the amount by which the security measures reduce security risks.

On the quality side, the CMM (both capability and maturity models) and MITO maturity model were studied. Regarding the CMM, both capability and maturity models were taken into account to analyse security process maturity. The capability and maturity levels of the process are very closely related since the capability model is related to the objectives in terms of security processes. The CMM maturity levels then take into account those objectives and use the content-related information to define the maturity levels. In that way the *level 1* of the capability model, identified as performed, corresponds to the level 1 of the maturity model, where the processes are considered as being chaotic. The second level identified as Managed corresponds to the *level 2* of the maturity model, where the security process are planned and executed according to certain objectives. The third level identified as Defined corresponds to the *level 3* of the maturity model, where the information security human-related aspects are addressed through awareness activities. The fourth level of capability identified as quantitatively managed corresponds to the *level 4* of the maturity model, where information security controls measures are controlled and measured. Finally, the *fifth level* of capability, identified as optimised, includes the idea of continual improvement with respect to the maturity model. In the same way MITO identifies its five levels, following the same logic, moreover basing it on Maslow's hierarchy, which is: stochastic, repeatable, tracked, measured and optimised.

28   ISM³, "Information Security Management Maturity Model," ISM3 Consortium, Madrid, Spain 2007. Available at http://www.ism3.com/index.php?option=com_docman&task=cat_view&gid=1&Itemid=9

29   ISO/IEC 15408-2:2008, Information technology – Security techniques – Evaluation criteria for IT security – Part 2: Security functional components, International Organization for Standardization (ISO), Switzerland, 2008.

30   (a) ISSEA. Systems Security Engineering Capability Maturity Model (SSE-CMM), International Systems Security Engineering Association (ISSEA), 2003; (b) M. Lamnabhi, Evaluer avec CMMI – Etape par étape Paris, France: AFNOR Editions 2008; (c) G. J. v. d. Pijl, G. J. P. Swinkels, and J. G. Verrijdt, "ISO 9000 versus CMM: Standardization and certification of IS development," *Information & Management*, vol. 32 (6), pp. 267-274, 1997.

31   A. Q. Scheuing, K. Frühauf, and W. Schwarz, "Maturity Model for IT Operations (MITO)," in Proceeding of the 2nd World Congress on Software Quality, Yokohama, Japan, 2000.

Moreover, Gartner[32] proposes a de facto mechanism for measuring process and program maturity based on the CMMI.[33]

On the technical and operational side, we based our reflection on the Common Criteria Evaluation Assurance Levels (EAL). There are seven assurance levels defined within these. Without analyzing them in detail, three groups of actions could be distinguished in order to pass from one level to another. The first one considers the degree of knowledge regarding the security target, which constitutes the very first indicator of the protection level to be provided. The second group is about the structure and the inherent features of the security mechanism, that is to say the security system that will provide the necessary level of protection level for the target. The third group, which deals with the upper levels, takes into consideration attributes such as the testing, review and in depth analysis of the security mechanisms.

NIST in its assessment framework concerning security based on an assessment scope, commonly known as FITSAF,[34] categorizes the information security in five levels, and proposes a framework allowing the assessment of information security as shown in Figure 3.11.

The first and the second levels concern respectively a kind of baseline, which is some documented policy and procedures. By placing these two main requirements, NIST confirms the idea that a minimum basis should be put in place in order to allow an evaluation of the security function. Concerning the policy, the existence of the document is not even discussed; what is relevant in FITSAF's point of view is the fact that the policy should contain at least the general scope of information security as well as a framework which should concern the responsibilities and the compliance. A documented procedure should go more into depth on these three general focus points by specifying the IT security responsibilities as well as the structure of controls/measures in order to satisfy the scope of the information security policy.

The third level concerns the implementation of the controls and procedures. Evidence that proves the achievement of the implementation stage are, among others, the awareness

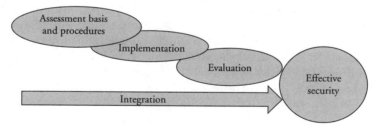

Fig. 3.11 Example of a conceptual assessment pathway – Adapted from NIST, *Federal Information Technology Security Assessment Framework (FITSAF)* Computer Security Division – National Institute of Standards and Technology – US Department of Commerce, 2000.

---

32   T. Scholtz and B. Burke, "Understanding the Maturity of Your Security Architecture Process "Gartner 2009. Available at http://www.gartner.com/technology/

33   See the following sources for more information related to maturity models of the information security architecture: T. Scholtz and B. Burke, "Understanding the Maturity of Your Security Architecture Process," Gartner 2009, http://www.gartner.com/technology/; T. Scholtz, "Toolkit Best Practices: Assessing Security and Risk Management Process Maturity," Gartner 2007, http://www.gartner.com/technology/

34   NIST, *Federal Information Technology Security Assessment Framework (FITSAF)*, Computer Security Division – National Institute of Standards and Technology – US Department of Commerce, 2000. [Online] Available at http://csrc.nist.gov/drivers/documents/Federal-IT-Security-Assessment-Framework.pdf

and education activities, meaning that the personnel consider the policy requirements. Another piece of evidence concerning the third level is the fact that security practices are adopted throughout the lifecycle of the system.

The fourth level is about the evaluation and test of the organizational aspects. Evidence is provided by an effective "evaluation program" based on the above-mentioned security requirements and characterized by their frequency. Another level of evidence concerns the reporting system and its industrialized nature. It is evident that an evaluation program could not be efficient without a reporting system in place capable of analyzing and reporting to the top levels all relevant security concerns. Besides these two aspects of evaluation, some proactive investigation activities related to vulnerabilities, risks and security incidents have to be adopted.

The fifth level of the FITSAF's organizational assessment framework concerns the full integration of the procedures and controls through all the organizational levels. Evidence could derive from the fact that the security program is spread out all over the organization and it is continually improved. In principle, according to NIST,[35] every important asset should have integrated security practices, and metrics concerning the security program should be established and met.

3.7.2 The holistic Information Security Assurance Assessment Model (ISAAM) maturity levels

The maturity model proposed is composed of five levels in order to match with the existing maturity models. The five levels defined by our ISAMM are: *fortuitous, structured, functional, analyzed,* and *effective*. It is important to underline at this stage that the proposed ISAMM is strictly related to the evaluation model itself, using the same variables that are utilized inside. The ISAMM does not include a "non-existent" level for two principal reasons. The first one is that because, as has been mentioned before, the maturity level has to be coherent with the model. It has already been specified that the proposed model can only be applied when some pre-requisites are achieved. The second reason is that a "non-existent" level would mean that the organization in question might have a risky attitude based on its own business objectives (profitability objectives). As such, there is no interest in applying such an evaluation model to fix a security level when no security is applied. For each level of maturity, considerations about the evaluation model components are defined in order to provide a homogenous maturity model. Level 1 and level 2 are characterized by the structure of the components of the security efforts and from level 3 the attention is mostly focused on the way the security activities are performed.

Level 1: Fortuitous

Existence of at least one dimension, but at a bare minimum the existence of the operational dimension is required. There are no identifiable and formal structures of focus areas that really exist, although some isolated specific factors may be perceived. This means that the existing security activities are instinctively performed within the organization. These security

---

35   NIST, *Federal Information Technology Security Assessment Framework (FITSAF)*, Computer Security Division – National Institute of Standards and Technology – US Department of Commerce, 2000. Available at http://csrc.nist.gov/drivers/documents/Federal-IT-Security-Assessment-Framework.pdf

activities take the form of some security measures applied as a result of mandatory requirements or basic needs for protection. Consequently information security is not at the managed process level; and as such no quality specification can be made. Generally speaking, an
organization which finds itself in a level 1 position does not display any proactive behaviour
regarding the protection of its assets.

Level 2: Structured

There is a clear and formal existence of all four information security dimensions, as shown
within the evaluation model. The formal existence of the security dimensions could be
claimed if some precise objectives regarding the dimensions were specified. Consequently,
the elements of the focus area mostly exist, as demanded by the best practices, as baseline
approaches and are described by the evaluation model. To each focus area, a minimum of
two specific factors are dedicated; often the "procedure/controls" and "resource" attributes
are assigned. The quality level reaches the first stage; that is to say, each dimension forms a
part of, and is considered within, the information security policy or any other information
security related document. Generally speaking, an organization that finds itself in a level 2
position may claim the existence of a security program.

Level 3: Functional

There is a complete information security architecture as described by the evaluation model.
That means that a clear structure exists in terms of the organizational, operational human
and legal dimensions. For each of the aforementioned criteria, the major parts of the focus
area are identified. This brings the organization to an accountability stage, where the organization has a clear understanding of the risks it may face and the related issues. Regarding the
specific factors, those related to the "procedure/controls" and "resources" must exist, because
of the accountability level claimed by the functional level. As mentioned before, from this
level information security is not only considered as an ensemble of countermeasures but as an
operational system composed of some defined and complete processes and procedures. For
this reason the average quality weighting level equals two, that is to say, for each dimension a
responsible person could be found.

Level 4: Analyzable

Organizations judged as having reached the fourth level of this maturity model should present
a completed architecture in terms of dimension and focus area. Based on the construction of
the evaluation model, it could be claimed that the organizations that have reached the fourth
level apply the major part of the requirements expected by the well-known information security standards and best practices. In that way it could be stated that the fourth level organization possesses a discernible managed information security system. Based on this, the average
quality weighting level clearly equals three, which means that specific factors are minimally
documented and monitored.

Level 5: Effective

This is the ultimate stage that the organizational information security system could reach,
incorporating continual improvement. As such, a completed architecture in terms of dimensions and focus area fully exists. Regarding the specific factors, all three attributes can be
discerned, namely the operational measures, appropriate human resources and the appropri-

ate procedures, as described in Section 3.2.5. The average quality weighting level attains the fourth level, meaning that a measurement system is running inside the organization. Reviews and audits are regularly performed to fix the current situation and future ones in information security terms, thus filling any existing gaps. A continual improvement procedure is imputed to each focus area.

This evaluation model might be implemented in cases where an organization has already deployed a set of well-documented control objectives, and controls and policies. For that, the processes and the security safeguards should necessarily and effectively be performed within the organization. The model proposed within the context of this chapter aims to be a semi-formal one, which means that a natural language is used. This is based on a specific method, imposing a rigorous structure on the processes. In the first stage, we chose to structure the information security program according to the Common Criteria modelling concept. This is because our objective is to evaluate the information security function, including the afore-mentioned four principal dimensions. The information security level of a given organization will derive from the performance quality of each one of these dimensions. In that way the objective to provide a holistic evaluation will be fulfilled.

As mentioned above, the assurance argument regarding a system under evaluation could be derived from a nested structure. For that reason the information security program is struc-tured in a nested manner including dimensions, focus areas for each dimension, and specific factors for each focus area. As we have seen above, the structural assurance is one of the condi-tions regarding the trust in a given system. This means that in order to gain assurance over the system, a formal structure describing all the components of the system is needed. This has to be performed from a general view of the system down to the most specific evidence compo-nents, which are the roots-of-trust corresponding to the different attributes within our model.

From a conceptual point of view, the information security program is the variable under evaluation. The different levels resulting from the evaluation will define the protection level of the organizational values. This variable has to be evaluated and assessed holistically. For that, the four dimensions of the variable are identified and analyzed.

Each of these dimensions includes different tools, namely the focus areas that are sets of activities corresponding to the same objective within the security program. Then a set of components for each focus area is identified representing the mechanism that permits the achievement of the security objective of the family, according to the classification made by the common criteria (Figure 3.12). Trust may be definded as the belief that proper impersonal structures are in place in order to enable one to anticipate a successful future endeavour.

This model fulfils the requirements of the IEEE standard for a software quality metrics methodology[36] as a basis to build up a measurement process. Moreover, in order to trust a given system based on the elements discussed, the model takes into account the main require-ments in order to understand a hierarchically structured system. For that purpose three views are needed:

- *Structural view:* concerning the architecture of the system and its interrelated ele-ments. In our case it concerns assured structure of the evaluation model;
- *Piecewise view:* concerning the smallest relevant parts of a system for a particular problem. In our case it concerns the specific factors considered also as being the roots-of-trust;

---

36   IEEE-Std. 1061, IEEE Standard for a Software Quality Metrics Methodology, IEEE, USA 1998.

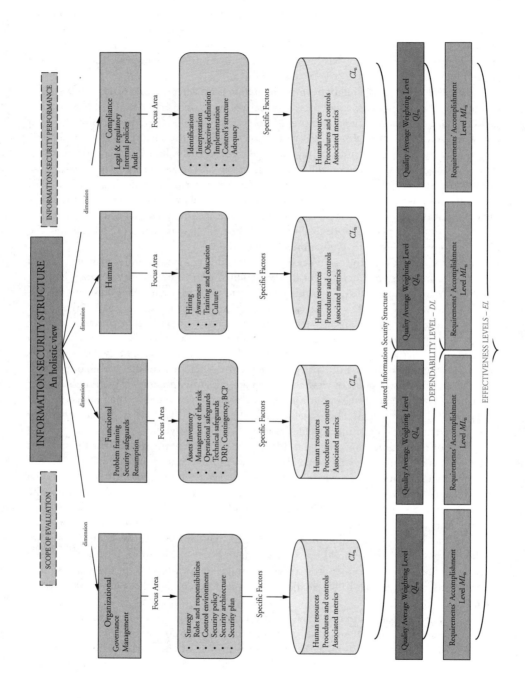

Fig. 3.12 An assured structure for the information security function.

- *Synoptic view:* treating the system as a whole. In our case it concerns the whole information security system evaluated from a three-dimensional point of view.

A similar structure based on the security dimensions was adapted from the Organization for Economic Cooperation and Development guide, published in July 2002, which included some guidelines for security information systems and networks.[37] Within this publication, information security is considered in a very broad sense and elements enumerated inside it consider the domain of information security in a holistic way. This means that under the assumption that the security level will only be as strong as the weakest link, the idea of evaluating all security components (technical or not) contributes to minimizing the likelihood of the existence of the weakest link causing the breach and leading to harm. Following the model's structure presented in Figure 3.12, for each dimension the following focus areas are identified:

- *Organizational dimension* (divided into two sub-dimensions, *management* and *governance*) is made up of the following focus areas: strategy, roles and responsibilities, control environment, information security policy, information security architecture and info-sec plan.
- *Functional dimension* (divided into three sub-dimensions, *problem framing, security safeguards,* and *resumption*) is made up of the following focus areas: assets inventory, risk identification, risk assessment, operational safeguards, technical safeguards, business continuity and disaster recovery planning.
- *Human dimension* is made up of the following focus areas: hiring and staffing, awareness, training and education and the overall security culture.
- *Compliance dimension* (divided into three sub-dimensions, *legal and regulatory, internal policies* and *audit*) is made up of the following focus areas: identification, interpretation, objectives definition, implementation, structure of controls, adequacy.

Each of the issues contained within the focus areas is addressed by some specific factors (in other words, *roots of trust*) that within the model are gathered into three groups: information security measures and activities, information security procedures, and information security human resources. The "assured structure" made up of these three elements allows the calculation of the information security completeness level index that aims to evaluate the assurance level of the information security program structure.

$$ISCL = \sum_{i=1}^{n} \left\{ SF_{attr} / N_{FA} \right\} \div 3$$

where:
- *ISCL* is the information-security completeness-level index;
- SF_{attr} is the number of effective specific factors for each focus area;
- N_{FA} is the number of such focus areas for each dimension.

If we take an example of the organizational dimension and assume that:

---

37   OECD Guidelines for the Security of Information Systems and Networks: Towards a Culture of Security, available at http://www.oecd.org

1. *FA* (strategy) possesses two effective specific factors;
2. *FA* (roles and responsibilities) possesses three effective specific factors;
3. *FA* (control environment) possesses one effective specific factor;
4. *FA* (security policy) possesses three effective specific factors;
5. *FA* (security architecture) possesses two effective specific factors;
6. *FA* (security plan) possesses one effective specific factor;

then the *ISCL* would be:

$$ISCL = \sum_{i=1}^{n}\{12/6\} \div 3 = 0.67 = (67\%)$$

This model allows the calculation of two main holistic information security assurance indices, namely the Dependability level (*DL*) and the Effectiveness level (*EL*). The first index includes and captures two main aspects; trustworthiness on the information security program structure, by including the appropriate index calculated before, and quality assurance, by including as a weighting factor the quality level QL_N where, for the condition mentioned in Section 3.6,

$$QL_N \in [1 \rightarrow 4]$$

we can write

$$DL_i = \sum_{i=1}^{n}(ISCL_i \times QL_i)$$

where:
- $ISCL_i$ is the information security completeness level of each dimension;
- QL_i is the quality assurance level of each dimension ranging from 1 to 4;
- *DL* is the dependability level calculated by weighting the information security completeness index (architectural assurance) with the quality assurance level (procedural assurance).

If we now take the example of the organizational dimension and assume that
- the information security completeness level is equal to 0.67; and
- the quality assurance level is equal to 3;

then the dependability level would be 2.01 for a maximum of 4, representing almost 50% of a fully dependable situation.

The second index, concerning the information security program's effectiveness, is calculated as shown here:

$$EL = \sum_{i=1}^{n}\frac{DL_i}{ML_i}$$

In fact, based on the definition of effectiveness, our index incorporates two parameters: the dependability and the maturity. The dependability represents the state of the overall information security program at time *t*, while the maturity, as defined by the model, serves as the reference point for information security requirements, and consequently for the objectives to be accomplished.

If we take the example of the organizational dimension and assume that the dependability level DL is equal to 2.01, then according to the maturity model proposed in the following chapters, the maturity level defining the objectives to be reached in security terms equals $ML_i = 3$. The effectiveness level EL would then be 0.7 (or 70%, meaning that the organization has achieved their security objectives to within a 70% level). Given the fact that an effective maturity level ($ML_i = 5$) is reached when the organization has an exhaustive architecture ($ISCL = 1$), and that each architecture component's quality assurance level has reached the highest level ($QL_i = 4$), additional continuous effort for improvement is called for.

3.8 Chapter summary

The objective of this chapter has been to introduce an ISAAM evaluation model that aims to evaluate holistically the health state of an information security program. This evaluation model should respond to two interrelated notions, assurance and trust. The underlying idea is to provide a means of evaluation that is capable of measuring the real health state of a given information security program, which means a model capable of providing "reliable" results. In general, the measurement's accuracy – in other word the confidence – will depend on three main factors:

- Who measures it?
- What is measured?
- How is it measured?

Among these three elements, the first could not be inherent to the evaluation system. Nevertheless our model can be performed, as we have mentioned it, by both external and internal evaluators. Our model is focused on the second and third points by specifying what has to be measured and how. This is done through the structure of the evaluation discussed throughout the chapter and through the different specifications proposed in order to gain a multidisciplinary view of the information security posture by introducing the notions of quality and the fulfilment of requirements. A confident evaluation providing a clear and true panorama of the system makes it possible to trust the outputs of the evaluation model, which consequently induces stakeholders to trust the information security system itself.

Chapter 4

Evaluating the Organizational Dimension

Within the framework of the evaluation of information security, this chapter clarifies and puts into a defined context two main aspects of the organizational dimension, the *governance aspect* and the *management aspect*.

4.1 Introduction

Information security governance, and more generally the organizational aspect of information security, plays a crucial role in the effectiveness and the quality of the information security program/system. This is mainly for three main reasons:

- Information security has increasingly become a business issue as information has become one of the main productivity factors;
- Information security has become a multidimensional and complex discipline due to the business environment;
- The technological side of information security is considered as being reasonably mature, so that the focus has now moved onto the human side. In fact the human side of the security is widely held to be the weakest link, so capabilities to overcome the technology have become more decisive than the technology itself.

The governance aspect and the management aspect are two overlapping activities but are specifically driven by different objectives. The governance aspect is more focused on orientational directives related to topics such as objective setting, strategic alignment, leadership or controlling, whereas management activities in comparison with governance assume a more operational nature since they rely on the governance outputs to be in charge of, or to produce the basis of, the information security system/program. Governance and management activities can also be distinguished by the fact that usually different staffs hold responsibilities for them. For the sake of the principle of the segregation of duties, the governance aspect will be strongly focused on the control and the evaluation issues of the information security system/program.

4.2 The information security governance concept

According to the Oxford English Dictionary, "to govern" means ... to direct and control the actions and affairs of a people, a state or its members…" So information security governance is strongly related to information security management and responds to the same objectives. In this context, the notion of governance will include the activities of controlling and directing (as would be expected for the management aspect) that are performed by the board of directors and executives. This definition of the information security governance takes into account the fact that information security governance is a high-level commitment and responsibility regarding the information security and requires a solid understanding of business in order to transpose business objectives into information security objectives.

Overall, information security governance is the process of establishing and maintaining a framework and supporting management structure and processes in order to provide assurance that information security strategies

- are aligned with and support business objectives;
- are consistent with applicable laws and regulations through adherence to policies and internal controls;
- provide assignment of responsibility.

Information security governance responds to the same objectives and is a part of corporate governance, which is the system by which corporations are directed and controlled. It concerns a set of responsibilities and practices exercised by the board and executive management with the goal of providing strategic direction, ensuring that objectives are achieved, ascertaining that risks are appropriately managed and verifying that the organization's resources are used responsibly.[1]

When discussing information technology governance architecture, a reference model defined by three principal outputs, the *cultural environment, accountability* and the *decision-making process* can be drawn. In this sense information security governance will be the load-bearing structure that will provide the very first indications about the expected quality of the information security system in place. Information security governance will thus provide the basis for deploying more explicit and specific information security measures and controls, in order to reach the desirable and appropriate security level.

By definition, governance activities are placed at the highest hierarchical levels of the organization. The highest levels carry the ultimate responsibility for the continued existence of the organization, and through a governance approach will express the effective needs in function of this central objective (Figure 4.1). Those needs, and consequently the information security requirements resulting from them, will constitute the foundation for the information security system/program as well as the direction of the priorities to be fixed.

From a responsibility point of view, the term "information security governance" describes the process of how information security is addressed at an executive level, or the overall way in which information security is handled, which results directly from the most commonly used compliance-based approach. Furthermore, the pairing of governance with high level (senior) managers can focus attention on the risk awareness attribute in respect of the top management level.

The information security governance role allows the consideration of information security as a business issue. At the same time, information security governance means the estab-

---

1   IFAC, *Enterprise Governance: Getting the Balance Right*, International Federations of Accountants, Professional Accountants in Business Committee (PAIB), 2004. Available at http://www.ifac.org/MediaCenter/files/EnterpriseGovernance.pdf

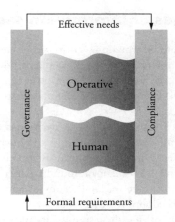

Fig. 4.1 Information security governance positioning between other information security domains.

lishment of a control environment, valid for all three levels of management, strategic, tactical and operational. Information security governance holds an integrative role by raising the information security issue at the top level, thus allowing information security concerns to be discussed and operated through all levels of the organization. This responds from a functional point of view to two fundamental principles of the Generally Accepted Information Security Principle (GAISP)[2], namely the *multidisciplinary principle* and the *integration principle*, which state that information security "should address the considerations and the viewpoints of all interested parties" as a "coordinated and integrated function". In spite of the fact that similarities and overlaps do exist between them, it is evident that governance and management are driven by two distinct objectives, namely direction and control (Figure 4.2).

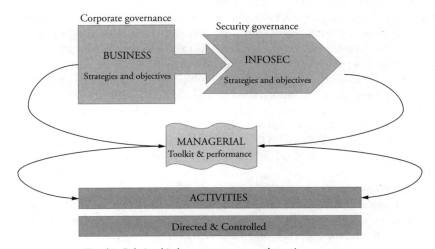

Fig. 4.2 Relationship between corporate and security governance.

2   ISSA, "Generally Accepted Information Security Principles V3.0," Information Systems Security Association USA 2003. [Online] Available at http://all.net/books/standards/GAISP-v30.pdf

4.3 The advantages of information security governance

Many advantages are imputed to information security governance, but from an assurance and trust point of view the most important advantages could be one of the following:

- The governance approach focuses on the problem of due care and consequently on the human (personnel) issues which are identified as being a big concern in security matters;
- A governance approach focuses also on the decision-making issues, thus transforming information security from a techno-centric to a business-centric activity, a change that helps to legitimise the information security function within the organization;
- Based on the commitment mechanism, founding documents like information security policies for example, take on another importance. Their implementation and more particularly their adoption are significant on an enterprise-wide basis;
- From a pragmatic point of view the resource allocation will be more optimal since the pressure for an efficient use of resources will derive from the executive levels;
- Finally, information security governance should create an environment capable of integrating information security through the organizational process life cycle as information becomes an increasingly important asset.

4.4 Relationship between information security and governance

The linkage between information security and governance ensues directly from the role that information security assumes within an organization. Both functions are related to the same end objective, which is the sustainability of the organization. The discipline of information security mainly ensures the availability, integrity and confidentiality of electronic assets, which are an important concern for strategic management. The strongest element of the relationship between information security and governance is that the latter is directly related to the role of the board of directors, being therefore the constituent that could upgrade information security to a strategic level and consider it as a priority business issue.

High-level management commitment and full support is required in the first place for all external and internal documents related to the information security function, following thus the requirement of the international standards relating to information security, ISO/IEC 27002 and ISO/IEC 27001. The implementation of the information security strongly depends on organizational factors. High-level management involvement and commitment is one of the most important elements and it could be evidenced by top management's participation, guidance and positive attitude with respect to Information Security. This can be justified by two main factors:

- The nature of the assets, considering the importance that the informational assets have within the totality of the organizational assets. Informational assets are those assets that promise future economic benefits for a given organization. Indeed, informational assets are taking an increasingly important place among the assets of an organization. They assume different positions, starting from an active position directly involved in production activities to a supporting position ensuring the good direction of business activities;

- The nature of risk, directly linked to the previous point. Considering the notion of risk, ($Risk = F[Vulnerability, Threat, Impact]$), and the importance of the informational assets pointed out above, the damage and, consequently, the impact harming the security state of the informational assets are of great importance to the organization.

Some other reasons for the importance of the high-level management involvement, come from the facts that:

- The high-level management is legally responsible for risk management;
- The ICT environment is increasingly becoming the subject of governance issues;
- Information security plays an ever-increasing role in the success of the organization.

Information security is strategically very important, and consequently senior management should play a crucial role in establishing and managing information security. The Board is responsible and accountable for the stakeholders' comfort and the board must ensure that their organization produces business value and delivers a suitable return on investment to the shareholders.

The existence of a document called "Corporate information security policy" legitimizes the information security approach to be implemented within the organization. That is also very useful since the objective is to evaluate the security posture of a given organization. From a "Sarbanes-Oxley (SOX)" perspective, on the one hand internal control is a responsibility of the board, and on the other hand internal control relies on information technologies. In this way the relationship between corporate governance and information security becomes clear. It should be underlined that the use and the development of information technologies have helped to create a new paradigm where control is decentralized along with IT systems and organizations are everything but hierarchical. Consequently information security governance is a good tool in a manager's hands to bring the hierarchical relationship into position.

Evaluating information security governance means providing an acceptable level of predictability for operations by limiting the impact of adverse events.[3] This can be done based on some high-level documentation from high-level management, as required by *The Standard of Good Practice for Information Security*,[4] such as:

- Information security strategy;
- Information security policy;
- Information security architecture.

In terms of information security organization, a top-down approach through an information security authority (or committee) should be followed. This authority includes members of top management, principal heads of departments, and representatives of security related functions. Furthermore a dedicated information security function should be put into place, having the responsibility to promote information security good practices across

---

[3]   ITGI, *Information Security Governance: Guidance for Boards of Directors and Executive Management*, 2nd ed., IT Governance Institute 2006.
      http://www.itgi.org/template_ITGI.cfm?template=/ContentManagement/ContentDisplay.cfm&ContentID=24384

[4]   ISF-std. *The Standard of Good Practice for Information Security*, Information Security Forum, 2007.

the organization. In practical terms governing the information security function means in practical terms that information security is managed in the highest managerial level of the organization.

The evaluation model adopts the viewpoint expressed throughout this section that to govern information security means having first of all a strategy that allows the organization to devise a supervising system, as well as assigning the appropriate responsibilities in order to meet the strategy's objectives. As such the above-mentioned elements will constitute our target of evaluation with respect to the governance sub-dimension.

4.4.1 Information security strategy as a road map for governance issues

The information security strategy outlines in general terms how an organization will achieve its objectives for security,[5] and is considered as being a road map that will drive organizations where they need to go with respect to information security. The information security strategy is a plan to mitigate risks based on the compliance efforts with regard to external and internal requirements[6] specifying the security budget in terms of each dollar spent compared to the cost of losses or damage if the budget is not spent.

The strategy is a concern of the highest managerial levels, and it is the primary source of the information security policy. The strategy directly results from the leadership and governance role of the executive level. The information security strategy, by considering the information security processes and activities, should convey the security vision and objectives as the board level in its guidance role has expressed them. This is a question of the integration of a managerial approach within the information security domain.

Based on the ISO's definition of the strategy, the latter should address general and fundamental topics such as:
- Indicate the method to be used in order to perform an effective risk analysis on an organizational-wide basis;
- Specify some security objectives as an input to the information security policy. The information security objectives (i.e. availability, integrity and confidentiality) should result from different sources. It might be the case that a risk posture will emerge from the risk analysis, as well as from the vision of the future of the organization. The vision of the future allows information security objectives to be prioritized. While the risk analysis based on the sensitivity criterion of the assets will prioritize the actions to be taken (safeguards, security measures, security controls), the vision has to incorporate the business needs and at the same time some performance targets have to be clearly articulated;
- Other inputs should be considered when designing the security strategy, such as the regulatory environment and the time schedule requirement.

---

[5]   ISO/IEC TR 13335-3:1998 Information technology – Guidelines for the management of IT Security – Part 3: Techniques for the management of IT Security (this part of the standard has been withdrawn and replaced by ISO/IEC 27005).

[6]   FFIEC, IT Examination Handbook – Information Security Federal Financial Institution Examination Council, 2006. Available at http://www.ffiec.gov/ffiecinfobase/html_pages/It_01.html

The security strategy plays a fundamental role in clarifying and giving a formal direction on what security will consist of, based on the priorities that have been set by the board level. The strategy focuses security efforts onto some well-defined projects to be completed in a specified period of time. This has to be considered as the output of such a strategy. To summarize, the quality and the added value of an information security strategy should be evaluated based on it clarity, scope and relevance to overall business.

4.5 People, roles, responsibilities and processes

4.5.1 People involved in the processes

Considering the use and the importance that information has in present business organizations, the whole hierarchical structure has to be involved in the information security function. From the perspective of the organizational dimension, if a single dimension solution improves a single security component, then something else may become the new weakest link. Hence there is a real necessity for a centralized view of information security, which means a transversal and managerial approach arising from information security governance. In general three principal positions can be distinguished in terms of role and responsibilities, namely:

- Top management (senior management, board, executives etc.) (CEO);
- Chief information officer (CIO);
- Chief information security officer (CISO).

Figure 4.3 gives an example of a conceptual information security governance framework. According to this figure, the three aforementioned positions have different responsibilities in

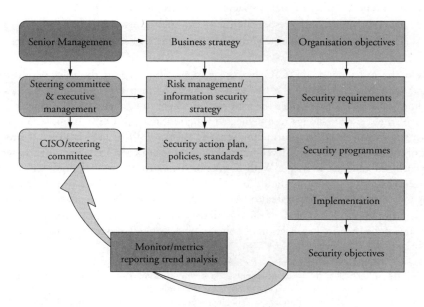

Fig. 4.3 Example of a conceptual security governance approach.

terms of information security governance. While the CEO's and CIO's roles and responsibilities within the information security remain clear and mostly relate to a strategic involvement, the CISO's role continues to evolve. Something important to underline in this context is the fact that based on the responsibilities assigned to the CISO, which is the position that is directly responsible for the security of the informational assets, it could be deduced that the CISO should interact directly with the highest level of the management rather than through an intermediary, for example the CIO.

4.5.2 The Role of top management

The CEO and CIO belong to the board of directors, having a definite impact on security concerns and especially on security governance topics. Belonging to the top-management level, there are two main responsibilities that should be assigned to them, vision and support. Responsibilities related to the definition of the information security vision come from the fact that top management is ultimately responsible for the organization's continued existence, and thus has the ultimate responsibility for the organizational values (assets) and at the same time for the risk posture directly related to those assets. In order to do so, top management has to have a deep understanding of both risks and the organizational values. This is in general terms. In more specific terms the security responsibilities regarding this category do differ somewhat from each other.

Looking at the CEO level, as has been said above it impacts the security purpose by deciding upon the risk posture and the internal control system to be adopted. The standard of good practices for information security (ISF) assigns the following tasks to the top management in terms of information security governance:

- Ultimate responsibility for the internal controls and the power of the evaluation of the proportionality of such a system with respect to the risk posture;
- The assignment of the responsibilities regarding the assets;
- The segregation of duties regarding the assignment of security responsibilities.

On the other hand, the CIO has the responsibility to lead the information-related projects and thus to manage the financial resources of such a project, including security spending. This is also true under the assumption where the direct and operational responsibility of the security belongs to a dedicated function, like CISO for example. Some well-known standards related to information security such as ISO or ISF[7] advance the requirement of the existence of a high-level group or committee to coordinate information security (or security in general) activities. With respect to the above-mentioned arguments, the top management-related positions should be represented within this group or committee, thus giving information security a strategic place and adopting a top-down management structure.

Another important mission of the top management in governance terms is their role as guarantor of the practical application of policies, by defining the tone at the top as advocated

---

7   ISF-std. The standard of Good Practice for Information Security Information, Security Forum, 2007.
      ISO/IEC 27002:2005, Information technology – Security techniques – Code of practice for information
      security management, International Organization for Standardization (ISO), Switzerland, 2005.
      ISO/IEC 27001:2005 (E), Information Technology – Security Techniques – Information Security Management
      Systems – Requirements, International Organization for Standardization (ISO), Switzerland, 2005.

by the IT Governance Institute in *Information Security Governance: Guidance for Boards of Directors and Executive Management.*[8] Evidence of the guarantor's role is provided by the commitment of the top management regarding information security.

Top management's commitment is perhaps one of the most meaningful aspects for ensuring that the information security really is governed. By "governed" we mean that the information security issues are discussed, considered and analyzed at the board level, giving thus the assurance that at a minimum:

- Security issues are considered as critical issues;
- Security issues are addressed in an enterprise-wide manner.

The top management's commitment is required and considered as being a cornerstone of security effectiveness in almost all well-known security standards, such as ISO/IEC 27002:2005 or The *ISF Standard of Good Practice for Information Security.* Top management's support directly affects some important information security variables such as accountability level (awareness, training) and the policy related topics (relevance, enforcement). Top management's commitment encompasses several duties or actions that should be performed. The actions to be performed merely correspond to a main objective, which is to visibly declare that the top management not only supports information security activities, giving to them a high importance, but that they also are the source of information security activities, enabling the security behaviour to be seen as a mandatory task.

Tangible evidence of this commitment is given for example by the fact that the information security policy is signed by the chief executive officer, which will clearly proclaim top management's support for the information security objectives and requirements. Another piece of evidence for the top management's commitment is also the participation of the latter in all security forums or meetings regarding security issues, in the risk and security management activities as well as the control activities. A clear positioning of top management concerning security issues should be declared and communicated throughout the organization. In this way information security tasks will be performed in a coordinated manner, thereby taking advantage of a centralized view and of decentralized functioning. Accordingly the high-level business objectives such as effectiveness and efficiency have a good chance of being achieved.

4.5.3 The chief information security officer (CISO)

Under this title is meant all the responsibilities that should be assigned to a functional position at an operational level concerning information security. It should be noted that the CISO's involvement follows the same pattern as the focus on information security, going from a technical focus to a business related one. The CISO becomes a kind of interface between the operational needs for information security and the decision-making process.

There are many existing models and real-life examples placing the CISO in different hierarchical positions. Some of them put the position under the CIO, which still remains the most common solution currently used. This schema considers the CISO's function to be technically oriented. It has to be underlined that within this dissertation framework, we

---

[8]   ITGI, Information Security Governance: Guidance for Boards of Directors and Executive Management (2006), cited.

are not arguing that giving a technical orientation to the CISO is wrong. On the contrary, it might be a feasible solution for small organizations. Nonetheless, regardless of the hierarchical position, the CISO or the person that will lead the information security activities should necessarily possess managerial skills and understand the organizational business strategy. In fact, due to the frequent changes in information security positioning, the person in charge of security has to deal with managerial activities (policies, procedures, audits, reporting, awareness) as well as with operational and traditional technical activities. At the same time, business managers also have to acquire a minimum of understanding of ICT limitations and constraints.

The CISO's role changes radically when the level of the complexity or the size of the organization changes. The CISO has to be considered as a senior-level person who possesses both technical and managerial skills. Within the security department can be identified multiple profiles which should be present, namely security managers, security architects, security engineers, security specialists and security analysts of whom the CISO will be the leader. Of course this will be the case for large organizations capable of affording such a heavy administrative hierarchy and for which these specific competencies could be very beneficial. Nevertheless the CISO should be capable of performing in three distinguished domains: managerial, technical and compliance. In such a security environment the CISO has to have a multidimensional professional profile.

A chief risk/security officer is liable for a large range of functions, including the overall leadership and the implementation of metrics and resource allocations. For example, the CISO can have the role of a liaison link between the two skill prerequisites of an effective information security function, the managerial and the technological.

Assigning the role of linchpin means giving to the CISO the opportunity and the possibility to interact with all the hierarchical levels in order to develop, as part of his responsibilities, a holistic information security program. To do that he should

- oversee the risk assessment processes;
- develop policies, standards and procedures according to risk; and
- test and report upon the effectiveness of the security processes.

A local security organization should be created, with a member of each unit having the responsibility to perform information security tasks in a timely and accurate manner.

4.5.4 The supervision environment

By supervision environment is meant all the available processes and activities that will allow the top management to verify that the information security duties are performed in a desirable way and, more importantly, to ensure that the security objectives are achieved. Furthermore, the supervision systems will be the principal tool on which the decision-making process will be based. If a reference is made to the ISO 27001 PDCA model to localize the notion of the supervision environment it will mostly concern the last two phases, namely the *check phase* and the *act phase*. The check phase will concern all the surveillance-related activities aiming to achieve a double objective, the effectiveness and the compliance of the whole information security system. The act phase is based on the gaps eventually brought to light by the check phase and the corrective, preventive and improvement actions to be undertaken.

There are two main tools to be assessed in order to evaluate the capability of the relevant authorities to control and review the information security program/system in place. These are:

- The control system (internal and external);
- The measurement system.

According to many regulations, such as SOX for example, it is the responsibility of the CEO and CFO to make it sure that the internal control system is operated effectively, which clarifies the idea that the control environment should be a part of information security governance dimension. Nevertheless, in order to have an independent view about the quality level of the security system, an external control system has to consider:

- *Strategic level control*, which means verifying compliance and conformity issues as well as the risk situation;
- *Tactical level control* allowing the organization to verify measurements and monitoring reports;
- *Operational level control* to verify the accuracy of the security controls performed on a daily basis and mostly focused on performance variances.

The supervision environment will be one of the tools from which the top management could benefit in order to accomplish the second duty they hold, that is to say controlling, because as has been mentioned above, governance is a matter of directing and controlling.

4.5.5 The internal and external control system

According to the well known integrated framework proposed by COSO (Committee of Sponsoring Organizations)[9] an internal control system is a process, implemented by high level management, to provide reasonable assurance over the achievement of objectives on a permanent basis. It is characterized by several components and a well-defined framework of interactions between them, presented graphically by the COSO cube.[10]

To summarize the COSO framework, it includes:

- A categorization of the subjects of evaluation, based on the organizational functional structure;
- A set of objectives for each functional element, namely:
  - Strategic – high-level goals, aligned with and supporting its mission;
  - Operations – effective and efficient use of the resources;
  - Reporting – reliability of reporting;
  - Compliance – compliance with applicable laws and regulations.

---

[9] COSO, "Internal Control – Integrated Framework," Committee of Sponsoring Organizations of the Treadway Commission 1994. Available at
http://www.snai.edu/cn/service/library/book/0-Framework-final.pdf

[10] For more information related to COSO see: "Strengthening enterprise risk management for strategic advantage," Committee of Sponsoring Organizations 2009; available at
http://www.coso.org/documents/COSO_09_board_position_final102309PRINTandWEBFINAL.pdf.

- A set of supervising control criteria to reach each objective independently of the functional granularity level. The control criteria based on the extended and updated COSO framework are:
  - Internal environment;
  - Objective setting;
  - Event identification;
  - Risk assessment;
  - Control activities;
  - Information and communication;
  - Monitoring.

From a functional perspective the structure of the internal controls should follow the same logic as the security system. For example, we find here the importance of the human dimension within the internal environment. Indeed the cultural aspect of the Information Security, through the integrity and ethical values, plays an important role not only in performing information security tasks but also in allowing assessments to take place.

On the subject of internal controls (audits or assessment activities), it is very important that the task should be performed by entities that that are not involved in the implementation and operation of the information security system, applying thus the independence principle. The main objective of an internal audit is to promote internal controls by developing cost-effective solutions to address security issues. On the other hand, an external audit is usually focused on two main objectives: the assessment of the internal controls; and the assessment in economical terms of the efficiency and effectiveness of the ICT environment. The audit activities pass through the "defence-in-depth" logic since the external one is a means of verifying the reliability and the accuracy of the internal control system. The results of the internal and external audits should be the inputs for the reviewing phase. The high-level reviewing phase should concern topics such as:

- The outcomes of the audit activities;
- The current state of security activities;
- Risk posture assessment;
- Possible recent changes that have concerned the organization.

4.6 Information security measurement system

Multiple strategic decisions concerning information security have to be taken at the top management level in order to address information security issues. Answering the following questions is a real challenge for the management:

- How many resources should be allocated?
- What are the risks that the organization is ready for and prepared to face?
- What are the organization's security needs?

At the same time it is difficult to assess the effectiveness of organizations' security installations because of the lack of integrated measurement managerial tools.

For the sake of cost control, the investments related to security resources have to be cost effective. Security objectives have to be associated with the critical values for the organization. Moreover, the role of each resource related to each security objective should be clearly identified. Evaluating a level of security preparedness is a very difficult task because of the interactions between, and chaotic natures of, multiple security measures that are in place. To fulfil protection requirements for a given asset, different security measures are requested that are related to different proficiencies, such as technical, organizational and judicial. Very often the same security measures are used to protect other assets with a specific weighting. In such a panorama, with "n-to-n" interconnected relations, evaluating the security preparedness level is not the most difficult task. The most difficult one is to ensure an overall level of security assurance, which seems to be almost impossible.

In order to size up the information security effectiveness and efficiency in such "n-to-n" interconnected relationships, it is necessary to rely upon a formalized and widely understandable information security measurement and metric approach.

4.6.1 Information security measurement and metric approach

The focus of security measurement has to depend on the ICT security approach of understanding and maturity for a given organization. Metrics could be seen as consistent standards for measurement, having as their primary goal the quantification of a problem or some particular characteristics of a chosen subject area. An information security metrics program, according to National Institute of Standards and Technology (NIST), is a tool facilitating decision-making and improving the performance of systems for a specific organization or situation.[11] In this context, information security metrics should be a set of quantitative and qualitative measurements that should be placed and interpreted according to the organizational context of a series of previous measurements and related to a structure of recurrent measurement. The output of such a measurement should be used to take decisions better about designing security countermeasures and improving security architecture during design and operation. Alongside the use of security metrics for decision-making, they could be required by laws, regulations or even by governmental administrations. To satisfy regulations and conformity requirements, and to facilitate decision making, a security metrics approach should rely upon the information security goals of the organization.

As the improvement of the organization's overall performance is the main objective of the executive managers, the IT security metrics should consider the risk situation and the risk perception of the organization as shown in Figure 4.4.

Everything indicates that, for the same risk, two different organizations could have different perceptions. The same risk could have different impacts and could thus be treated in several ways. Intuitively a security breach, harming the confidentiality criterion, will not have the same impact for a bank as for a company in the manufacturing industry. So it will not be prioritized and considered in the same way. It should be re-emphasized that what really matters is to minimize losses by implementing security measures and controls, based on their

---

[11]   E. Chew, M. Swanson, Kevin Stine, N. Bartol, A. Brown, and W. Robinson, "Performance Measurement Guide for Information Security (SP 800-55 – Revision 1)," U.S. Department of Commerce, National Institute of Standards and Technology, Computer Security Division 2008. [Online] Available at http://csrc.nist.gov/publications/nistpubs/800-55-Rev1/SP800-55-rev1.pdf

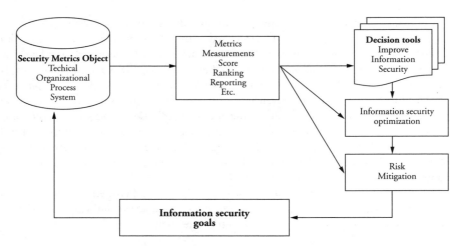

Fig. 4.4 Information security metrics as a management decision-making tool.

security objectives. It is important to underline that any impact generates losses, and that losses are not only caused by malevolent actions but also by errors or accidents.

To reduce the complexity of the evaluation of the level of security preparedness, we propose measuring the conformity of the implemented and managed security controls to the organization's risk positioning. To do that, a security program including certain specific elements should exist:

- Security flowchart;
- Security policies;
- Security procedures;
- Security implementation;
- Security tests;
- Security internal and external audit trails.

Thus, the security metrics measuring the security level could be classified as:

- *First level security metrics*: To evaluate the existence of certain appropriate security measures and controls;
- *Second level security metrics*: To evaluate how the security measures and controls are implemented and managed. This contributes to building up a measurement of quality.

Information security is a process designed to counter the relevant informational risks. A general approach to managing risks within an organization is composed of two main steps (Figure 4.5):

- STEP 1: Positioning of the organization in relation to the security objectives related to a level of comfort judged appropriate by the management;
- STEP 2: Translation of information security needs into measures, proceedings and actions to be taken in order to reach the required comfort level.

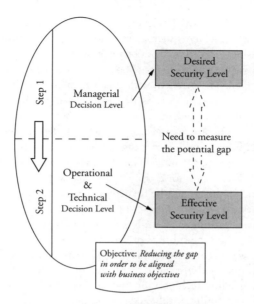

Fig. 4.5 Organizational metrics framework.

4.6.2 A measurement framework in the scope of improvement and decision-making

To use metrics in a decision-making context, security professionals have to simplify the proceedings and the results. This allows for better evaluation and communication of the relevant message, in a fully understandable way, to the higher management levels. Let us take the example of an intrusion detection system that has stopped thirty intrusion attempts. This could be seen as a good result from a technical point of view. What could be more interesting for the managerial level, however, is to show how many intrusion attempts were successful and what was their impact. It allows the assessment of whether the result is acceptable or not. If not, the existing controls in place have to be evaluated in order to assess and improve the situation.

Once the kind of metrics to provide and the scope of the information security metrics program have been decided upon, the next decision is to find out the reference point for the measurements. It is equivalent to determining the nature of the resulting statistics. Some basic indicators are needed that allow the evaluation of the overall security situation for the entire information security program and these will depend on the motivation for the measurement. The measurements will be formulated differently if the output is to be addressed to a technical expert, a decision-maker, an external authority, or stakeholders.

To avoid getting lost in a huge volume of measurements, the approach is focused on the critical assets to be protected. A critical asset could be a single component such as a system including several single components. This is why it is better to use the concept of "value" rather than that of "component or asset." The inherent assumption is that a well-protected asset could resist specific attacks and thus protect all the related assets. The organization's values are the organization's assets, both tangible and intangible, including the computer data. A comprehensive and meaningful assessment of all security dimensions concerning each critical asset is required. The overall security level should not be limited to attacks such as viruses or theft but should also cover incidents such as fire and flood; everything that could harm the business or prevent business objectives from being attained.

Information security measurements based on attack scenarios state that all relevant scenarios should be identified. The problem with this way of considering information security metrics in a decision-making framework is that in practice one has to go too far into the details of the scenario and to make some assumptions about the way the attack would be performed. In reality the outcome of a genuine attack will depend on the attacker's capacities, motivation and skilfulness and hence it can prove to be too difficult to identify a typical point of attack. The principal target and collateral damages scenario will be based principally on the classification of threats and, for classifying threats, some specific information such as source, the mode of attack, the target, the frequency of occurrences, the severity and a set of countermeasures are needed.

Some of these characteristics are the subject of statistics, some others are the subjects of perception, and yet others are the subjects of very subjective calculations. In the absence of statistics, the different ways of perceiving losses or severity and the difficulty of calculating hidden costs such as reputational cost mean that this whole manner of discussing security levels could be inadequate at a non-technical top management level. Moreover it is impossible to foresee and anticipate every future unsolicited event and possible scenario.

Each asset is subject to some protection measures related to security criteria that have been implemented by its owners. An asset could be concerned by several security criteria and to satisfy each of them several security measures could be needed. The underlying concept is that the activities within an organization are defined at the basis of "beneficial interest" based on a business model. To carry out this business model, some assets (including more and more informational assets) are needed and these assets are subject to the protection measures. Previously information security was very "techno-centric" because assets requiring protection were also highly technical. This behaviour has changed nowadays. Measurement is considered as a decision and the object of the measurement will depend on the decision; in this way it will be up to the owners to state such decisions. Nevertheless the only reasonable manner to measure the security of an entire organization is to measure the quality of its risk management.

4.6.3 Answering some fundamental questions

In order to assess the security status of the organization, once it has been decided how this program will be set up and what will be included in it, some fundamental questions should be answered.

Why measure? This is the fundamental question for determining the scope of the mission and the important variables to be taken into account. There will be quite different ways to address the question of investment in a new technology or a resource to be employed, which will be based on a Return on Investment (ROI) approach, rather than an evaluation of the effectiveness of the security program running in the organization. It will be quite different again to address the question of whether the program in place really meets the organizational security objectives. Perhaps the measures in place are effective but are these measures sufficient or insufficient according to the objectives fixed and expressed by the top-level management? If we make a diagram of the security steps as described, the scope of the measurements will also define the variables and methodologies to be used (Figure 4.6).

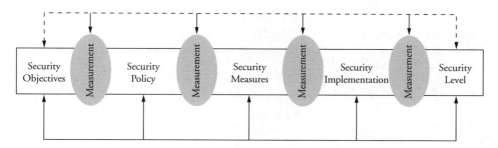

Fig. 4.6 Measurement basis within an IT security metrics system.

Every measurement effort should necessarily be put into a well-defined circumstance or situation. To evaluate the overall information security preparedness level, the measurement of the fulfilment of the security tasks according to the security steps and processes is mandatory.

What to measure? Once the scope and the subject of the measurement have been identified, the next step is to decide what kind of measurement applies to a specific context or circumstance. If the task is to assess the security level in an improvement scope, the best approach is to take into account all the dimensions of the security program linked to the decision making level. For specific local purposes, some technical aspects may have to be assessed. In a higher level control system, some organizational aspects may have to be assessed, and for operational purposes some parameters relating to the day to day functioning of security controls may have to be evaluated.

How to measure? Until now, we have limited the perimeter of the measurement in order to simplify the outputs. The objective is to obtain some reliable and understandable measurement outputs according to the strategic objectives required by the managerial level. But the task still remains complex with many measurements to be taken in several areas. From a decision-making point of view, the measurement has to be related to the object of the assessment. The object of the assessment is the organizational security status composed of security controls, procedures and operational tasks to protect organizational assets. So, to assess the security level of a system, we propose using a top-down risk analysis approach, considering as a reference point the value (asset) to be protected, starting from the most critical. In this way we place the security metrics program into an information security and information risk governance approach.

To adopt our approach to measurement, the first step to be undertaken is to assign a degree of criticality to all the assets that the organization aims to protect. Each asset will be the subject of some security objectives in terms of availability, confidentiality, integrity and conformity. Legal risk is becoming increasingly relevant in today's environment and considering the fact that an instance of non-conformity could leave the organization liable to penalties, we propose adding conformity as a security criterion in this approach. Every exploited security breach could affect the security criteria and generate security incidents. Every security incident is liable to create losses. According to this deductive reasoning, in order to assess the security level, two crucial variables have to be identified:

- What is the value requiring protection?
- Against which kind of incident?

Once the asset and the incident have been identified, risk components such as threat, vulnerability and impact have to be determined. According to these components we can evaluate the existing security measures and controls countering the risk. At this stage two kinds of judgements can be made:

- If the security objectives are met, the security level is judged as being sufficient;
- If not, the security professionals and the managers have to identify why and then determine what the organization has to do to improve the unsatisfactory security level, deciding upon the actions to be taken.

4.7 The information security management perspective

4.7.1 Components subject to evaluation

Information security management, when compared to information security governance, is more of an operational activity while still retaining an organizational scope. Information security management is used to establish and maintain a secure information environment by implementing and maintaining processes and procedures. The aim of information security management is to create a framework within which information security operates as expected. If it could be summarized in a few words, both information security governance and management are domains driven by directing activities but there is a conceptual difference, which is that governance mostly focuses its intention on control activities. The latter is directly related to the predominant role of the top management within governance. The quality of the control level by the top management will be strongly affected by the capacity of managerial levels to create a measurement (metrics) system capable of giving a reliable representation of the security posture.

There are five principal missions (outputs) directly assigned to information security management:

- A risk and security measures cartography based on the criticality and sensitivity of informational assets;
- A comprehensive protection framework mapping risks to the appropriate security measures;
- A deployment platform (according to the organizational maturity level) striving to standardize and automate as far as possible security practices and behaviours;
- An information security program or system operating the security capacities to provide a protection level based on a system management model (i.e. PDCA);
- A monitoring system that can capture the state of health of the information security program/system and is capable of ensuring continual improvement.

Based on these objectives, and in order to structure information security management under an organizational umbrella for evaluation purpose, focus is placed on the three following information security management components:

- The information security policy – the source of the security goals and requirements;
- The information security architecture – the source of the information security program/system structure;
- The information security plan – the source of the information security activities and procedures to be performed.

4.7.2 Information security policy

The information security policy is the cornerstone and one of the most important elements of the information security program or system. It contains fundamental guiding statements on how information security should be designed within the organization by specifying the goals or the objectives, as well as the actions or behaviours, to be adopted in order to ensure a certain level of protection for the organizational values. As an important reference point, the information security policy should be related to the business objectives by specifying how these objectives could be reached and by taking into account the risks introduced by the use of ICT Technologies.

In general, policies are "management instructions" on how an organization should be run. The information security policy is a statement on protecting an identified resource from unauthorized use and more generally speaking, on showing what should be protected, by defining what "secure" means for the organization. According to the NIST special publication on *recommended security controls,*[12] the information security policy is an aggregate of directives, regulations, rules and practices that prescribes how an organization manages, protects and distributes the information, and should be considered as the starting and reference point on which the information security must be based.

The information security policy is a direction-giving document for information security and is part of an organization's strategy, implying principally two main objectives:

• Indicating management's commitment;
• Defining the role of information security with respect to the vision and the mission of the organization.

This is the direction proposed by the ISO code of practice for information security management,[13] concerning the security policy, where the policy meets two main objectives, the first of providing support and the second of giving guidance on information security. In practical terms, the information security policy is the document that is intended for the deployment and the implementation of the information security functions.

There are two distinct forms of policies related to information security, namely the Information Security Management System (ISMS) policy and the information security policy. The first is derived directly from ISO/IEC 27001:2005 and from the information security management system considered within. This document, according to the author, and as also required by ISO/IEC 2002:2005 itself,[14] is concerned with the management's commitment.

Three main types of information security policies can exist, in the following forms:

• General security policies – this category concerns the overall goals as well as the resources and the responsibilities regarding the information security program. One

---

12   NIST, "Recommended Security Controls for Federal Information Systems and Organizations (SP 800-53, Revision 3)," U.S. Department of Commerce, National Institute of Standards and Technology, Computer Security Division 2009. Available at
     http://csrc.nist.gov/publications/nistpubs/800-53-Rev3/sp800-53-rev3-final.pdf
13   ISO/IEC 27002:2005, Information technology – Security techniques – Code of practice for information security management, International Organization for Standardization (ISO), Switzerland, 2005.
14   ISO/IEC 27001:2005, Information Technology – Security Techniques – Information Security Management Systems – Requirements, International Organization for Standardization (ISO), Switzerland, 2005.

of the topics of such a global security policy is also the compliance issues concerning the legal and regulatory requirements.

- Issue-specific security policies – this is a more detailed category of the policy, which is more focused on specific statements and relevance regarding a given specific issue, such as privacy policy.
- System-specific security policies – this category specifies the security actions concerning a preponderant security objective for the system in question. Within this category operational rules (for example by job category) and policy implementation actions are specified.

Independently of the type of policy, some basic and indispensable elements of the information security policy are put forward in ISO/IEC 27002:2005,[15] within its first chapter entitled "information security policy."

The elements without which a security policy could not be effective, or even could not be taken into consideration, are listed here:

- The scope of information security, its objectives and a clear definition of the security, in order to clarify the need and the objectives, as well as to provide a general basis of understanding.
- The management's commitment. The latter is widely recognized as a cornerstone of information security effectiveness since it is the main element forcing employees to pay attention to information security issues.

Moreover, the other indispensable element of an information security policy is the "raison d'être," in other words the security goals. Its precise content will depend on the level of granularity of the policy, but generally the security goals will cover the protection of the availability, integrity and confidentiality information security objectives.

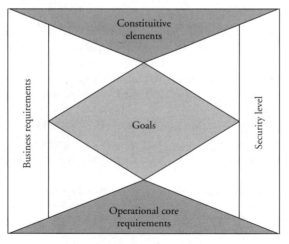

Fig. 4.7 Information security policy framework.

---

15   ISO/IEC 27002:2005, cited above.

As shown in Figure 4.7, the operational core of the policy, which is the specific requirements regarding different security issues or concerns, should also constitute any information security policy. The operational core element is the element that could often differ from one organization to another. Nevertheless in this category, ISO/IEC 27002:2005[16] provides a baseline, including issues to be addressed such as: compliance, awareness, continuity planning, violation of the policy requirements, and specific responsibilities with respect to Information Security.

According to the standard of good practices for information security (ISF),[17] an information security policy requires at a minimum:

- The classification of the information;
- The owner of the information;
- Mandatory risk analysis for important information;
- Information security awareness;
- Compliance;
- Reporting of incidents and security breaches;
- Security objectives to be satisfied (availability, confidentiality, integrity).

In order to be effective such a policy has to be communicated, reviewed, and revised. It should be underlined that the requirements within the security policy can be expressed as a function:

IS requirements = F [Business vision, CIF]

Operational excellence, customer knowledge and product leadership characterize business vision, while Critical Impact Factors (CIF) concern the different damages that security incidents cause for the organization. By critical impact factors is meant financial losses, productivity (capacity losses), reputational damages and legal liabilities.

An information security policy, in order to be fully implemented, needs to coexist with specific tools such as organizational standards or procedures. In fact, as we have already discussed, the information security policy contains directives, regulations and rules on how to address the security issues. In order to correctly implement those elements, dedicated tools explaining how to do so are necessary. On the one hand, standards show what should be done, and on the other hand, the procedures specify how to perform the steps in order to implement what is specified within the information security policy. In fact, procedures specify the operational steps to be undertaken to appropriately achieve the policy's requirements. Considering the policy's life cycle, the effectiveness of such a policy will be measured through, for example, development, styling, presentation, commitment, dissemination and maintenance.

To summarize, the effectiveness of the security policy will depend on three principal processes:

- The development of the policy document;
- The communication process;
- The enforcement process.

---

16   ISO/IEC 27002:2005, cited above.
17   ISF-std. *The Standard of Good Practice for Information Security*, Information Security Forum, 2007.

ISO/IEC 27001:2005[18] identifies two baseline controls related to the effectiveness of the information security policy, namely:

- A policy document that is approved, published, and communicated;
- A policy that is reviewed at planned intervals.

The effectiveness of the security policy, and thus the achievement of the security level claimed by the policy, will be a function of two coordinated efforts proposed hereafter. The first will be the effort of the "issuing authorities" belonging to the decision-making level of the organization. The trust element concerning this category will be the applicability conditions illustrated or measured by the granularity level of the security policy. By "granularity" level is meant the way the security policy is detailed in more operational documents such as organizational standards, and procedures, or even in more specific security objective related policies such as confidentiality policies or integrity policies. The second category concerns the ability of the organization to enforce the aforementioned security policy. This could be measured by the deployed means within the organization to communicate the policy's requirements enterprise-wide. Awareness and training activities play a crucial role in this issue.

4.8 Information security architecture

Information security architecture is another important element of information security management regarding the effectiveness of the information security function. It is defined by the standard of good practices for information security (ISF) as being the framework for the application of some standard security controls. This is from a conceptual point of view. On the other hand, from an operational point of view the information security architecture is a process to ensure that all individuals recognize their responsibilities with regard to information security and are aware of how they need to act in order to protect informational resources.[19] It should be underlined that here "responsibility" means the responsibilities of every employee with respect to the information security practices. This is to be distinguished from responsibilities from a governance point of view dealing with the responsibilities with respect to the information security system itself.

As we can deduce from these two definitions, and based on a primary meaning of the word architecture, the art or science of building or constructing edifices of any kind for human use, the information security architecture will concern the way the security program will be conceived, developed and maintained, by considering the information security elements and the interrelationships between them. One of the primary goals of the security architecture is to clearly provide some defined control solutions. On the other hand, the notion of the *Enterprise Information Security Architecture* (EISA) is to provide mechanisms that enable the organization to translate business requirements for security along with general principles and best practices or to connect business drivers with technical implementation guidance.[20] So any information security architecture should focus its intention on three constitutive elements, namely:

---

[18]   ISO/IEC 27001:2005, Information Technology – Security Techniques – Information Security Management Systems – Requirements, International Organization for Standardization (ISO), Switzerland, 2005.

[19]   J. H. P. Eloff and M. M. Eloff, "Information Security Architecture" *Computer Fraud & Security,* vol. 2005 (11), pp. 10-16, 2005.

[20]   T. Scholtz, "The Structure and Content of an Information Security Architecture Framework," Gartner 2008. [Online] Available at http://www.gartner.com/technology/

- Business functions through policies, standards and procedures;
- Operations through the technical safeguards and different tests;
- Assurance processes such as internal and external audits or every control activity.

There are two principal styles of architecture related to information security. The first one considers information security as a process and bases the security infrastructure principally on the Plan-Do-Check-Act (PDCA) approach. Other approaches based on the process feature could be similarly adopted, such as the Policy Framework for Interpreting Risk in E-Business Security (PFIRES) which is very close to the PDCA but is based on the product development lifecycle and consists of the four following phases: assess, plan, deliver and operate. The second style of architectural construction is principally based on the nature of information security controls, based on an ISO/IEC 27002:2005-like structure. This architecture can include five main components:
- The security organization and the infrastructure;
- The security policies, standards and procedures;
- The security baselines and risk assessment;
- The security awareness and training programs;
- The compliance.

Other security architecture models could exist to answer special needs and situations or focus for example on a more logical data-centric modelling. This kind of security architecture is derived from a *data classification model* based on criticality and sensitivity called "classification criteria" and on the data security model including the security requirements resulting from the classification. It should be noted that the security requirements might originate both from well-known standards or best practices and from regulatory requirements, such as privacy rules. Each of these methods has its own advantages and disadvantages and responds to different managerial objectives. For example a PDCA or PFIRES approach to developing an information security architecture mostly responds to a life-cycle approach to managing security, whereas an ISO-like architecture mostly responds to a standardized framework offering an easier way to perform

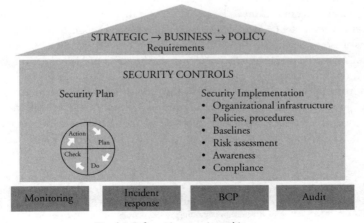

Fig. 4.8 Information security architecture.

measurements, thus allowing better evaluations of the effectiveness of the whole system. In order to include information security architecture in our model, we present it as shown in Figure 4.8.

This way of considering the matter does not only include the security measures controls resulting from the four different dimensions, but puts them into a specific context according to their functional role. Conceptually, the information security architecture results from the information security policy, which is the direction-giving document concerning the security requirements. Consequently, the information security architecture should respond to policy requirements and have the same structure as the policy. To do that, in a more general way the architecture should be designed as a construction based on three main blocks; that is to say the requirements block, the security controls block and the security management specific activities blocks.

In Figure 4.8, the *upper level* specifies the security goals deriving from the policy requirements, where the policy requirements themselves derive from the visions and security objectives expressed by the top-management level. It is very important to assess this continuum because a positive affirmation will provide evidence of a coherent organizational attitude. The *middle level*, independently of the categorization of the security controls, provides the assurance structure of Information Security. Some basic elements regarding the controls should obligatorily appear, for example the security measures such as physical, procedural and logical ones as well as the interrelationships between them. The *lower level* concerns all the activities that will enhance the quality of the information security system and will put the information security system on a solid improvement basis. It is about monitoring, incident response, the Business Continuity Plan (BCP) and auditing. This construction corresponds to our model's primary assumption, which is the evaluation of the information security system/program based on a triple perspective: structure, quality, and requirements.

4.9 Information security plan: the road-map of security operational activities

To summarize elements of information security management, it could be stated that the main output of the information security policy is to specify the information security objectives, or more specifically information security goals, and from them to produce some verifiable information security requirements to be satisfied. After that, and based on the policy requirements, a security architecture should be drawn up as a mechanism that will contain all the security measures and security controls to be applied in order to satisfy such requirements. A security plan should be prepared in order to specify the actions to be taken in relation to the implementation of those security measures and security controls.

The information security plan concerns the "coordinated actions to be undertaken to implement the security policy".[21] For that reason it is one of the specific factors related to the information security policy, and thus one of the elements of information security management. The actions should basically concern the topics covered by the security policy,

---

21   As also specified by P. Bowen, J. Hash, and M. Wilson, *Information Security Handbook: A Guide for Managers (NIST Special Publications 800-100)* National Institute of Standards and Technology, 2006. Available at http://csrc.nist.gov/publications/nistpubs/800-100/SP800-100-Mar07-2007.pdf
ISO/IEC TR 13335-2:1997, Information technology – Guidelines for the management of IT Security – Part 2: Managing and planning IT Security (this part 2 was combined into the revised ISO/IEC 13335-1:2004).

principally the awareness activities, the security enhancement issues, the policy enforcement and of course all the oversight tasks. An important place within the security plan should be taken by the assignment of security responsibilities regarding all the entities interacting with the organization.

First of all, an information security action as a component of the information security process should be identified and defined. This has to be done based on the result the security action has to achieve. To achieve such a result a given action may incorporate one or more security measures and controls. The actions incorporated within the plan should reflect the security vision and the security objectives pronounced by the board level within the security strategy and meet the security requirements as defined within the security policy. The coherence between these different elements will clearly indicate the effectiveness level of the security actions to be undertaken. Once the actions are identified and defined, for each a work-plan for the implementation should exist, as recommended by the ISO security related standards. This work-plan should incorporate priorities related to the security action to be performed, as well as a detailed budget and time schedule.

Another function of the information security plan is to make an assessment of the security measures and controls. As mentioned before, the security plan will transform the high level requirements into some tangible procedures to be undertaken in order to reach the security objectives. At this stage the information security program/system is ready to be put in production, which means that the plan will describe and document the way the system will practically be run. For that reason the assessment of the security measures and controls will provide an accurate panorama of both existing and future situations. The security controls, in order to be assessed, should be categorized and inventoried, according to their function in relation to the security objective they serve, or to any other categorization criterion. The criterion is not really of great importance; what is important is the coherence of the categorization and the meaning the categorization will give to the different categories.

The information security plan will be the road map of the operational activities and tasks regarding security. The plan will directly depend on the quality and above all will depend on the coherence of all the components of the organizational dimension that are documented within the plan. The existence itself of such a plan will show that the information security program (or system in place) is running according to a certain structure and logical development and responds to some well-identified prerequisites.

4.10 Evaluating the organizational dimension

Governance and management sub-dimensions characterize the *organizational dimension* of the information security. As was explained above, the choice to theoretically and conceptually divide the organizational dimension between governance and management was made because of the different objectives and different responsibilities of each. From an evaluation point of view the distinction between these two sub-dimensions has been made more specific and detailed in order to bring out a clear picture of assurance elements. From a conceptual point of view the governance sub-dimension is characterized by direct and control activities, while the management sub-dimension is characterized by operate and perform activities. The organizational dimension aims to obviate risks related to a breach within the security system of the organization that could directly or indirectly be imputed to a management failure

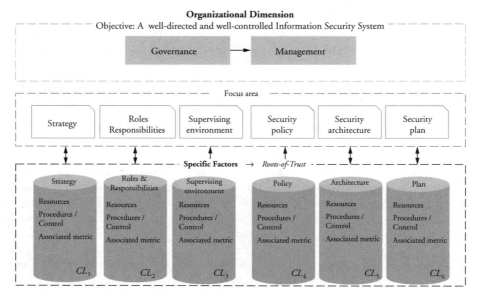

Fig. 4.9 The evaluation assurance structure related to the organizational dimension.

having an incidence in both functional and human dimensions. Figure 4.9 proposes the assurance structure specific to the evaluation of the organizational dimension of information security.

4.10.1 Analysis of the governance sub-dimension

As we can see in Figure 4.9, the governance processes are not only the inputs for managerial processes but also for other dimensions of the information security program, since the information security high-level objectives are established and enforced through governance processes. Evaluating or judging the governance sub-dimension as being of good quality may mean that a priori the managerial activities have been put on a solid basis.

The governance sub-dimension can be divided into three focus-areas, representing thus the security issues to be resolved. The first focus area concerns the *security strategy*, giving the high level directions on what the information security will be based on and will rely upon. The lack of a security strategy will show that an organization has no defined objectives in security terms, which means that the security function either does not exist or is performed informally and is driven by the daily needs for protection. As we have already mentioned, without a strategy a security policy cannot be credible. By using the same deductive reasoning we should say that without a security policy we could not speak of a security program capable of achieving effectiveness and efficiency objectives, but only about some security measures that are applied regularly.

The root-of-trust (specific factors) elements regarding the strategy focus area will principally be based on the existence of the following:

- A document named *security strategy*. This document might be an individual one or even incorporated into the overall strategy document. The existence of a clear statement mapping business objectives with security objectives should exist.
- A high level person responsible not only for the document but also for the coherence of the security objectives based on the business perspective. The responsible person should obligatorily be involved in developing the information security policy since this should detail the high-level objectives of the strategy.

Once the strategy has promulgated the security vision and traced the direction in which the security should be oriented, one of the security issues (focus areas) that are addressed by the governance sub-dimension is the assignment of *roles and responsibilities*. The assignment of roles and responsibilities within the governance sub-dimension could be divided into three categories:

- Strategic, represented by the board-level members, who are responsible for the setting of security objectives as well as the framework for supervising security;
- Executive, represented by the CIO or even by the security committee, who are responsible for the financial aspects as well as the coordination activities;
- Operational, represented by the CISO who is responsible for the operational management of the security activities.

The specific factors concerning the roles and responsibilities focus area could be of a different nature. First of all, the three above-mentioned levels should be present in two fundamental protection processes, namely the risk and security management as defined within this framework. Their participation has to be effective and has to provide a formal commitment to those activities by demonstrating their participation and, most importantly, by validating the outputs of such processes: the risk posture and the appropriate security level. Another important specific factor of the roles and responsibilities focus area concerns the financial resources. The executive level has a clear responsibility for the financial resources for the security activities. After that, a distinct budget for the information security activities should be calculated. By providing appropriate resources to the security function, the security function becomes more responsible for the protection level it has to provide.

At a more operational level regarding the CISO function, a clear position within the hierarchy should be assigned. Placing the CISO at the board level will legitimize and facilitate his performance. The CISO should possess a formal job specification that should be coherent with the position he may hold within the hierarchy. Moreover, the CISO's profile (whether it is multidisciplinary or technical) will also give some indicators about his attitude to the information security function.

Here we reach our last focus area in governance terms, which is the *supervising environment*. At this stage the high-level managers have announced their vision and the overall objectives and have assigned the appropriate roles and responsibilities to make it function. Now, in order to ensure the achievement of objectives and continual improvement, some internal and external control processes, together with a measurement system, are needed. The control processes will be focused on the information security measures to ensure that they are effective, while the measurement processes will be focused on the information security results to ensure that an improvement perspective is adopted.

Regarding the *internal control system*, one of the most important specific factors is that the function should be allocated to a dedicated and independent person. This person is very often included within the financial department and of course has as a primary objective the internal control system around accounting. Based on the importance that information data have nowadays, the internal control entity should clearly incorporate the information security control dimension and embrace well-known best practices or methodologies to carry out this task. Regarding the *external control system* there are three principal elements, or roots-of-trust, to be evaluated that directly derive from the organizational behaviour. Legal or regulatory texts, with their mandatory character, often require an external audit. In order to correctly perform the check phase, as required by the PDCA model, the organization should

- organize the prior-audit phase, based on a well-defined process, with some well-defined objectives and expectations;
- plan regular timetables for the audits; and
- build up a formal process for the post audit phase, having the goal of analyzing the audit results and findings, which is also the process that brings the more important part of the added value in audit terms.

The last specific factors of the supervising environment focus area according to our model are those related to the measurement system. As we have already described, the measurement system is a powerful tool for managers to better evaluate the performance of the security system in place, allowing thus a more effective decision-making system. To reach those objectives there are some steps to be undertaken in order to provide a useful and meaningful measurement system. Evidence of direct involvement of the board level within the measurement system should be identified. It might be the permanent presence of a member as well as an automated system delivering the measurement's results. The latter could be integrated also into an overall reporting mechanism, but this is not a crucial element. The measurement system will embrace a multidisciplinary character by the use of a large range of measurements enclosing all the security dimensions, organizational, operational, technical, legal, and human. A strong trust element is the evidence showing whether the measurement efforts are institutionalized or not. An institutionalized measurement system means that all activities are performed based on a prior plan regarding goals and the scope of the measurement and its use.

4.10.2 Analysis of the management sub-dimension

Information security management is concerned by three categories of issues and composed thus of three focus areas, namely the information security policy, the information security architecture and the information security plan. The information security management used within this paragraph does not totally correspond to the same definition proposed by international standards. In fact by information security management from an organizational point of view, we mean only those elements that will create the conditions for the adequate operational functioning of the information security system.

Information security policy

The first focus area and one of the elements widely recognized by the literature and practitioners as the cornerstone of the information security management is the *information security policy*. As was mentioned before, the information security policy is the reference point of the overall information security program, offering guidance on how the information security should be operated, which are the security goals to be reached, and what it is permissible to do or not with respect to Information Security. The assessment of the policy focus-area should be based on three specific-factors.

The first concerns the existence of such a document and the importance this document has within the organization. It is very important that a formal document identified as security policy exists, because the credibility of the security approach depends upon it. This document has to be the result of a deep reflection performed by a dedicated group. Having a tangible document with some tangible and well-defined requirements in it will certainly be better than the same requirements spread over multiple documents. Information security has become a critical issue so a central security policy will obviate possible misunderstandings or contradictory messages. Regarding the importance given to the security policy, commitment at the board level is the most eloquent form of evidence but is not the only one. Another important piece of evidence is the relevance this policy has to the business objectives.

The second group of specific factors concerns the constitutive elements, and the third group of specific factors is related to the elements internally provided to implement the information security policy, including means of communication and distribution.

The assessment of the security policy should include the following characteristics:

- Existence;
- Completeness;
- Format;
- Supporting documents;
- Policy management program, to continually have an up to date and improved document.

Information security architecture

The second focus area within the information security management sub-dimension considered within our model was the *information security architecture*, based on the information security policy requirements specifying the framework of the application. An information security program cannot be effective if it is not based on a solid architecture able to incorporate a wide range of security controls in order to achieve policy requirements. The evidence of a trusted information security architecture should be provided with regard to these following elements:

- The coherence of the architecture with regard to the policy. Evidence is shown when each security goal specified within the information security policy corresponds to some dedicated information security control measures or a group of information security control measures;
- The configuration of the security architecture.

Information security plan

The last focus area of the security management sub-dimension, the *information security plan*, follows the same logic as the information security architecture in the sense that it has also the duty of condensing objectives, goals and requirements into some applied procedures. Both focus areas are anchored to the information security policy and apply it in two different ways. The architecture is focused on the controls to be implemented whereas the security plan is focused on the actions to be taken. Based on this appreciation of management's reasoning, the specific factors regarding the plan should be categorized in the existence of the plan itself and its structure.

The existence of the plan provides the evidence that an evaluation might use. On the other side the high level-plan should be contextualized to every department. In that way information security issues will concern all the representative professions existing within the organization. The fact of contextualizing information security plans will enhance accountability and will strongly decrease the potential for their being ignored. Of course, in order to be effectively implemented, and based also on the inherent characteristics of the plan (measurable objective), an evaluation of the achievement of the information security plan should be performed on a regular basis.

4.11 The maturity model related to the organizational dimension

Based on these previous considerations, and the maturity model structure presented in Chapter 3, the following maturity model regarding the compliance dimension should be used as a basis for the evaluation of effectiveness (Figure 4.10).

Fig. 4.10 The maturity model related to the organizational dimension.

Level 1 Fortuitous	• *Existence of at least one dimension:* Generally the management dimension can be identified with some informal security practices susceptible of being enforced. • *No existing focus area structure:* This implies that elements of strategy and policy exist (for example, objectives, goals or expected behavior) but are not formally sanctioned. • *Isolated specific factors:* These are generally situated at the procedures/controls level. *No quality specification can be done.*
Level 2 Structured	• *A clear and formal existence of the dimension:* The two sub-dimensions of governance and management are identifiable. • *Focus area structure mostly exists:* This could be verified, but minimally. Security strategy, policy and responsibility assignments are in place. • *Specific factors include two attributes:* For each identified focus area, the specific factors procedure/controls and human resource could be assigned. *The quality level has reached the first level,* which means that issues related to the governance and management sub-dimensions are included within the information security policy and in other strategic documents related to information security.
Level 3 Functional	• *The architecture is complete:* The two dimensions and the six focus areas exist, as described within the model. • *Specific factors:* In general, the attributes for procedure/controls and human resources are identifiable for each related focus area. *The quality level* is characterized by an average weighting of two, which means that the governance and management aspects are the responsibility of a specific person (organizational function, job function).
Level 4 Analyzable	• *The architecture is complete:* The two dimensions and the six focus areas exist, as described within the model. • *Specific factors:* The three general attributes are identifiable for each related focus area, which means that the level of metrics is reached for each focus area. *The quality level* is characterized by an average weighting level that equals three, which means that the that specific factors are minimally documented and/or monitored.
Level 5 Effective	• *The architecture is complete:* The two dimensions and the six focus areas exist, as described within the model. • *Specific factors:* The three general attributes are identifiable for each related focus area, which means that the level of metrics is reached for each specific factor. *The quality level* has an average weight that clearly equals four, signaling that a procedure for continual improvement is imputed to each focus area, where internal/external reviews and audits are regularly performed.

4.12 Chapter summary

This chapter has focused on the organizational aspects of the information security dimension, currently one of those most discussed. The expected output of this dimension is a security system that includes within its framework the business perspective of the organization. From a technical related element, information security turns out to be an element capable of improving the business posture. For that reason the high and medium hierarchical levels of the organization become the main actors of the organizational dimension. Each level plays its specific role within the dimension, with the highest levels mostly concerned with the governance issues and the middle levels concerned with managerial issues. The difference between these two important notions was specified, allowing the definition of the focus areas and their related specific factors. The identification of these contributes to understanding the different relationships between the components of the organizational dimension in order to build up the assurance structure of the dimension and then apply the evaluation model.

Chapter 5

Evaluating the Functional Dimension

The aims of this chapter are to describe the functional dimension in detail, to show the link that this has to risk management and to the design of preventive and detective measures, and to categorise the elements within the dimension.

5.1 What is the functional dimension in relation to information security?

The functional dimension of information security is composed of several processes based on the security measures or safeguards to be implemented that respond to a common objective, the mitigation of risk. By risk mitigation we mean all the processes that directly contribute to reducing either the likelihood of the risk concretising or the impact of the risk.

The functional dimension thus has a direct impact on risk and will be one of the first elements of response that an organization will formulate to confront a wide range of risks. From our perspective, the functional dimension is the information security dimension that links information risk management and information security activities. Both these activities allow the organization to implement a complete system for securing its assets.

This chapter proposes a categorization of the elements of the functional dimension based on a timescale with respect to these functional activities. The activities need to be performed in a way that provides a maximum of coherence; this is key for offering an adequate protection level. Functional dimension activities will include:

- *Problem framing,* focused on the identification, evaluation and the analysis of the relevant risks with which the organization is concerned;
- *Information security safeguard selection and implementation,* composed of different security control measures focused on the threats or vulnerabilities;
- *Resumption activities,* corresponding to the issue and based on the idea that zero risk does not exist and hence focused on preventive activities mitigating the impact of an occurrence of risk.

5.2 Framing the Problem

Framing the problem results from structuring basic knowledge of the information security program/system. The result of the problem framing process is the definition of the protection needs and requirements that will influence the structure of the information security program.

The problem framing consists of the following activities:

- The identification of the organizational values and their classification according to their importance, based on valuation criteria;
- The identification of the risks harming those values as well as the risk assessment processes;
- The selection of protection strategies.

The problem framing relies heavily on the risk management strategy in place within the organization. Through this chapter we will go into more depth on risk issues with respect to the considerations set out in Chapter 2 in relation to the identification of elements of information risk and security management, in order to point out their differences and similarities. Nevertheless a broader conception of the risk management could usefully be considered, rather than the specific one strictly related to the informational risk discussed in Chapter 2. It relates to overall enterprise risk strategies of which informational risks form only a part. In this way, an Enterprise Risk Management (ERM) process is a sequential process that supports the reduction of uncertainty and promotes the exploitation of opportunities.

It is composed of five steps:

- The identification of the root causes that could degrade organizational goals in security terms;
- The risk assessment based on the evaluation criteria (impact, likelihood, control measure effectiveness) in order to determine the risk level;
- The evaluation of risk tolerance to determine acceptable risks;
- The risk mitigation, either by trying to reduce the uncertainty related factors or by reducing the potential losses;
- The monitoring of the process effectiveness and the timeliness.

This enterprise-wide risk management takes into account not only informational risk but all the risks susceptible to damaging informational assets. This is not only a list of risks that could come into play, but also a list of assets that could suffer damage. In this way there are two variables playing a crucial role within the problem framing, namely the *risk appetite* and the *risk tolerance*. The risk appetite concerns the boundaries of what an organization considers as acceptable risks, while risk tolerance concerns variations in the measuring of the risk appetite.

According to COSO,[1] four elements should principally be taken into account in order to determinate the risk appetite, namely:

- The existing risk profile, which means the distribution of risks according to risk categories (financial risks, market risks, operational risks, reputational risks, etc.);
- The risk capacity, representing the maximum risk an organization may bear;
- The risk tolerance, including the acceptable level of the variations;
- The desired level of the risk, representing the risk/return level.

---

[1]   COSO, "Strengthening Enterprise Risk Management for Strategic Advantage," Committee of Sponsoring Organizations 2009. Available at
http://www.coso.org/documents/COSO_09_board_position_final102309PRINTandWEBFINAL.pdf

The objective of the problem framing assessment is the evaluation of the enterprise-wide risk management process, by identifying the attributes of a successful enterprise risk management process.

5.2.1 Identification of critical systems

The quality of the identification of critical systems is essential to obtaining the best view of the risk profile, according to the NIST handbook on computer security.[2] We refer here again to enterprise wide risk with respect to the issues discussed in Chapter 2, which is the identification of the critical enterprise assets. For that, four invariant steps have to be undertaken regarding the identification of the critical systems:

- Establishing the protection perimeter;
- Identifying the assets within the perimeter by considering the tangible informational assets (hardware, software) as well as the less tangible ones (data);
- Establishing the level of importance of the assets;
- Identifying the duration of the chosen protection strategies according to the protection needs.

In order to identify critical systems or assets, the analysis should be based on the level of support provided by the system or the asset to the business objectives. Two methods are put forward for classifying the critical systems: the need for protection and the mission's criticality. Once the critical system has been identified, the identification of the assets making up that system is necessary.

An assets inventory list should be drawn up within the organization, specifying the analysis criteria and based on the most critical and the most sensitive assets. The list should be created based on a "classification scheme" as required by the ISF Standard of good practice for information security,[3] by using a double evaluation schema calculated from:

- The potential business impact;
- The potential loss of the dominant security objective with which the critical asset is mostly concerned.

Other valuation approaches could be considered that are based on the economic characteristics of the asset such as its cost, its market value or even its income value. A possible list of general assets is proposed that includes: information, equipment, inventories, personnel, services, facilities, and financial resources. Once the critical asset has been identified and listed, an asset owner should be designated, as recommended by main security related standards in order to allow accountability for the protection.

2   NIST, *An Introduction to Computer Security – The NIST Handbook (Special Publication 800-12)* National Institute of Standards and Technology – US Department of Commerce, 2004. [Online] Available at http://csrc.nist.gov/publications/nistpubs/800-12/

3   ISF-std. *The standard of Good Practice for Information Security,* Information Security Forum, 2007.

5.2.2 Risk control

Evaluating the risk management process takes on a double importance in our model. First of all, performing a risk management process within the organization will provide the assurance that security concerns are considered in a systematic and coherent manner. Moreover, the fact that the security needs are based on a realistic panorama allows the organization to set up a risk posture resulting from a deep analysis, resulting in an appropriate information security program. It is important that the risk activities correspond to the well-known concept of "bridging," which means that

- the technological context is understood, from both a risk and a security perspective;
- the implications of the safeguards to be used are known; and
- the impact on the business is also known.

From this perspective, and in order to evaluate the ability of the organization to manage its risks, we propose categorizing risk controls into three areas that will be considered by our evaluation model, namely:

- The risk constituents;
- The risk handling process;
- The selection of information security safeguards.

Of course, in order to be effective and efficient, the risk controls should be regularly monitored and reviewed. The objective of the evaluation will be to provide evidence to interested parties that an effective enterprise-wide risk management process runs within the organization and that it has a solid basis.

Risk constituents

Risk, as defined by the security management standard ISO/IEC 27005:2008[4], is the probability that a given threat may exploit vulnerabilities of an asset or a group of assets, and thereby cause harm to the organization. As can be noticed from this definition, there are two risk components to be considered in a risk assessment process, the threats and the assessment of vulnerabilities:

- *Threats* are defined within the request for comments (RFC 2828)[5] as the potential for violation of security, which exists when there are circumstances, capabilities, actions or events that could breach security and cause harm;
- *Vulnerabilities* are flaws or weaknesses in a system's design, implementation, operation or management that could be exploited to violate the system's security policy.

Threat Assessment

The threat assessment will give an accurate picture of the threats presenting a danger for the organization, allowing organizations to build up effective risk assessment. From an external perspective, there are two main elements to be appraised; firstly the identification of the pos-

---

4   ISO/IEC 27005:2008, Information technology – Security techniques – Information security risk management, International Organization for Standardization (ISO), Switzerland, 2008.

5   Network Working Group, "RFC2828 – Internet Security Glossary," The Internet Society 2000. Available at http://www.faqs.org/rfcs/rfc2828.html

sible threats that could harm the organization's assets, and secondly, the way they are put into the organizational context. The identification of the threats should principally be based on the identification of the threat agent as well as the undesirable event deriving from it. There are multiple checklists classifying the threat agents. Main threat categories could be identified according to their inherent character, demanding thus the use of different tools and practices:

- Human related;
- Nature related;
- Technology related.

Based on an economic logic, and in a context of security performance, a classification based on the distinction between unintentional or intentional events or threats is not particularly relevant. Organizations should worry about the damage that might be caused by a risk rather than whether it is intentional or not. Categorizing and listing the threats provides a solid basis to identify those threats that most significantly concern the organization, constituting thus the basis for an in-depth analysis. Organizations, based on their experience and the knowledge of the operational environment, should address threat–related issues according to their specific natures, keeping in mind the fact that threat identification will constitute the basis of the selection of safeguards.

General threats, put into the organizational context, should be assessed by specifying the preventive actions the organization should put in place, as well as identifying any possible amplifiers or catalysts. Amplifiers are elements that encourage the threat agent to carry out an attack. The reasons why a given organization would be chosen as a target can be seen as catalysts. ISO/IEC 27005:2005 – Code of Practice for Information Security Management requires that threats should be identified generically and by type, preventing organizations from overlooking them.

Another important element of the threat assessment is the threat statement, which links every relevant identified threat with the undesirable events and the relevant assets. In this way, the identification and the threat assessment are performed on a systematic basis by considering a wide range of sources such as experience, judgement and common sense. Performing such an analysis allows the choice of the best protection strategies that correspond to the specific needs of the organization. A set of security controls responding to threat requirements (but not to security requirements) should be identified, aiming to reduce the likelihood of each threat. For every threat, a number of security measures could be adopted, corresponding to different threat sources. This infrastructure of measures could be thus a source of protection but also a source of vulnerabilities.

Vulnerabilities Assessment

Vulnerabilities are flaws or weaknesses in a system's design or implementation, and include thus the control system. Vulnerabilities are the other side of the coin, concerning the exposure to risk of assets. While threats are mostly driven by factors external to the system (but not necessarily external agents), vulnerabilities find their sources in the internal and operational parts of the system. The vulnerability assessment follows the same logic as the threat assessment, except that it requires a more proactive investigation, due to the fact that vulnerabilities concern the current state of the system. Vulnerabilities could be identified in a number of areas, as shown by ISO/IEC 27005:2008 – Information Security Risk Management: these include organizational measures; procedural measures; personnel related measures; physical and environmental measures; as well as the hardware, software or communications equipment.

Due to their complex character, the most important element to be set up in order to better comprehend their nature (and the way to remedy them) is a prior classification of administrative, technical or physical vulnerabilities. Independent of the identification strategy, the most important evaluation related element to be addressed is that a given organization should specify whether it had made a proactive and regular identification of the vulnerabilities. In this sense the change of management phase takes an important place, obliging organizations to ask if a possible vulnerability could have been introduced after each system configuration change. Nevertheless, ascertaining the vulnerabilities within the organization does not necessarily mean providing a level of protection for the organizational assets that might be directly concerned by those vulnerabilities. It is clear that speaking about a real risk causing harm to the organizational value means that an existing vulnerability would be exploitable by a threat. For that reason the list of vulnerabilities identified within the organization does not constitute evidence that they are fixed. Those vulnerabilities should obligatorily be correlated and linked to the classified threats in order to provide meaningful information about the security issues to be faced and the security practices to be adopted.

The risk handling process

The risk handling process includes the risk assessment process and the risk treatment process. The risk assessment process is composed of the risk analysis and the risk evaluation. In the scope of evaluation, risk-handling tasks are the actions to be undertaken by the organization to identify, analyze, evaluate, and take decisions about those risks that principally concern the organization. After the identification and analysis of risk constituents presented in the preceeding section, the following steps should be performed:

- The determination of the objectives by defining the cost of the risk;
- A clear identification of key risks;
- An assessment of the business impacts;
- Recommendation of the actions to reduce the risk to an acceptable level.

To do that, the organization should rely on some structured methodologies. Numerous commercialized or free methods exist and are listed with meticulous care by ENISA in "Risk management: implementation principles and inventories for risk management/risk assessment method and tools".[6] Nevertheless, independent of those different methods, there are some invariants constituting the backbone of such a risk handling process.

The first element, as stated above, is the fact that the risk assessment process should be performed based on a structured methodology according to the *Standard of Good Practice for Information Security* (ISF).[7] The ISF's requirements are based on the argument that the risk analysis is one of the most important inputs to the whole security program, so that it should be assessed in a consistent and rigorous manner. Such conformity to some best practices and

---

6   ENISA, "Risk Management: Implementation principles and Inventories for Risk Management/Risk Assessment method and tools," European Network and information Security Agency – Technical Department Heraklion, Greece 2006. Available at http://www.enisa.europa.eu/rmra/files/D1_Inventory_of_Methods_Risk_Management_Final.pdf

7   ISF-std. *The Standard of Good Practice for Information Security,* Information Security Forum, 2007.

standards could ensure protection against negligence-based liability and be of a great added value in the short term.

The determination of the risk appetite, specifying which are the risks that are judged as acceptable for the organization and which is the degree of tolerance, was one of the cornerstones of risk control. As such, one of the elements defining the risk appetite of the organization is related to the losses resulting from the occurrence of a given risk. There are multiple loss categories concerning any particular risk, but just to take an example we have chosen the categorization of the losses made by the Information systems Audit Association (ISACA), in the CISA review manual:[8]

- Direct loss of money;
- Breach of legislation;
- Loss of reputation/goodwill;
- Endangering of staff or customers;
- Breach of confidence;
- Loss of business opportunity;
- Reduction in operational performance/efficiency;
- Interruption of activity.

Another element to be considered in our evaluation model regarding the risk handling process is the frequency of the risk handling procedure. We introduce this element in our evaluation, firstly based on the risk dynamics and secondly based on its mandatory nature resulting from different legal requirements. A risk assessment process should be conducted periodically (at least annually) for some of the critical systems or as required by specific legal or regulatory constraints. To resume, evaluating the risk handling process means evaluating the ability of the organization to:

- Rely on a well known and well accepted methodology;
- Provide a clear and accurate panorama of potential losses;
- Continuously perform and improve the process.

The selection of safeguards

The selection of safeguards is the last activity of the risk management process (and at the same time the first of the information security management process) and more generally of the problem framing sub-dimension. It is the element linking the activities of risk and information security that allows daily activities and permits thus the organization to pass from a program stage based on a silo approach, to a system stage opting for a more transversal approach. A safeguard may address different aspects such as, for example, threats, vulnerabilities, impacts, and consequently risks.

The selection of safeguards should necessarily be based on the risk analysis and should consider the threats associated with the vulnerabilities that should be obviated. A great number of possibilities do exist, based either on the analysis of the paired threats and vulnerabilities or on the safeguard catalogues published by several organizations, such as for example:

- BSI, "IT Baseline Protection Manual," Bundesamt für Sicherheit in der Informationstechnik (BSI) 1996.

---

8   ISACA, *CISA Review Manual 2006*. Rolling Meadows, Illinois, USA Information Systems Audit and Control Association (ISACA), 2006.

- ISF-std., *The Standard of Good Practice for Information Security*, Information Security Forum, 2007.
- ISO/IEC TR 13335-4, Information Technology – Guidelines for the Management of IT Security – Selection of Safeguards, International Organization for Standardization, 1996.
- ISO/IEC 27002:2005, Information Technology – Security Techniques – Code of Practice for Information Security Management, 2005.

The selection of safeguards should be a result of an analysis in which multiple features have been taken into consideration. There are three principal categories of safeguards, namely:
- Physical security safeguards including the security personnel;
- Procedural security safeguards related to the operating procedures, documentation, application, development and acceptance;
- Technical security safeguards focused on hardware and software related solutions.

A balance should be maintained between the non-technical safeguards and the technical ones (Figure 5.1).

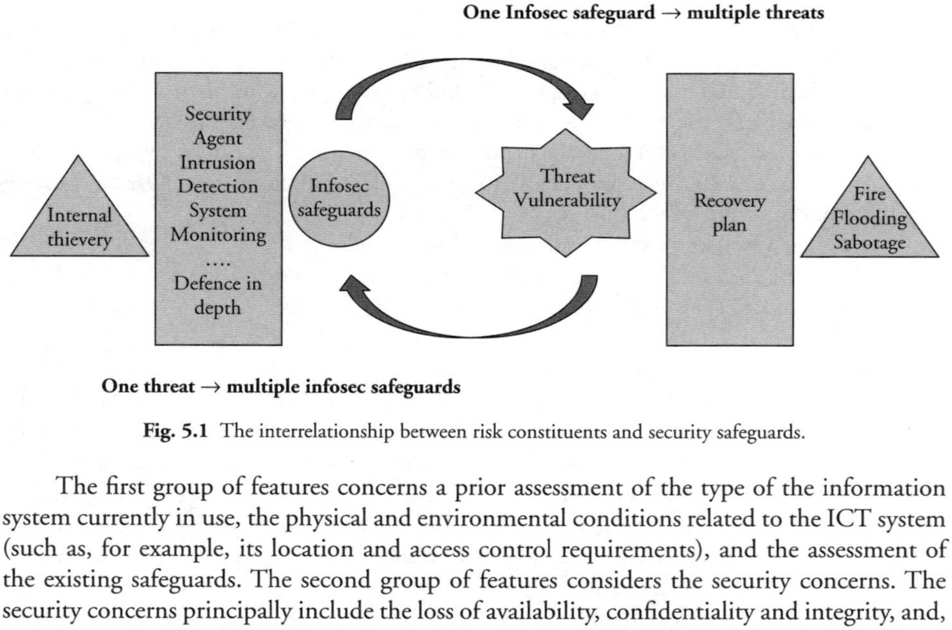

One Infosec safeguard → multiple threats

One threat → multiple infosec safeguards

Fig. 5.1 The interrelationship between risk constituents and security safeguards.

The first group of features concerns a prior assessment of the type of the information system currently in use, the physical and environmental conditions related to the ICT system (such as, for example, its location and access control requirements), and the assessment of the existing safeguards. The second group of features considers the security concerns. The security concerns principally include the loss of availability, confidentiality and integrity, and, going more into detail, the loss of accountability, authenticity and reliability might be considered. The third and the last feature concerns the choice of the safeguards to be implemented considering different constraints such as, for example, time, financial, technical, sociological, legal, and environmental constraints.

Evidence concerning these three features should be obtained in order to take a position on the "information security safeguard selection" issue. It is important to underline that once the information security safeguards are selected they have to be implemented and managed in order to provide the best possible security protection level along with a good return on investment.

5.3 Information security safeguards

The information security safeguards, as we have mentioned several times, are the practical information security measures and controls to be implemented, following the risk treatment strategies undertaken in the problem framing phase, in order to meet security specific needs. Information security specific needs include, but are not necessarily limited to, operational procedures, physical security, and hardware and software features. The following sections of this chapter will be focused on the key success factors enabling these safeguards to be successful. The analysis will not be focused on the different technologies to be implemented, but rather on the concept and the added value that the safeguards will provide in terms of the overall protection level.

The functional security safeguards are categorized throughout this book into two main groups:

- Technical safeguards, directly ensuing from the use of technological tools;
- Operational safeguards, enhancing the quality and the effectiveness of the technical ones, allowing thus the improvement of the protection level.

The analysis regarding the technical and operational safeguards throughout this section is carried out based on two approaches:

- The analysis of the topics discussed in various information security evaluation related resources such as the CISA review manual, the NIST handbook on security and the CISSP (Certified Information Systems Security) official guide[9]; and
- The security requirements stipulated within well-known information security related standards, such as ISO/IEC 27002:2005 and the ISF standard of good practice for information security information.[10]

It should be underlined that the highlighted elements discussed in this section will be the subject of the evaluation process. The highlighted elements will be examined based on the relevance of each to the topic under discussion.

5.3.1 Technical information security safeguards

By Technical security safeguards should be understood the information security safeguards that will ensue from the implementation of a given technology or control measure. The implementation of information security technologies helps to enhance the protection level based on the principal information security criteria, namely availability, integrity and confidentiality. In general terms, the technological solutions, from a functional evaluation point

---

[9]   Respectively: ISACA, *CISA Review Manual 2006*, Rolling Meadows, Illinois, USA Information Systems Audit and Control Association (ISACA), 2006. NIST, *An Introduction to Computer Security – The NIST Handbook (Special Publication 800-12)* National Institute of Standards and Technology – US Department of Commerce, 2004. [Online] Available at http://csrc.nist.gov/publications/nistpubs/800-12/. H. Tipton and K. Henry, "Official (ISC2) Guide to the CISSP CBK," ISC2, Auerbach Publications, 2007.

[10]   Respectively: ISO/IEC 27002:2005, Information technology – Security techniques – Code of practice for information security management, International Organization for Standardization (ISO), Switzerland, 2005. ISF-std. *The Standard of Good Practice for Information Security, Information Security Forum*, 2007.

of view, have to respond to three assurance attributes: existence, completeness, and the effectiveness and efficiency of the deliverables. It is important to underline that the technological measures capabilities, and their accuracy in the strictest sense of the word, are the subject of the evaluation of multiple dedicated standards, the most well-known in this domain being ISO/IEC 15408, commonly known as the Common Criteria (CC).[11] The evaluation of the security technologies is, however, outside the scope of this book.

We chose to focus the evaluation model on three areas that we consider to constitute the main source (entry points) of risk damage. These are:

- The protection against physical and environmental risks;
- The protection against logical unauthorized access;
- The protection against malicious code principally introduced through communication technologies such as e-mail for example.

This choice is motivated by the fact that the security technologies relating to these three areas represent the most important part of the security technologies, so we focus our intention solely on the main characteristics of security technologies from a functional point of view, not on the technology itself.

Physical and environmental security

Physical and environmental security principally aim to prevent unauthorized physical access, as well as any kind of damage or intrusion inside the established perimeter of protection. Based on this definition it can be stated that the information security criterion that is most concerned by these safeguards is the availability of the resources. Physical and environmental protection is mostly focused on the buildings, the information systems, and the related supporting infrastructure. Two main objectives are taken into consideration by the physical and environmental security: the first objective is to create *secure areas* and the second one to provide *secure equipment*. In order to reach these objectives, the first concern is a previously established perimeter encompassing the valuable assets that are subject to protection. A distinction can be made between different safeguards to be implemented inside the established perimeter based on protection objectives such as deterrence, prevention, detection and reaction. The second concern of the physical and environmental protection is the protection of targets. Principally there are two main areas to be taken into consideration:

- Physical access to the valuable resources;
- Protection against environmental threats.

When considering physical access, it is important to identify the critical assets requiring protection, as well as the vulnerable access points to those assets. Evidence should be delivered to show that for each of the access points physical access controls have been imple-

---

[11]   ISO/IEC 15408-1:2009, Information technology – Security techniques – Evaluation criteria for IT security – Part 1: Introduction and general model, International Organization for Standardization (ISO), Switzerland, 2009. ISO/IEC 15408-2:2008, Information technology – Security techniques – Evaluation criteria for IT security – Part 2: Security functional components International Organization for Standardization (ISO), Switzerland, 2008. ISO-Std. ISO/IEC 15408-3:2008, Information technology – Security techniques – Evaluation criteria for IT security – Part 3: Security assurance components, International Organization for Standardization (ISO), Switzerland, 2008.

mented. Those access controls should correspond to a defence in depth logic, enabling a physical access control for every access level (e.g. building, offices or dedicated locations).

The *environmental threats* principally concern fire, flooding, electrical infrastructure or any other environmental threat harming the availability of the organizational assets. Without going into detail on the means of response to each threat, four main areas should be considered during the analysis, each dedicated to one of the identified relevant threats, such as the perpetrator and the amplifiers, the detection and alarm mechanisms, the means of protection, and the testing activities related to each of the means of protection.

To summarize, evaluating the physical and environmental from a functional point of view according to our evaluation model means showing evidence of:

- the identification of the areas requiring environmental and physical protection, as well as the identification of the protection targets within the area; and
- the establishment of a secure environment, where each protection target corresponds to an environmental and physical risk, and appropriate security technology against these risks is assigned.

Information access control

Information access control, contrary to physical access control, is focused on the unauthorized access to intangible assets such as data or electronic systems. Information access control ensures that only authorised entities may gain access to the restricted resources. As such, it will be mostly focused on the issues of identification and authentication. The information control function can be seen as:

Information access control = F [*Users, Resources, Specific use of resources, Accountability related to the use of resources*].

The first element to be taken into consideration regarding information access control is focused on user *privileges*. Organizations should take into consideration the multiple categories of the users (e.g. employees, contractors, partners, clients, consultants) and specify the access rights according to the needs of each. In all cases user privileges, in terms of access rights, should correspond to two main principles, which are the separation of duties and the least privilege principle. Segregation of duties concerns the dissemination of tasks and the associated privileges for a specific process among multiple users. The least privilege principle requires that a user (or a process) be given no more privilege than necessary. The achievement of these two principles should be two important points of control for our evaluation model, providing evidence of the effectiveness of the access control procedures. The evidence will be given by a formal procedure regarding the needs assessment in terms of access rights including the identification of the users as well as the distribution of the access utilities.

A definition of the resources to be accessed should parallel the user privilege identification. For each resource, classes of users authorized to access it should be assigned. To do that, a user role assessment must be performed, linking each of the user categories to the data they might access.

As a matter of identification, every user should possess a specific and individual means of identification and authentication. Different technologies could be used for identification and authentication, such as for example passwords, token or even biometric means. Many elements have to be taken into account to determine the strength of these technologies. This is, however, outside the scope of this book, which is based on the assumption that an organization that is motivated to construct a reliable information security system already possesses the engineering resources that allow it to chose between the different propositions existing within the market. In this context, the evaluation will be focused on the procedural rules managing the technology selected. The administrative tasks involve the implementation, monitoring and tests of these access control technologies. In terms of user privileges, for example, a user access list should be created documenting the type of permitted access to a particular resource.

Another aspect to be considered while evaluating the information access control will be the ongoing practices to access the information once the access rights have been established. The evaluation of this aspect should focus on two main features:

- The first feature is the accuracy of the identification and authentication processes;
- The second feature is the establishment of the formal rules regarding the subject that will potentially be accessed.

The first feature, when considering the sign-on process, requires a rigorous process in terms of the configuration of the security mechanism offering this service. A rigorous process might be produced by implementing some controls such as, for example, the limitation of the number of unsuccessful sign-on attempts, the limitation of the duration of a sign in process, or the fact that during the sign-on process authentication data are not stored or displayed as clear text. Storage of the sign-on logs can help in providing evidence of the resources being accessed and the attributes of the entity having accessed those resources.

Regarding the second element of the authentication, the same rigorous process is required. In the authentication field, the rigour concerns not only the process itself but also the strength of the technology being used. A clear distinction should be made between a classical authentication, characterized by IDs and passwords, and the strong authentication characterized by some cutting-edge technological mechanisms such as smartcards or biometric devices. Considering the cost of the latter, these technologies would normally only be implemented to protect access to critical information resources. Hence a preliminary analysis should be performed in order to define the criticality of the information resources.

More generally, the evaluation features related to identification and authentication should consider the following topics:

- The quality of the IDs and passwords (unique IDs, concealed passwords, temporary passwords, strength level of passwords, changing frequencies);
- The way that identification and authentication means are used.

To summarize, the main difficulty still remains the correct assignment of the access rights to user categories. One of the first steps an organization should undertake is the identification of such user categories and the duration of the access rights.

Finally, the coverage of the different layers forming part of the identification and the authentication efforts should be subject to evaluation. ISO/IEC 27002:2005[12] recognizes three main levels to be taken into consideration from this perspective: the network, the operating systems, and applications and electronic data. Information access control is the subject of preliminary decision-making activities in terms of access privileges and access rights related to

---

12   ISO/IEC 27002:2005, Information technology – Security techniques – Code of practice for information security management, International Organization for Standardization (ISO), Switzerland, 2005.

these privileges. As such, and as it is also required by ISO/IEC 27002:2005 – Code of practice for information security management, an access control policy should be devised to provide evidence that the question of information access has been addressed within the organization and to present organizational requirements focused on all the features discussed above.

Protection against malicious code

The protection against malicious code should be based on two main streams. The first one is the behaviour of the employees, notably focused on the use of informational resources and social engineering practices, which is the subject of Chapter 6 where we address the human dimension of information security. The second one is related to the technology being used to stop the malicious code from penetrating the system or to reduce the likelihood of its impact. The technology being used to stop malware should be the subject of an in-depth analysis in order to justify the choices. Our evaluation model does not aim to provide a technical evaluation scale but to functionally evaluate the technology.

The main technical related evidence to be provided concerns antivirus solutions, including not only protection against viruses but also protection against a wider range of malware, such as Trojan horses, spyware, adware, and so on. As well as antivirus tools, other technologies such as tools examining file integrity and intrusion detection systems could be used to contribute to preventing malware penetration. As has already been described in the case of a specific technology, the technology related to the protection against malware should be evaluated based on two main aspects:

- The context and the way this technology is used in respect of technical controls;
- The way this technology is maintained and managed in respect of procedural controls.

The use of this technology aims to ensure the detection of malware infections, starting with the identification of the risks the organization could face and the identification of the resources that would be concerned by those risks. The systems that are mostly susceptible to malware are those systems that are, or could be, connected to the Internet. These include servers, messaging resources, computers and even hand-held computing devices such as PDAs. ISO/IEC 27002:2005 recommends a policy regarding the use of the different informational resources in order to decrease the likelihood of being affected with malware.

Independently of the existence of such a policy, the following topics should be considered during the evaluation:

- Protection technologies (such as, for example, antivirus, firewalls or Intrusion Detection Systems (IDS)) to be implemented and the context of their use;
- The way internal resources, such as e-mail, web services, etc. should be used;
- The way external software resources might be introduced and/or operated (e.g. installation of unusual programs in the internal IT environment);
- A clear assignment of liability in the case of malware introduction independent of its character (error or a malevolent action).

At the same time the maintenance aspect, especially related to the configuration and update of the specific technological solutions, is of the utmost importance. As a first and imperative stage we could mention a regular and automatic scan of risky subjects or the systematic scan before external storage media or software are installed. A clear procedure (that could be eventually transformed into a policy or even a standardized procedure) should determine that the update of the (antivirus) software is planned at regular intervals and a specific control evidencing the fact that the update has been performed should also be foreseen. The technological solution should be configured to scan or monitor relevant targets[13] and each of these targets should be the subject of periodic review in order to ensure that, for example, the protection is not disabled by another procedure, the configuration is correct, and appropriate emergency procedures are in place. As well as the technological capacities regarding the devices used to detect, stop or quarantine malware, other supporting measures should be applied to reduce the risk of downloading malware. The standard of good practices for information security (ISF) and ISO/IEC 27002:2005 put forward different controls to be implemented. Alongside these specific topics, it should be underlined that in order to provide an adequate level of protection against malware, two procedures should be operated in parallel:

- Those related to the technology; and
- Those related to the procedures specifying the appropriate behaviour that should be provided by the different stakeholders.

Such a logical path is key for the evaluation of particular technologies such as, for example, encryption technologies. These technologies are widely used by organizations for which confidentiality is a great concern. From a technological point of view progress has been made to produce new methods of encryption, as for example in the field of quantum cryptography. The use of the cryptography should also be the subject of a usage policy and correspond to well-documented standards or procedures. The policies or standards should include

- the definition of the circumstances in which cryptography is used;
- the selection of the cryptographic solutions; and
- an assessment of the suitability of the solutions, as well as of the possible restrictions related to this technology.

Generally speaking, it is important to underline that for every technology, as Gartner recognizes when discussing encryption solutions,[14] the technology itself is not the perfect solution but has to be supplemented with other controls.

5.3.2 Operational security safeguards

Operational security safeguards cover those measures that will enhance the quality of all the other technical, organizational, legal and human related safeguards and control measures. Within this book those safeguards are enumerated based on a logical ongoing path that implies:

- The identification and the management of the valuable assets as a prerequisite for the formulation of security requirements;
- The performance of operational activities focused on supervision of the protection systems; monitoring processes to detect anomalies and reveal possible structural changes to be taken into account;
- Successful incident management capable of handling incidents and avoiding the escalation from an operational incident to a major crisis situation.

---

13   As, for example, executable files, removable storage media, network traffic or even computer memory.
14   E. Oullet and J. Wheatman, "Typical Elements of an Enterprise Data Security Program," Gartner 2009. Available at http://www.gartner.com/technology/

Asset Management

Asset management is one of the basic needs within information security since the assets (in a broader sense, including tangible and intangible resources) represent the raw material of the whole information security program/system. The assets represent the target of the protection; and so deep knowledge about their nature and their importance should be acquired within the organization. The main objective is to implement the "appropriate protection" of the assets. The definition of *appropriate* follows directly from the importance (sensitivity, criticality, influence, and importance) a valuable asset has throughout the business processes. Three main organizational issues are touched upon here: the classification of assets, their use, and the related responsibility. As such, the first step to undertake is the inventory of the important assets. This is one of the most frequently requested tasks and at the same time the most neglected. The main reason for this is inherent to the complexity of contemporary business structures and the fact that intangible assets often take a more important place in the organizational environment than tangible ones.

The identification of the important business assets is the first step of the risk management process and constitutes the basis for the identification of the relevant risks regarding the asset. From a security point of view, asset management, and more specifically the fact of building up an inventory, puts the assets into a functional and dynamic perspective. The inventory will not only offer a current view of the ensemble of the assets to be protected, but also an historic view raising the different interrelationships that might exist between them. As such the asset inventory will provide a holistic view of the organizational values that will better allow appropriate protection.

The *portfolio of IT assets* allows the taking into account of all asset interactions as well as the optimality of the asset's use and investment. However, ISO/IEC 27002:2005 put forward a list of asset categories to be taken into account when drawing up an asset inventory. In these are included the information, software, hardware, services and the related infrastructure, the personnel and their qualifications, as well as the intangible assets such as the corporate image or reputation. The fact of inventorying the valuable assets of the organization allows both the classification of these assets and the assignation of formal responsibility to an entity or a person that will control the different aspects, including the protection.

The classification of the information should be the first step that will lead to the protection requirements. The classification should consider the classified asset in terms of value, legal and regulatory requirements, sensitivity and criticality. The classification of the information accentuates the need to assign formal responsibilities related to the assets. Those responsibilities are assigned to the asset's owner as the person who should be in charge of the management of the different protection measures required to secure the asset. Consequently the asset's owner is also responsible for defining the appropriate rules regarding the use of the asset.

To summarize, the CISA review manual[15] recommends the following records for each one of the information assets:
- Distinct identification of the asset and its location;
- Asset security/risk classification;
- Asset owner.

---

15   ISACA, *CISA Review Manual 2006*, Rolling Meadows, Illinois, USA Information Systems Audit and Control Association (ISACA), 2006.

As can be noticed, after this first step of asset management the result is an ensemble of assets to be protected, bringing a certain number of specific factors that will define a number of protection requirements related to the security concerns that themselves will consequently define a number of information security measures or procedures to be implemented. Once all these efforts in terms of surveillance have been provided, it will be necessary to ensure that the implemented safeguards are operating as intended and that the different changes rising from the scalable needs are addressed. This could be done through an effective monitoring system.

Information security monitoring

The concept of monitoring is used in a broad sense including the close observation of the security practices (information security safeguards, measures, and procedures) in order to ensure that the security practices:

- Are well performed;
- Take into account the need for continual improvement.

The monitoring activities should survey and report information security conditions to provide to top management an accurate and comprehensive situation of information security. Schneier, in arguing that information security is increasingly a people issue, considers that monitoring is the activity that will give immediate feedback about the efficacy of the security[16]. On the other hand, security monitoring can be considered as a process providing assurance that a certain security posture exists.

Technologies such as firewalls offering a continuous audit, or incident detection systems that send messages when they detect an anomaly, are not sufficient. The highest achievement of these technological efforts is reached when interpretation capacities are available to respond to such alert signals and to analyse abnormal behaviour. As such the monitoring activities should be based on a monitoring strategy specifying the information security controls to be monitored as well as the frequency of the monitoring. Regarding the information security accreditation of the federal information systems, NIST identifies three tasks regarding monitoring, namely:

- The configuration management and control;[17]
- Security control monitoring;
- Status reporting and documentation.

This current section is focused on security control monitoring and the reporting issues. Nevertheless, a monitoring process would essentially not be possible if a pre-defined level of configuration did not exist. From a defence in depth analysis, the monitoring activities are supplementary to the information security control measures to identify probable security problems that would not be identified during the risk management activities, more specifically during the impact analysis stage.

The security monitoring processes could be classified in two main groups. The first group is called *security state monitoring*, which is essentially concerned with the configuration

---

[16]   B. Schneier, "Managed Security Monitoring: Network Security for the 21st Century," *Computers & Security*, vol. 20 ((2001)), pp. 491-503, 2001.

[17]   The configuration management and control is related to the problem of change management.

system, and it might serve as starting point for problem management.[18] The second group is called the *security event monitoring* and it is mostly concerned with real-time reporting of the security events, which serves as a starting point for the incident management.

For example, in respect of system monitoring, and especially the IDS technology that might be used, the standard of good practices for information security (ISF) envisages the performance (Section CI 1.4 of the standard) of

- detection of known attack characteristics;
- detection of unusual system behaviour;
- a process to incorporate new attack characteristics;
- documentation on how to alert personnel of the suspicious activities; and
- protection of the IDS software itself.

Independently of the tools being used to perform those two facets of the information security monitoring, both should be relying on some predefined rules on how the different subjects of the monitoring would behave or by defining some common features related to them. For example, ISO/IEC 27002:2005 describes several measures that should be implemented in order to monitor the operation of a given system such as the access rights, the processes necessitating an access control, unauthorized access attempts, the appropriate means of alarm, and so on.

A qualitative monitoring system should foresee the performance of three main tasks:

- *The selection of the information security controls* or processes to monitor. Obviously it is impossible to closely monitor all the implemented security measures. The selection should reflect the priorities and importance of the information system to the organization;
- *The measurement system,* which will be used to depict the situation and to be used as a tool for decision-making. The metrics have to be focused on the implementation, operation, and desired outcome issues regarding the monitored information security controls;
- *The reporting system* to be put in place without which the monitoring would be considered valueless.

The monitoring activities will locate such vulnerabilities or eventual nonconformities (in a broadest sense) likely to give rise to problems. Once those vulnerabilities or nonconformities have been identified, a plan of critical updates, along with a plan of actions and milestones, should be established in order to put monitoring on an effective basis.[19] Besides this, the standard of good practices for information security (ISF) recommends that

---

[18]   More information about this notion can be found within the *ITIL method* (http://www.itil-officialsite.com/Publications/Core.asp)

[19]   NIST, "Guide for the Security Certification and Accreditation of Federal Information Systems (NIST Special Publication 800-37)," U.S. Departement of Commerce, National Institute of Standards and Technology, Computer Security Division 2004. Available at
http://csrc.nist.gov/publications/nistpubs/800-37/SP800-37-final.pdf
NIST, "DRAFT Guide for Applying the Risk Management Framework to Federal Information Systems: A Security Life Cycle Approach (NIST Special Publication 800-37 Revision 1)," U.S. Department of Commerce, National Institute of Standards and Technology, Computer Security Division 2009. Available at
http://csrc.nist.gov/publications/drafts/800-37-Rev1/SP800-37-rev1-FPD.pdf

monitoring activities should include the reporting of the financial information related to the security practices, such as the cost of security controls, financial impacts of the security incidents, and the return on investments of the deployed security controls.

The monitoring activities will be a strict prerequisite in respect of change management, which will ensure that that the continuous improvement is derived from a solid basis. As such it should pertain to the whole information security element, going from the strategy related issues through architectural issues to the technological ones. The monitoring process brings into focus a wide number of changes introduced to the system, either from new risk concerns or from organic modifications within the technology being used or within the different processes.

Change management

Change management is one of the most important processes that should be operated within the organization to allow the enhancement of the quality of the information security posture. This discipline, historically exclusively used by *quality personnel*, is becoming more and more relevant for security personnel. Throughout this book, the quality issues are considered as an inseparable aspect of information security having a direct impact on the protection level provided by the implementation of the information security program. Change management ensures that necessary changes are applied correctly and do not compromise the security of the assets or business processes. As such, change management is mostly related to the procedural side of information security rather than the technological one. Most of the incidents are directly related to a change. The change could rise from different sources such as user needs, improvement necessities, laws, new security requirements, obsolescence of the hardware and software infrastructure, etc. What is important in this context is to administer and manage the potential change. It means establishing a fair compromise between the different factors liable to arise during a change. As a crucial process focused on quality issues, change management should strive to become a standardized process characterized by its traceability, legibility, and identity.

In the first place, any potential change should be the subject of a *request for change* including precise structural details about the change.[20] The details provided will allow the prioritization of the change based on its potential impact or its urgency. After that, based on the prioritization order, a categorization order is established. The categories are based on the standard or nonstandard character of the change. A standard change follows a predetermined path, while a nonstandard change could be categorized in three sub-categories, namely: major change, significant change, and minor change.

Once the descriptive step is completed, an important phase of change handling has to be considered. This phase is based on an analysis regarding:

- The ecosystem, which means: the identification of the processes, information resources, organizational and human capacities on which the change will have impact or with which it will interact;
- The change's lifecycle starting from the change recording and going up to the closing date. To each one of the life cycle phases some specific activities should be assigned;
- The change planning in terms of timescale.

---

20   Information related to its management, follow-up handling and descriptive information.

The third evaluation facet related to the change management evaluation concerns the responsibility related to the change process. The ITIL method[21] recognizes that for every change procedure there should be a "change manager" who is the person responsible for the change process management as well as the consistency of the process. After the change has been applied, the process is not yet finished. In order to avoid, or address, potential problems related to the change, a follow-up procedure should be devised including:

- The change recording and details;
- The communication about the new situation documenting the before and after states;
- The checks to be performed in order to confirm the effectiveness of the change process.

CISA and the standard of good practices for information security (ISF)[22] require a formalized and documented process of change request, authorization testing implementation and communication to the users. As such it has to be embodied in policies, information security plans and operational practices.

Incident Management

The organizational capability to manage security incidents is the trigger element of the functional dimension of the information security program. The management of an incident is determined on the one hand by the detection of the threat activity and on the other hand by the appropriate response to such an incident, in order to contain the activity and to avoid the security incident turning into a disaster. An incident is characterized by a revenue loss and a negative business impact caused by the failure of a given activity or by the lowering of the expected result of the activity. For ISO/IEC 27002:2005[23] the incident management should include the communication of security incidents as well as security holes. As such the crucial activity that should obligatorily be considered is the reporting upwards of the relevant information. Generally the incident management related issues are based on two dimensions:

- The incident handling;
- The incident response.

An incident is any adverse event or situation that poses a threat to the security objectives of availability, integrity and confidentiality; information incident management is considered as a key protective measure with the goal of limiting negative activities. On a practical basis, the organization should draw up an event list establishing some *identifying factors* characterizing a distinguishable incident. The latter is an important basis for the detection phase of the incident management focus area. The *incident management process* should be able to provide three kinds of services:

- Proactive services, the assistance provided to anticipate the security incident;

21   *ITIL method* (http://www.itil-officialsite.com/Publications/Core.asp).
22   ISACA, *CISA Review Manual 2006*, Rolling Meadows, Illinois, USA Information Systems Audit and Control Association (ISACA), 2006.
      ISF-std. *The Standard of Good Practice for Information Security*, Information Security Forum, 2007.
23   ISO/IEC 27002:2005, Information technology – Security techniques – Code of practice for information security management, International Organization for Standardization (ISO), Switzerland, 2005.

- Reactive services, the activities to be initiated when there is an indication that an event is occurring;
- Security quality management services considering activities such as risk analysis, business continuity, awareness raising etc.

Incident management can be handled with a five-step procedure, including:
- Incident identification and notification;
- Incident containment limiting the scope and the magnitude of the incident;
- Incident eradication ensuring that the cause of the incident is eliminated;
- Recovery restoring the IT environment;
- Follow-up on an improvement scope.

The response phase aims to contain the incident, prevent its escalation and, if possible, preserve of evidence of what happened for future investigation. ISO/IEC 13355-3[24] recommends that an IT incident analysis scheme be constructed and organized to support risk analysis and other security related activities. A successful incident handling capacity, according to NIST,[25] demonstrates the following characteristics:
- The understanding and the education of the constituency (including computer users and program managers);
- Centralized means of communication;
- Expertise in the requisite technologies;
- Links between the other groups to assist in incident handling.

At the same time the incident response function should contain the capacities to address the following issues:
- Reporting of the security incident;
- Triage in order to prioritize incidents susceptible of causing the most significant damage;
- Formal identification of the key details of the incident (sources, severity);
- Coordination of the recovery efforts;
- Containment of propagation;
- Eradication of the incident;
- Recovery phase;
- Notification phase.

Then the same steps as described for the change management should be applied from a quality point of view based on ITIL, including the ecosystem, the life cycle, and planning.

---

24   ISO/IEC TR 13335-3, Information Technology – Guidelines for the management of IT Security – Techniques for the management of IT Security, International Organization for Standardization (ISO), Switzerland, 1996.

25   NIST, *An Introduction to Computer Security – The NIST Handbook (Special Publication 800-12)* National Institute of Standards and Technology – US Department of Commerce, 2004. Available at http://csrc.nist.gov/publications/nistpubs/800-12/

Incident response management is one of the key success factors for resumption, specifically for the Business Continuity Plan (BCP). This is particularly true for incident detection, which is the basis of the initiation of the business continuity plan procedures[26].

5.4 Resumption and continuity

The resumption and continuity focus area is the last area of the functional protection mechanisms from which an organization could benefit. Within this phase, it is assumed that all the other protection efforts have failed and consequently the risk has been, or is imminently going to be, exploited. This is the first distinguishing feature capable of differentiating the overall information security efforts from those of resumption. Within this evaluation framework, the resumption and continuity related efforts are considered as one of the multiple components constituting the information security program. The second distinguishing feature, when discussing resumption and continuity activities or procedures, is the severity and the target of the risk coming to fruition. It has to be underlined that numerous categories of risk are potentially harmful for the organizational values and the current organization is not able in practice to cover each of them. Consequently, it might so happen that a risk will be exploited thus disrupting the ongoing processes and damaging the organization. The disruptions could be categorized as:
- Non-disaster stemming from a business malfunction;
- Disaster, where a disruption causes the entire facility to be inoperative for a lengthy period of time;
- Catastrophe, where a major disruption to the facility causes destruction of the data.

In these cases the resumption-related activities would consider any risk event that potentially could result in a disaster or catastrophe. The principal resumption and continuity related processes are the Business Continuity and Disaster Recovery Planning (BCP/DRP).

Before analyzing business continuity and disaster recovery planning, a specific risk evaluation procedure, dedicated to the BCP/DRP scope, should be initiated. The risk evaluation process related to a BCP/DRP is more specific, with reference to the overall risk evaluation process and belonging to the overall risk management process. Nevertheless, the approaches remain similar, with an identification of the exposures, the determination of the probabilities, and the identification of the controls. But this risk evaluation process related to the BCP/DRP will mostly be focused on specific features such as the vital records, the evaluation of the backups, and the cost of the downtime, all of these having as an objective to provide a risk prioritization grid. At this stage, it is necessary for the organization to strictly prioritize which of the parameters, among criticality or loss extent, will be the determinant variable motivating the future action to be undertaken. There are two parameters that practically are used either as synonyms or as counterparts. In a BCP/DRP scope, it is important that a clear distinction be made between them. This is because only one of them will be the starting point and/or the focus point of the entire BCP/DRP. The difference between the criticality and the loss extent will be discussed in depth within the section related to the business impact analysis.

---

26   ISACA, *CISA Review Manual 2006*. Rolling Meadows, Illinois, USA Information Systems Audit and Control Association (ISACA), 2006.

5.4.1 Business continuity planning constituents

The CISA (Certified Information Systems Auditor) review manual[26] defines the overall process of the business continuity as being the activity that could:

- Enable business to continue offering critical services;
- Ensure business will survive a disastrous event.

The business continuity plan is the ensemble of preparative processes and practices that ensure the preservation of the business in the face of major disruptions. Continuity, in the form of a normal state of a business, is ensured based on two main processes incorporated into resumption and continuity related activities, namely the disaster recovery and the contingency planning, which together make up the overall process of business continuity planning.

The BCP is designed to avoid or mitigate risks and their impact, thus reducing the time to restore the normal state of business by safeguarding the organizational assets and hence ensuring the continued existence of the entire organization. The main risk that is considered in a BCP is the interruption of business. The standard of good practices for information security (ISF) expects an effective BCP to cover the unavailability of critical information and systems such as the business areas, business applications and IT facilities. It results from the two predecessor procedures, the Recovery and Contingency (Figure 5.2).

Disaster recovery planning specifies procedures to enact when a disaster occurs. More specifically a DRP is an action plan document, designed to assist the organization in recovering from data losses and restoring data assets resulting from the catastrophic events. As we can see in the definition given below, the DRP is for the recovery of the Information Systems Department of a given organization. With respect to the BCP, the very closely related and interdependent element of the DRP is more focused on IT systems, while the BCP is concerned with the stability of the critical business processes. The scope of the DRP is the restoration of the availability of the IT systems. To summarize, and at the same time clarify the positioning of the BCP with respect to the DRP, it can be stated that: the immediate output of the DRP is the prompt restoration of the infrastructure capacities allowing the subsequent attainment of the second objective belonging to the BCP, which is the reduction of the impact and the return to normality.

On the other hand, the concept of the contingency is a *middle zone* concept that is often used as a synonym for business continuity in general. In fact, in our understanding it

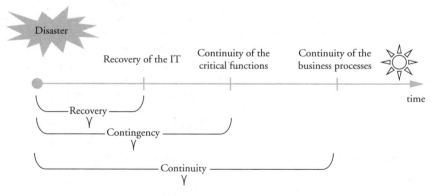

Fig. 5.2 Business continuity and resumption's activities timescale and role.

is a transition phase going from the immediate reaction the organization should provide in response to a disaster to the actions to be undertaken to ensure the ultimate objective of the whole resumption and continuity dimension, which is the return to normality. With respect to business continuity, contingency planning is a process assuring the continuity at a local level. According to the same author, the principal scope of contingency planning is to manage the very important issue of downtime costs. NIST in "Contingency planning guide for information technology systems"[27] discusses the same idea of the continuity scope at a local level and specifies that the contingency planning is a user manual for executing the continuity strategy. Contingency planning is to make provision for continuing business processes in a disaster situation. It is based on three processes: the identification of the critical functions, the possible disaster scenarios, and the development of the procedures to address these concerns.

Five elements should be considered in order to establish successful contingency planning:
- Conditions for initiation;
- Critical timescale;
- Schedule of key tasks;
- Detailed procedures;
- Security controls to be applied.

Other elements could be mentioned and the list proposed below could contain even more detail. What is most important, though, and is brought out by this classification, is the fact that contingency planning is a procedure that absolutely requires accuracy in the way its procedures will be performed.

The very first key success factor for BC/DR planning is to consider the organization as a complex and ever-changing entity comprising a wide range of constituent elements (equipment, people, tasks, departments, communication methods, interfaces etc.) and to understand all of these intricacies and their interrelationships. As we can notice here, we are involved in preventive efforts in order to ensure the continued existence of the organization, even in the case of a catastrophic event. This is the main reason for the inclusion of the BCP into the overall information security program and more specifically to consider it as a fully-fledged element of an information security management system. We think that the achievement of BCP/DRP objectives is conditioned by
- the use of pertinent information;
- the creation of a solid structure in terms of needs assessment and disaster management;
- the basing of continuity strategies on a realistic panorama of the organization's concerns; and
- the culture of change management.

A successful BCP thus hinges on four main pillars:
- Crisis management;
- Collection of documents;
- Backup strategy;
- Emergency solutions.

---

27   NIST, "Contingency Planning Guide for Information Technology Systems (SP 800-34)," U.S. Department of Commerce, National Institute of Standards and Technology 2002. Available at http://csrc.nist.gov/publications/nistpubs/800-34/sp800-34.pdf

Lifecycle processes of the business continuity plan

There are some invariable activities within a business continuity process. These activities present more or less the same characteristics as the whole information security program. The business continuity plan is based on three main groups of processes focused on the initiation and formalization of the project, its design, development, and implementation, and the managerial control activities dedicated to it.

Initiation and formalization

The first group of initiation and formalization could be split into two sections. The first concerns the knowledge of the organization and aims to provide an accurate business impact analysis that is based on risk management outputs. The second section is related to the strategic decisions that should be taken based on the knowledge of the organization. The first section, namely the knowledge of the organization, aims to provide a faithful panorama of the organization, its structure, its working conditions and requirements, and its interdependencies to consequently set up the critical components to be worthy of a particular attention. This first section will therefore be focused on the following issues:

- The establishment of the scope and objectives for the BCP;
- The definition and the acquisition of the resource requirements;
- The constitution of a team responsible for carrying out the whole project;
- The support and commitment of management should be gained and demonstrated (as indeed it should be for the overall information security program).

Within the Business Impact Analysis (BIA), the knowledge of the organization goes deeper than the risk management process, by identifying and analyzing all kinds of risks the organization might face and those are liable to have a catastrophic effect upon the organization. In the second section of the first group of BCP processes, the expected result should first of all be the BCP scope and objectives criteria, as well as the management's commitment and involvement in the different project phases. An important element needing to be addressed during the first group of activities of initiation and formalization is the project's resource requirements. It is a key element that is closely correlated with the effectiveness of the whole project of the BCP. But in more general terms, BCP's first group of initiation and formalization is about all the preparatory activities in order to avoid catastrophic effects.

Design, development and implementation

The second group of the design, development, and implementation effort is about the implementation of the continuity plan and the strategies related to it, in order to devise the action plans on how to react in a crisis situation. This is performed through a formal planning of the activities, resources and procedures necessary to overcome a crisis situation and the impacts of the disaster. The standard of good practices for information security (ISF) identifies the three most necessary elements for an effective BCP.

- The first elements concern the list of services subject to the BCP. It determines the essential services that should be kept operational in spite of the disaster and its extent. It should be noticed here that from a BCP perspective, the important feature to be taken into account is the service, or more precisely the output that the given service provides. The identification of the service itself will be considered as a selection criterion to then identify the resources to be recovered.

- The second central group of elements concerns the list of tasks to be performed in the event that the BCP plan is activated. In fact, if it does prove necessary to activate the plan, the "stress" factor should not be neglected. In this case the knowledge of the tasks to be undertaken, as well the degree of ease of becoming familiar with them, becomes a necessity rather than a simple success factor.
- The third group of central elements of a BCP includes the guidelines. The idea is that all the procedures and tasks will be managed and run by human elements. As such a deep knowledge of the why and how should be ensured in order to take appropriate actions in a stressful situation.

Managerial and control activities

The third group of the managerial and control activities is directly related to the quality of the expected output of the whole BCP program. This group includes the activities of monitoring, reviewing and testing that are vital for the BCP. In fact, "when the time to respond is at hand, the time to plan is over", wrote Jeff Morgan, a Delta Airlines emergency response manager. In that sense, the managerial and control activities are engaged throughout the whole process from the beginning to the end. In the beginning a continuity planning policy will be the point of reference, as was the case for the information security program. This is because within the continuity planning policy are included the continuity requirements, roles and responsibilities that are the backbone of the whole process. Once the operational part is developed, all the BCP processes, procedures and activities should be regularly controlled[28] because the smooth running of the BCP processes is more stressful than the performance of security activities trying to fix a security breach or event. By definition the organization stands here in a crisis situation, where it is important that the response should not only be quick but also precise in terms of capability and expected results.

To summarize, as the dependence on the information systems increases, the BCP/DRP has to be increasingly integrated with information security planning. For that matter, the BCP is fully considered as one of the links of the security chain. The business continuity plan is the tangible evidence that a business continuity management system exists within the traditional integrated management system.

Business Impact Analysis (BIA) – A crucial and specific stage of the BCP

Business Impact Analysis (BIA) is one of the most important and the most specific steps of BCP. In the analogy made below, that the BCP is an information security program *in miniature* specific to a small part of the overall security concern dedicated to a crisis situation,[29] the BIA should be analogously considered as being the risk analysis function. The "BCP Good Practice Guidelines"[30] define the business impact analysis as a mandatory process for evaluating the impact over time of a disruption to an organization's ability to operate. Resources that are absolutely essential for the organization should be identified and the time during which the company may continue the business without these resources should be estimated.

---

28 Controlled in this context means: reviewed, updated, improved and tested.
29 Especially harming the availability of the organizational resources.
30 BCI, "Business Continuity Management – Good Practice Guidelines 2008," Business Continuity Institute 2008. [Online] Available at http://www.thebci.org/gpgdownloadpage.htm

The criterion of criticality is the one that will define the business processes that have to be taken into consideration by the BCP program. By "critical" should be understood all these functions that cannot be performed unless they are replaced by identical capabilities and that have a low tolerance to the interruption. Multiple selection criteria could be used, particularly the geographical or functional criteria advised by the *good practices for BCP*. Nevertheless, the most important element in the selection criteria is not which of the criteria it is better to choose, but rather remaining coherent among them. That means that for a large organization the final criteria should be the same all over the organizational boundaries.

There are three questions a Business Impact Analysis should answer:
- What are the critical business processes?
- What are the critical information resources related to those critical business resources?
- What is the critical recovery time?

Furthermore, there are three areas to be assessed in the case of a Business Analysis Impact, namely:
- The business interruption;
- The revenue losses;
- The costs of embarrassment.

The attribute to be evaluated when performing a business impact analysis is the impact that a given disaster scenario will have because of the interruption of a business process judged as critical for the organization. As might be deduced, the main concern of a business impact analysis is the availability of the process. It seems that there are two main moments that have to be clearly distinguished in a business impact analysis scope. The first is the identification and the second is the prioritization. Both have to define a very important subject worthy of being taken in consideration by the business continuity plan. These two moments specifically correspond to two main attributes, respectively criticality and impact.

In this way, the criticality attribute should be used to identify among numerous business processes the most critical ones, those whose disruption might prove to be catastrophic. Given the fact that ICTs are more and more integrated into the business processes and constitute a non-negligible component of the organizational business environment, the risk is that the organization might have a tendency to consider all IT processes as being critical. In fact, in order to choose among a great number of critical processes, the attribute of the impact should be introduced. It is clear that the processes and resources presenting a probability of great impact should be prioritized and should be the subject of recovery and contingency countermeasures. Furthermore the embarrassment cost resulting from a public-relations exposure is a crucial attribute distinguishing a crisis situation. A crisis situation should be managed as driven from two matters of interest, the internal and the external. The internal-related concerns involve the extent of the damage as well as the technical fixes. The external ones, which seem to be the most distinctive attribute when speaking about a disaster, concern the activities related to the customers and public relations management.

Here should be underlined the idea that, from a business impact analysis point of view, the concept of the business process is used instead of the concept of the assets that has usually been used up to now. In fact it arises from making a clear distinction between what is *important* and what is *critical.* In fact something being considered as critical is inevitably important but the opposite might not be true; something could be considered as important without being necessarily considered as critical. Considering the security objectives, availability, integrity and confidentiality, the concept of critical assets is strongly related to the availability objective. The lack of availability leads to an interruption of the service directly related to its physical (tangible) existence. Availability is the security objective that is specifically required by the standard of good practices for information security (ISF) to denote a critical situation. In fact ISF imposes on business continuity planning the objective of covering the prolonged unavailability of different resources such as key individuals, business information, system or application software as well as network services and office utilities. The other security objectives that do not have an impact on the direct existence of the asset are not considered as being important. In this sense there are three mandatory processes to be considered when performing a business impact analysis:[31]

- The identification of the critical business processes to identify the IT critical resources related to them;
- The identification of the disruption impacts related to these resources;
- The development of the recovery priorities.

There are three objectives a business impact analysis should achieve with respect to each activity:[32]

- The documentation of the impact;
- The determination of the Recovery Point Objective (RPO) and of the Recovery Time Objective (RTO). RPO is the amount of data loss that is deemed acceptable and RTO is the amount of time it takes, from initial disaster declaration, to having critical business processes available;
- The identification of the dependencies.

Concerning the identification of the impact, an exhaustive identification of the business processes should be performed in order to provide a solid basis in order to settle critical business processes. During the impact assessment the organization should pay attention to the selection criteria, that is to say the business processes and the methodology used to identify them. Organizations should remain coherent when choosing the criteria categorizing business processes. Two criteria could be used to identify the business processes, namely the geographical criterion and the functional criterion. On the other hand coherence is also required when calculating the impact. The use of a homogenous criterion is needed. The organization should decide between the use of the operational criterion to assess the impact or the use of the financial criterion. By operational should be understood the impact that the interruption of the critical business process will generate with respect to the internal and external dependencies.

Backup
Once the critical processes and the resources related to them are identified, the first operational step to be undertaken is the constitution of backups, either in capacity-related terms or as important electronic data to be safeguarded, in order to enable the continuity of the business

---

31   NIST, "Contingency Planning Guide for Information Technology Systems (SP 800-34)," U.S. Department of Commerce, National Institute of Standards and Technology 2002. [Online] Available at http://csrc.nist.gov/publications/nistpubs/800-34/sp800-34.pdf

32   BCI, "Business Continuity Management – Good Practice Guidelines 2008," Business Continuity Institute 2008. [Online] Available at http://www.thebci.org/gpgdownloadpage.htm

processes. The back up strategy is one of the DRP activities aiming to speed up the process of disaster recovery and, as such, the cornerstone of the entire business continuity plan. It is about short-term alternatives allowing the organization to recover from a major disruption and take up essential activities again. As such, it will be one of the elements of the DRP that will allow prompt recovery, ensuring that contingency activities are progressing as smoothly as planned. A distinction can be made between the recovery backup and operational backup. The latter concerns daily activities and has the objective of overcoming ordinary and common incidents. The recovery backup is the one that allows an organization to handle a major disruption.

A great part of the success of backups relies on the offsite libraries. This element is a subject of evaluation within our model, examining the backup quality of the organization. In general, the analysis related to the recovery issues should be oriented on three main elements:

- Materials, including hardware, software or any other tangible asset necessary to successfully perform the backup mission;
- Electronic data that should be available in order to continue the business processes;
- Personnel to operate these resources.

The first step regarding the backup solution is to choose the appropriate solution according to the organizational needs. There are some criteria to be considered when choosing backup solutions such as:

- Capacity;
- Technical compatibility;
- Shelf life;
- Restoration time;
- Software solution;
- Regulatory requirements.

Once the analysis is completed a multilayered backup method should be implemented in order to be able to ensure the continuity of the basic business processes. Physical backup, logical backup and application backup can usually be proposed.

5.4.2 Disaster Recovery Planning

The Disaster Recovery Plan (DRP) is a plan set up to enable an organization, and specifically its computer installation, to quickly restore operations and resume business in the event of a disaster. It consists of procedures to implement immediately following a significant event, while the business continuity planning is more a long-term strategy for organizational survival.

The disaster recovery plan involves three processes:

- Construction involves a planning committee that performs a risk analysis for all functional areas. The output is a plan of actions that has to be approved by the top management;
- Adoption;
- Evaluation.

As mentioned previously, the disaster recovery plan plays the role of a *buffer zone* between the disruption of the normal business processes and the return to normality. The recovery procedure will address the restoration of the lost or damaged facilities. As such, the disaster recovery plan has to take the form of a very formal procedure sustained by a written plan and a clear mission statement. The plan incorporates the procedures to be undertaken in the case of a business disruption in terms of actions to be taken, persons to be involved, infrastructure to be employed and resources to be available. The main challenge to be addressed by an organization in terms of disaster recovery plan is to pass from a recovery procedure to a formal plan, which means that all the employees must be familiar with the aforementioned plan. At the same time the recovery plan should be based on some clear and identifiable objectives, thus resembling the mission statement.

There is another important aspect to be evaluated when talking about the disaster recovery plan, namely the test of such a plan. The aim is to perform regular tests in order to improve the plan and to perfect employees' reactions in the event of a disaster. Regular testing of the plan is of the utmost importance because the plan is designed to be activated under stress. This means that there is no time to dedicate to other tasks outside the plan. Everyone should know clearly what they have to do in an emergency, and what is right to do during a given period of time. The following availability-related technology attributes should be assessed in order to offer an adequate recovery level:

- Timeline;
- Mainframes;
- Arrays;
- Distributed architectures;
- Instant backup;
- Redundant infrastructure.

5.4.3 Business continuity planning as a coherent process

The business continuity plan is the activity allowing organizations to identify their critical infrastructure by identifying the critical missions within the overall diagram of the business functions. The identification of the critical missions brings up the identification of the supporting resources, which could be human resources, process capability, applications and data, and physical infrastructure. The output of such a BCP will be the internal controls in place allowing organizations to:

- develop an emergency response designed to protect lives and limit damage;
- set up an appropriate recovery phase as specified within the recovery objectives of the business continuity plan; and
- provide a prompt resumption to return to normality as fast as possible.

To do that the disaster recovery plan should rest on a five-phase methodology, allowing staff to administer and manage the plan.

The first phase concerns knowledge of the organization, its primary purpose and critical factors. This phase, as mentioned above, concerns identification of the critical processes and identification of the potential risks related to those processes. Consequently, knowledge of the organization allows determination of a crisis mapping, as well as the recovery objectives, based on the eventual points of failure. The result of this first phase should be a plan of action capable of reducing the risk impacts on critical processes.

The second phase concerns the disaster recovery plan strategy. This strategy, based on the first phase results, will enable alternative methods and means regarding the continuity of the organization's activity. This BCP strategy might be devised based on different levels of granularity such as, for example, a global strategy or a local one. The result of the strategy will allow the choice of the most appropriate technical recovery solutions.

The third phase concerns the establishment of the disaster recovery plan with respect to the second phase. This phase requires first of all the acquisition of a technical infrastructure. In order to be correctly operated, this technical infrastructure will need firstly to be tested and secondly to be enhanced by organizational procedures in terms of personnel and tasks.

The fourth phase concerns the development of the disaster recovery plan. After having considered the risks, needs and resources, the organization then needs to apply this information to a real situation. The real situation will concern a potential crisis situation and for this a number of elements should be analysed. First of all, certain features should be decided in order to be sure of the nature and gravity of the event that would require the activation of the disaster recovery plan. Around this notion of crisis there are two features to be addressed: the way the crisis will be managed including the reaction modes and responsiveness criteria; and the organizational resources in terms of teams that will handle the crisis, including the crisis units or response team. Each one of these teams will possess its own organizational schema and dedicated infrastructure.

The fifth phase concerns the disaster recovery plan awareness related activities as well as the tests of the BCP and its regular review. Almost all authorities consider that testing is essential to determine whether the disaster recovery plan is adequate to address critical risks.

Several times in the BCP related section we have compared the latter to the whole information security program/system. Going in the same direction and to ensure that the whole process remains coherent and controllable, a disaster recovery plan policy and a BCP itself should be devised. The disaster recovery plan policy addresses issues such as the definition of the different concepts (more specifically, what might constitute a crisis situation), the top management's commitment, guiding principles, plan-related objectives and related requirements. The BCP itself will specify the goals, the organizational aspects, the procedures allowing achieving the goals and the improvement-related means and tasks.

5.5 Evaluating the functional dimension

Based on the evaluation model proposed within Chapter 3, the evaluation assurance structure of the functional dimension of the information security is as presented in Figure 5.3.

In order to appropriately evaluate the functional dimension, the assurance evaluation structure was put into a timescale focused on the *protection targets* and categorized into three performing periods regarding the potential risks: ex-ante, ongoing and ex-post. The protection targets of the first and second period are the organizational valuable assets, while the protection target related to the third period concerns the critical organizational assets.

The first sub-dimension of problem framing concerns all the activities focused on the assets and the risks these assets might face. Practically speaking the risk management process is aiming to mitigate risks by the implementation of some appropriate information security safeguards. Evaluating the capacity of the organization to manage its risk includes different tasks.

The first evidence is provided by the existence of a risk management policy as an important document guiding the organization to become aware of the different impacts. The risk policy should specify the logical path to follow, based on identification efforts of the assets and the related risks to come up with implementable solutions based on the security safe-

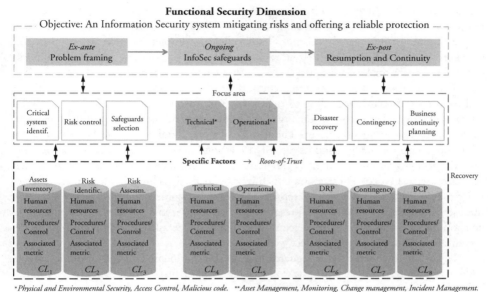

Fig. 5.3 The evaluation assurance structure related to the functional dimension.

guards. In that sense, evidence is given by the existence of asset lists along with the different risks that might concern those assets. This pair of features having been established, risk treatment and mitigation strategies regarding every risk should feature in the policy. As we can notice here, once the assets have been identified, the target of the analysis changes to focus exclusively on risks. The mitigation strategies have to be based on formal methodologies in order to be as exhaustive and efficient as possible. From an effectiveness point of view, the risk policy should be elaborated upon in a risk management plan and a responsible person be assigned to both of them, thus ensuring consistency and quality.

It should be highlighted that the three above-mentioned activities constituting the problem framing (risk constituents, risk handling process, risk monitoring) should be performed almost in parallel, because each could represent a very useful input to the others. Based on this point, the person who will evaluate the organization from a risk perspective should differentiate between organizations that have already been performing such processes for a certain time and those that are just beginning the implementation. This is true even if the processes or the elements described above that provide the assurance that risks are correctly addressed, are being performed in both situations. The experienced organization possesses an important advantage over the beginner because performing such activities in parallel should be less of a problem as it could leverage previous efforts and base the analysis on the previous scenarios.

From a measurement point of view, metrics related to the problem framing issues should be focused on the accomplishment of the objectives stated within the policy. To take an example, a potential metric to be used is the number of the identified important assets that are accompanied by at least two procedural or control measures. This kind of metrics might be established for all three focus areas.

The second sub-dimension of ongoing activities concerns the information security safeguards that have already been chosen. The aim is to enable effective results and hence considerable risk reduction. Independent of their technical or operational character, the implementation quality feature is common and evidence of their existence will be provided by the outputs of the related processes. The evidence of implementation will be provided based on the availability of the different resources that each one of these processes requires in order to be operational, and the effective duty assigned to these resources.

The evaluation model takes into account the functional difference between operational and technical safeguards according to their goals and their nature. As such, technical safeguards will mostly depend on the quality of the technology and the accuracy of their selection based on the risk mitigation needs. The quality of the technology should be evidenced by the prior-acquisition analysis and its capacity to respond to situational concerns. At the same time the accuracy of the selection is evidenced by the coherence of the arguments on which the selection was based. Those arguments might be focused exclusively on financial characteristics or on risk protection characteristics. Nevertheless contractual agreements regarding the use of support for the technical resource as well as after-sale services agreements could be good indicators to show that the acquisition followed a detailed reflection concerning the organizational intentions with respect to the technology.

Regarding the operational safeguards, they are mostly focused on the procedural aspect and consequently will depend on the evidence based on quality-related issues such as standardized procedures, communication about the procedural features and review of the achievement of objectives. Evidence of the accuracy of the operational safeguards can be obtained when all the related concepts are clearly defined by the use of formal attributes. This statement is applicable with respect to asset management, monitoring practices, change or incident management. A procedure should exist for each operational focus area and specialized entities should also exist to administer and manage them.

From a metrics point of view, technical measures will be affected by the success rate with respect to their expected or planned outputs. For example, regarding the antivirus solutions the penetration rate with respect to the number of instances of malware stopped might be a good indicator of the success rate of this technology. Regarding the operational safeguards metrics, the emphasis should be placed on the knowledge of the procedural tasks. As such, a potential metric could be the number of the employees concerned by a given procedure compared with the number of employees that really master the procedure. In addition, objective achievement related metrics should also be used, such as for example the number of changes that were subject to a change management procedure as the model's previous sections described it.

The third sub-dimension concerns the ex-post activities based on the resumption and continuity processes. This third sub-dimension was also structured on a time-scale basis. The particularity of this sub-dimension resides in the fact that within it are present both technical solutions and procedural ones. As such, the characteristics discussed above are relevant for this sub-dimension too. Nevertheless the resumption and continuity sub-dimension demonstrates some specific attributes such as the definition of the event (disaster or not) and the documentation of the conditions under which the plan will be activated. Since the resumption and continuity sub-dimension is related to hypothetical and infrequent events, the existence of the BCP itself is very strong evidence to be considered during the evaluation. On the other hand, based on the importance of the plan in the situations where it will be activated, tests and reviewing efforts are of a great importance from an evaluation point of view.

Regarding the metric side of the resumption and continuity sub-dimension, it will be focused on three main categories:

- The metrics focused on effectiveness issues such as the number of the potential events or identified critical assets considered by the plan;
- The metrics focused on the accuracy of the plan such as the number of potential events that could be handled with respect to the available recovery technologies;
- The metrics focused on the proficiency of the plan such as the number of employees mastering the plan with respect to the total number of employees.

5.6 The maturity model related to the functional dimension

Based on the analysis made above the following maturity model is proposed for the functional dimension of the information security (Figure 5.4).

Level 1 Fortuitous	• *Existence of at least one dimension:* In general situated within the current security practices characterized by some implemented InfoSec safeguards motivated by day-to-day protection needs. • *No existing focus area structure:* This implies current risk-related issues are addressed by baseline technical safeguards included in the backup for the critical applications and data. • *Isolated specific factors:* These are generally situated at the procedures/controls level, with some classical risk being addressed by the use of some technical safeguards. *No quality specification can be done*
Level 2 Structured	• *A clear and formal existence of the dimensions:* Efforts are made within the organization in terms of risk analysis and safeguards administration accorded to it. The residual risks as well as the potential natural disasters are the subject of a preventive plan. • *Focus area structure mostly exists:* Risk identification and evaluation, as well as technical and operational safeguards, are carried out; the objectives to be attained are defined. In terms of resumption and continuity, the efforts are mostly focused on the disaster recovery issues. • *Specific factors include two attributes:* For each identified focus area, the specific factors procedure/controls and human resource could be assigned. *The quality level has reached the first level,* which means that risk, security and resumption-related activities are included within the information security policy or any other strategic document related to the information security field.
Level 3 Functional	• *The architecture is complete:* The three dimensions and the eight focus areas exist, as described within the model, thus providing the risk-treatment strategies based on risk analysis and security-safeguard implementation. These take the operational processes into account, with resumption and continuity based on approved plans. • *Specific factors:* In general, the attributes for procedure/controls and human resources are identifiable for each related focus area. *The quality level* is characterized by an average weighting level of two, which means that risk, security and resumption-related activities aspects are the responsibility of a specific person (organizational function, job function).
Level 4 Analyzable	• *The architecture is complete:* The three dimensions and the eight focus areas exist, as described within the model. • *Specific factors:* The three general attributes are identifiable for each related focus area, which means that the level of metrics is reached for each focus area. *The quality level* is characterized by an average weighting level that equals three, which means that the that specific factors are minimally documented and/or monitored.
Level 5 Effective	• *The architecture is complete:* The three dimensions and the eight focus areas exist, as described within the model. • *Specific factors:* The three general attributes are identifiable for each related focus area, which means that the level of metrics is reached for each specific factor. *The quality level* has an average weight that clearly equals four, signaling that a procedure for continual improvement is imputed to each focus area, where internal/external reviews and audits are regularly performed.

Fig. 5.4 The maturity model related to the functional dimension.

5.7 Chapter summary

This chapter has focused on the functional dimension of information security, which is the dimension that will directly contribute to the diminuation of the probable risk damage. The expected output of these dimensions is to enable the information security system to mitigate risks and to offer reliable protection. Having risk as a reference point, we categorize the dimension based on a timescale approach and identify the ex-ante processes allowing the organization to obtain knowledge about risks and assets, terming this "framing the problem." We then identify the different information security safeguards for what we called ongoing processes, composed of technical and operational safeguards. Issues related to these safeguards have been discussed based on their functional characteristics. In addition to the measures taken to mitigate risks, we also introduce into the model what we called ex-post-processes. These are the processes and plans allowing the organization to better manage the situations where risks are exploited. For each of these three focus areas we identify the key success factors and the elements for which evidence should be provided in order to claim assurance. A specific maturity model of the functional dimension is proposed in order to allow the organization to identify and situate its specific security requirements.

Chapter 6

Evaluating the Human Dimension

The aims of this chapter are to identify areas in which the human dimension has a significant impact on information security within an organization; to discuss common weaknesses and failings, and to propose methods for measuring and improving compliance.

6.1 The main issues related to the human dimension of information security

Security specialists are often heard to claim that "the security chain is as strong as its weakest link," a statement that is very often followed by the suggestion that the weakest link involves humans. It is commonly admitted that more than three-quarters of security breaches result from inside activities.

In an evaluation context, the human dimension is the one that provides the evidence that information security issues related to personnel are well addressed, managed and controlled within the organization. This is important because humans are not only considered as the weakest link, but also as an important element that implements, operates and uses the technology and the procedures. As Lacey says within his work "Managing the Human Factor in Information Security,"[1] "people are not only the greatest assets but also the greatest liability." According to international standard on guidelines for the management of IT security, (ISO/IEC 13355-1), the security objectives in terms of availability confidentiality, and integrity could not be reached without taking into account the "human factor," their vision of security, their responsibilities, and the efforts being made regarding their education and training.

The goal of the *human dimension* is clearly and closely related to the concepts and the organizational focus area of the information security policy, or more generally to the established rules within the organization. The primary goal of the human dimension is to increase security awareness by ensuring that the employees not only understand the "what" and "how" of the policy but also understand the "why," by positioning information security as an important factor in the health of the organization. This statement stresses the ideas that information security awareness is another layer increasing the robustness of the security posture. Organizations often instinctively incorporate awareness, training and education

---

[1]   D. Lacey, *Managing the Human Factor in Information Security: How to Win over Staff and Influence Business Managers,* England: John Wiley and Sons, Ltd., 2009.

activities into their daily practices. To be more effective, these activities need to be coordinated. In order to claim the effectiveness of these activities, the quality of the coordination and its management have to be analyzed and evaluated.

The information security domain of the human dimension is related to the security activities related to the personnel issues. From this point of view the personnel are not only considered as a target of the risk but also as the source. As such, information security related to the personnel is a variety of ongoing measures to reduce the likelihood and severity of risk related to human weaknesses, meaning incurring intentional and accidental damage or losses as a result of actions undertaken or omitted by people inside the organization. In this context, this kind of security increases user acceptance of information security practices and behaviours and at the same time enhances the security posture.

Conceptually, the NIST handbook "An introduction to computer security"[2] makes a clear distinction between three main activities, awareness, training, and education, that are related to the information security human dimension:

- In terms of attributes: awareness concerns the "what," training concerns the "how," and education concerns the "why."
- In terms of impact timeframe: awareness activities have an impact in short-term, training in an intermediate perspective, and education in a long-term perspective.
- Based on these, the goal of the awareness activity is to recognize, the goal of training is to be fully skilled, and the objective of education is to understand.

The dependent variable to be evaluated when speaking about the human dimension is the personnel security status that corresponds to the following logic and parameters:

Personal Security Status = f (Accountability, Background investigation, Competence, Separation of duties, Worforce analysis)

Accountability is about making people responsible for their conduct; the background investigation activities concern the preventive efforts that should be provided by the organization focused on the personnel security status; the competence could be reached by providing internal conditions to better improve knowledge, assuming that the background investigation has already investigated the candidates' previous experiences; the separation of duties ensures that no single human resource has the control of a transaction from the beginning to the end; and the workforce analysis could be considered as the driver to improve all the previous aspects. At the same time personnel issues could be considered from an information security metrics-related focus. Responsibilities and background checking are two main concerns regarding personnel issues.

In the book *Schneier on Security*[3], the author emphasizes the role of the human dimension within the information security program, stating that only amateurs still target machines, while career criminals now target people. Based on this perspective, information security awareness takes an important place within information security management. The

---

2   NIST, *An Introduction to Computer Security – The NIST Handbook (Special Publication 800-12)* National Institute of Standards and Technology – US Department of Commerce, 2004. Available at http://csrc.nist. gov/publications/nistpubs/800-12/

3   B. Schneier, *Schneier on Security,* Wiley, 2009.

need to correlate the capability to manage the human resources within the information security domain with the strategic approach to be adopted is very important because a governed stage of information security cannot be attained if an adequate strategy regarding personnel does not exist.

6.2 Staffing

According to the ISO code of practice for information security management (ISO/IEC 27002:2005),[4] hiring practices aim to ensure that new entrants are acquainted with their responsibilities in terms of risk, fraud and misuse of resources. There are three aspects to be taken into account in the before-hiring phase according to this standard:

- The first aspect is to ensure that responsibilities are mentioned to each potential candidate. This requires formally defining and documenting all the responsibilities stemming from the information security policy of the organization;[5]
- The second concerns the procedure for selecting candidates. It requires an accurate and rigorous verification of the candidate's relevant details such as CV, references, and education;
- The third aspect concerns hiring conditions related to internal rules of conduct.

It is important to be conscious of the fact that those preventive before-hiring activities can never be completely foolproof.

A substantial issue regarding personnel security is closely related to the change management concept in terms of the actions to be taken whenever a modification arises or the contract comes to conclusion. Thus ISO/IEC 27002:2005 suggests that a clearly defined and assigned responsibility should exist within the organization in order to ensure that leavers depart the organization according to a well-defined procedure. There are also aspects to take into account in order to ensure that contract termination is performed according to organizational requirements. Clear responsibilities related to the existing job position should be assigned. In addition, ISO/IEC 27002:2005 suggests that each modification of roles and responsibilities should follow the same procedure, in terms of security, as a contract termination.

If we analyse the different human aspects related to information security outlined in the sources quoted above, it can be concluded that preliminary preparative processes should be performed within the organization in order to foster an information security perspective. Staffing analysed from a timeframe point of view will concern the significant following practices:

- The before-hiring practices should reflect *a foregoing organizational security culture* in order to better define the security requirement to be conveyed. It is the first condition to be fulfilled in order to enable the "staffing" related activities to provide beneficial results;

---

4   ISO/IEC 27002:2005, Information technology – Security techniques – Code of practice for information security management, International Organization for Standardization (ISO), Switzerland, 2005.

5   Additionally and in the same sense, the *Standard of Good Practices for Information Security* (ISF) suggests that staff agreements should be established to specify responsibilities.

- The ongoing practices should contribute to empowering employees to achieve their specific information security objectives. Requirements related to every job position should be formally documented and enforced. Appropriate available security tools and procedures enabling a good environment for employees to be involved in information security issues must accompany these requirements. Specifically in relation to the ongoing practices, the issue concerning change management should be emphasized, by creating a framework capable of detecting and handling all the changes in a real time, in order to adapt new responsibilities[6] with respect to the rights and restrictions;
- The practices related to the ending of an employment contract should involve formal means of interdepartmental communication. This is an element that is often neglected in reality, but based on its importance it should be a part of the overall awareness strategy.

6.3 Security awareness

6.3.1 Rights and duties

Security awareness is the extent to which staff understand the importance of information security and the security requirements and their individual responsibilities resulting from these requirements, as identified in the standard of good practices for information security.[7] But before reaching the understanding stage of the subject, in our case information security, efforts to acquire knowledge of the issues are necessary. In general terms awareness is the understanding that security is everyone's responsibility and organizations can focus everyone's attention on security concerns by raising user knowledge and commitment. Based on this definition it could be argued that information security awareness could be a tool to promote the information security policy and compliance. From a wider point of view information security awareness does not only mean getting introduced to the concept and obeying certain rules but rather also understanding the reasons behind those rules. This statement introduces the first two information security awareness independent variables; the communication and the efforts to be made in order to be sure that the message is understood.

Compared with the training activities, the awareness activities are mechanisms occurring through informal activities such as posters, themes and visual reminders. The idea is to pass from an accomplishment-oriented approach to a cognizance-related one. The OECD defines the concept of awareness as being aware of the need for security of information systems and networks and what can be done to enhance security.[8] Information security awareness underlines that a user is committed to their security mission within a given organiza-

---

[6] Going in both directions, upgrading (concerned with the segregation of duties) and downgrading (concerned with exaggerate access right for example)

[7] ISF-std. *The Standard of Good Practice for Information Security* (ISF 2007).

[8] "OECD Guidelines for the Security of Information Systems and Networks; Towards a culture of Security" Organization for Economic Co-operation and Development, Paris 2002.
Available at http://www.oecd.org/document/42/0,3343,en_21571361_36139259_15582250_1_1_1_1,00.html

tion since the concept considers the *human link* as the most vulnerable link and a source of breaches and damages.

The following objectives for the security awareness program can be identified:

- Employees recognize their responsibility for protecting international assets, which means that for each employee information security should be a part of the job;
- Employees understand the value of the information security by first of all understanding the value of the information itself and the role of this as a valuable asset of the organization;
- Employees recognize what constitutes a violation and are able to recognize the warning signs that could indicate a potential security breach;
- The current level of awareness remains high.

Based on this categorization, it could be argued that for each employee there is a mandatory duty to apply the policies and procedures that are outlined by the organization's decision-making bodies. The first step to create such a consciousness is the classification of the information by degrees of importance, sensibility or confidentiality in order to then define the significance of the violation.

Security awareness and its effectiveness are closely related to the security policy and security awareness is the first and most direct output of the information security policy implementation. This statement derives from the fact that the application of the security policy assists employees to follow the internal code of ethics, thus helping the development of the security culture and awareness. Based on the security policy a common body of knowledge based on the different international documents should be formed and divided into technical issues (firewalls, IDS, encryption, password protection, access control) and non-technical ones (security policies, legal aspects, ethics, information security culture).

6.3.2 Types of awareness problems

Two categories of awareness problems can be identified: awareness framework and awareness content. The awareness framework involves engineering disciplines whereas the awareness content category involves non-engineering ones. Based upon this, an organization should enhance the teams responsible for awareness with other competencies beyond those of standard security professionals. Nevertheless, the framework, with the intention of coherence and effectiveness, should consider the issues in order to create formal mechanisms for identifying and defining the four subjects that were specified as objectives. It seems a trivial task, but should it fail this could generate important misunderstandings and consequently could bring important problems into focus. The awareness activities aim to spread the desired message and to ensure that this message is well understood. As such, the preliminary duties of fixing the subject itself should be an important task that has to be included within the awareness agenda. It is then possible to come up with a double layer of control of the objectives and their pertinence.

6.3.3 Awareness program

Security awareness is largely dedicated to the end user. For that reason we think that the topic of the awareness program should involve non-technical topics such as ethics, legal issues and information security culture, for example, or even make technology more generally accessible. The most common awareness topics can be categorized into:

- Risk management and information security objectives focused on what is at stake:
  - threats, vulnerabilities;
  - availability, confidentiality, integrity.
- Regulatory requirements and accountability focused on accountability issues:
  - user responsibilities;
  - personal use and gain issues;
  - policies (e.g. password);
  - social engineering, phishing;
  - shoulder surfing.
- Different information security disciplines, focused on the security basic knowledge enhancement:
  - functional, communication, and procedural related security issues.
- Overview of the main information security controls concerning the end-users and their role, focused on user microenvironment issues e.g.:
  - protection from malware;
  - e-mail attachments;
  - cyber-slacking;
  - spam;
  - physical environment.
- Both incident handling and disaster recovery and contingency issues focused on how to react in the event of problems.

Security awareness should give people effective skills by enforcing:
- Knowledge responding to the question of what to do;
- Attitude responding to the question of what you think;
- Behaviour responding to the question of what you do.

The three aforementioned dimensions are divided into six focus areas, namely:
- Adherence to policies;
- Keeping passwords secret;
- Appropriate use of e-mail and internet;
- Use of mobile equipment;
- Reporting security incidents;
- Identification of the actions and their respective consequences.

According to the ISF good practices[9] the security awareness program should be enterprise-wide, endorsed by the top management and supported by a set of clearly defined and documented objectives in order to be effective. Awareness activities should be an ongoing process performed everywhere using different ways to reach the end user. At the same time, NIST[10] argues that if an attention-getter is used repeatedly it loses importance and becomes useless. Hence awareness topics must be periodically rotated in order to keep the attention of

---

9   ISF-std. *The Standard of Good Practice for Information Security* (ISF, 2007).
10   NIST, "Information Technology Security Training Requirements: A Role – and Performance – based Model (SP 800-16)," U.S. Department of Commerce, National Institute of Standards and Technology, Computer Security Division 1998. Available at http://csrc.nist.gov/publications/nistpubs/800-16/800-16.pdf

the stakeholders. For that, multiple methods have to be used in parallel in order to reach the objective. These methods are brought together in four main groups:
- In-person methods;
- In-writing methods;
- On system methods;
- Other methods.

Another categorization of methods to be used in an awareness program, could be:
- News;
- Discussions (e.g. courses, tests);
- Activities;
- Internal incident reports.

The latter requirement, with the argument that the message has be appropriate for the audience, allows us to categorize three main stakeholder groups:
- Top management concerned mostly with the endorsement of the information security policy, legal issues, business continuity, etc.;
- IT personnel concerned mostly with the practical side of information security, for example risk analysis, implementation and the follow up of safeguards, security recommendations etc.;
- End-users concerned with the daily security threats affecting them, such as viruses, e-mail concerns, protection of data, security policy knowledge.

It is a very important input to the awareness program to categorize stakeholder groups in order to assign roles and responsibilities clearly, allowing the organization to define for each group the right awareness activity. Stakeholder categorization will enhance incident reporting based on a bottom-up approach and security implementation based on a top-down approach. Moreover the stakeholder categorization allows the organization to optimise the whole awareness program in terms of costs, reuse and effectiveness.

The statistical data clearly indicate that the prevailing component for most security incidents is human behaviour; consequently information security awareness is one of the aspects that have to be subjected to evaluation. According to the European Network and information security Agency (ENISA)[11] there are four categories of measurement concerning information security awareness:
- Process improvement;
- Attack resistance;
- Efficiency and effectiveness;
- Internal protection.

6.3.4 An endless process

It has to be stressed that information security awareness is not a one-time effort. In order to achieve this goal, an established budget and long term planning prove to be necessary. Their

---

[11] ENISA, "A Users' Guide: How to Raise Information Security Awareness," European Network and Information Security Agency, Heraklion, Greece 2006. Available at:
http://www.enisa.europa.eu/doc/pdf/deliverables/enisa_a_users_guide_how_to_raise_IS_ awareness.pdf

existence or not will give the very first indication of which awareness activities are performed in an institutionalized manner within the organization. It is crucial for the effectiveness of security awareness, perhaps more so than for the other security processes, that it is operated on an ongoing basis. For that, a change management approach has to be applied to the awareness initiatives. It will help to close the gap between particular issues and the human response to the need for change. It can be produced by performing a periodic analysis of the effectiveness and the efficiency of the current practices in place.

The information security awareness program has to be considered as a prerequisite of the training and education program. In this context an intermediate stage has to be devised, performed and delivered. This is what NIST in the Federal Information Technology Security Assessment Framework (FITSAF)[12] identifies as "security basics and literacy." In more general terms, ISO/IEC 27002:2005[13] suggests that before starting training courses, a so called "formal integration period" should be undertaken covering security policy topics and organizational expectations for each employee. The use of such a standard could enable employees to provide due diligence and due care, which are basic outputs of an information security awareness program.

Awareness is an important aspect with respect to an organization aiming to be conscious of the importance of security-positive behaviour. This makes information security awareness an important component of the information security baseline.

6.4 Security training and education

6.4.1 Building human capacity

Strictly speaking, the awareness activities are concerned with the dissemination of protection needs among the personnel in order to give them good reasons to adhere to and to adopt the security practices during their professional activities. This is principally aimed to adjust personnel's attitude in terms of information security. The next stage of the whole *awareness program* is to enhance and perfect the information security knowledge directly related to the role and the responsibility an individual holds inside the organization. Information security training is considered as being the most critical element of success. It is a more specific, more formal and more interactive activity than awareness. Information security training has to be offered based on individual needs and responsibilities. Such a training program tailored to role is required by NIST and ENISA.[14]

---

[12]   NIST, "Information Technology Security Training Requirements: A Role – and Performance – based Model," cited above.

[13]   ISO/IEC 27002:2005, Information technology – Security techniques – Code of practice for information security management, International Organization for Standardization (ISO), Switzerland, 2005.

[14]   NIST, "Building an Information Technology Security Awareness and Training Program (SP 800-50)," U.S. Department of Commerce, National Institute of Standards and Technology, Computer Security Division 2003. Available at http://csrc.nist.gov/publications/nistpubs/800-50/NIST-SP800-50.pdf

ENISA, "Information Security Awareness Initiatives: Current Practice and the Measurement of Success," European Network and Information Security Agency, Heraklion, Greece 2007. Available at http://www.enisa.europa.eu/doc/pdf/deliverables/enisa_measuring_ awareness.pdf

The training scope will be the implementation of security in day-to-day procedures. In the same direction the objective of training and education activities for the standard of good practices for information security (ISF)[15] is how to run and develop systems correctly and how to apply security controls. During this intermediate stage, information security basics are often addressed. A detailed list of included topics is proposed by NIST "Information technology security training requirements."[16] What it is important to retain, from an evaluation process point of view, is that there are four categories of topics to be assimilated by the employees:

- The notion of value;
- What are the risk components?;
- What are the security components?;
- What are the responsibilities concerning each employee based on the identified risk and information security components specifically concerning the organization?

In addition three main categories of security training topics are suggested, specifically:
- Laws and regulations;
- Security program tools and procedures;
- System life cycle security.

As we can see from these categorizations, three main learning fields dominate information security training and education activities, namely those related to values, risks, and security context. Dealing with responsibilities and accountability issues needs a more specific approach and requires a deep knowledge of information security topics with respect to the position held by the employee within the organization.

Information security training strives to produce relevant and needed security skills. The training and education step has to be performed in order to allow employees to run systems correctly, to correctly develop and apply security controls, and to appropriately report information security incidents. This phase contributes to performing an evaluation of the effectiveness of security controls in place. Educating users means changing their behaviour related to information security. Educating people means giving them the skills to perform information security. So training and education follow the same objective, to better handle information security practices, but they are placed in two different stages of maturity namely, the knowledge and the behaviour.

6.4.2 Key success factors

The *information training program* makes it possible to pass from the stage of *being aware* to the stage of *knowing how to do it*. These two stages will be the key success factors for a third stage of *doing it*. For that, some hands-on activities are needed in order to actually achieve positive behaviour in security terms. Besides that, the fact of following a training program makes employees individually responsible for information security. As required by NIST, ENISA, ISO/IEC 27002:2005 and the standard of good practices for information security

15   ISF-std. *The Standard of Good Practice for Information Security*, (ISF, 2007).
16   NIST, "Information Technology Security Training Requirements: A Role – and Performance – based Model," cited above.

(ISF),[17] a process of needs assessment is necessary in order to claim an efficient training program. For that, speciality classes have to be determined and it is very important that training needs should be addressed as a minimum for the following roles:

- Executive management;
- Information security related personnel;
- Resources and data system owners;
- System administrator and information technologies personnel;
- Operational personnel.

It should be stressed that within the training task list, the internal end-users do not figure because their needs have to be assessed and satisfied through the awareness program. In respect of awareness, it is important to tailor the message to each person's actual role and responsibilities, rather than their hierarchical position. Now, within the training domain, it is the content and the extent of the role that take on more importance. In any case, the fact that information security training does not concern the end-user is not unanimously accepted.

Information security training emphasizes secure working practices, which are derived from a true assessment of need. This means that information security training concerns all grades of employees with respect to the needs of their role information security terms. Training can be defined as an activity guiding the employees on how to use the security functions and education as being the activity allowing the employees to understand the importance of security. Information security training and education might concern everybody, as such priority will be given to those employees who directly work within the information systems framework.

Considering the process, there exist some meta-requirements concerning the information security awareness program[18] and the training program.

The first one is that the training program corresponds specifically to a cognitive approach, which means that in order to provide secure behaviour, the employee has to understand what he is doing and what he has to do during his work. ISO/IEC 27002:2005 suggests that training activities must include

- security requirements;
- security related responsibilities including disciplinary actions;
- the correct use of informational resources; and
- incident handling.

---

[17]   NIST, "Contingency Planning Guide for Information Technology Systems (SP 800-34)," U.S. Department of Commerce, National Institute of Standards and Technology 2002. Available at http://csrc.nist.gov/publications/nistpubs/800-34/sp800-34.pdf
        ENISA, "Information Security Awareness in Financial Organizations," European Network and Information Security Agency Heraklion, Greece 2008. Available at http://www.enisa.europa.eu/doc/pdf/deliverables/is_awareness_financial_organizations.pdf
        ISO/IEC 27002:2005, Information technology – Security techniques – Code of practice for information security management, International Organization for Standardization (ISO), Switzerland, 2005.
        ISF-std. *The Standard of Good Practice for Information Security*, (ISF, 2007).
[18]   In this context the information-awareness program is used to describe the program encompassing the security awareness and training/education issues.

Based on this, cognitive processing is needed, implying that the special training topics the employee will face have to be related to his previous learning topics and knowledge. This is very important because the learning continuum, mentioned by many other authors before, is thereby ensured and the adherence of the employee to this secure behaviour required will be stronger.

Dissemination and enforcement of the policy are critical issues implemented through the training program. This fact gives a wider view of the training program than the one given by NIST in information technology security training requirements, imputing the training activities only to the information technologies department personnel. This is true since the use of computer resources nowadays involves all employees, not only the information technologies professionals. As such the training needs should be extended to all personnel grades with respect to their role and responsibility, as mentioned above.

6.4.3 Knowledge dissemination

Information security education is a deeper understanding of information security practices through a process of knowledge dissemination by long-term learning, specific seminars or other forms of transmission. It is intended for information technology security specialists in addition to their role-based training. But the cornerstone of the security capabilities at this stage remains experience. As was demonstrated by the literature research, training activities follow the same logic as the ones related to awareness, that is to say:

- The framework determining the objectives and the aim of the program;
- The content specifying which are the topics which require further attention;
- The process related controls in order to ensure a high quality and useful results regarding the program.

For both sides of the information security awareness program, security awareness activities and training/education activities, there is an important aspect playing a crucial role related to the motivation to consider information security during daily activities. This motivation should concern both top-managers and ordinary employees. The idea is to find effective means to really motivate both categories to be concerned by information security. For a long time putting forward the idea that information security reduces risk was the main motivational argument. This failed for a multitude of reasons, including the difficulty in measuring the risk reduction. In order to provide the appropriate motivation, tangible rewards should be foreseen. These tangible rewards might be included in the classical rewards (salary, commission, bonuses, perks, recognition, job advancement) by clearly indicating the part of the reward related to the security behaviour.

6.5 Security culture

6.5.1 A question of know-how

The security culture of an organization is a very important issue since the human factor is considered as being the resource that implements information security and is also considered as being the *weakest link* of the security chain. The security culture within a given organization is considered by ENISA as being a broad understanding and commitment to information security, while others consider the information security culture as the process of instilling the aspects of information security to each employee. Thus the security culture is the result of the efforts that have been made in awareness, training and education processes. In order to reach a security culture stage, all the previous activities related to the human dimension of the security have to be performed in a continuous framework.

6.5.2 A question of framework

The culture framework is defined based on three elements: firstly as being some shared, taken-for-granted assumptions; secondly that these assumptions address the way of solving problems; and thirdly these solutions should be perceived as a correct way of proceeding. Thus, the security culture is the ownership of the security principles by the employees, characterized by ongoing training, allowing employees to hold themselves accountable.

The effectiveness of the security culture can be characterised by the coherence of the messages passed over all the communications channels, but in fact a "security culture" consists of what people really do. In order to be effective the security culture has to be embedded into an overall organizational culture and be an entire part of it. The concept of the culture in general is considered as being a primary and crucial factor in the effectiveness of an organization, driving all its actions. But as could be noticed from the considerations proposed above, the culture is a matter of perception. As such the organization should concentrate its efforts not only on identifying the important topics and finding appropriate solutions, but also on trying to construct an adequate message and communication in order that those topics are perceived as such by all personnel grades. To do that a popularizing work effort is shown to be necessary and consequently a multi-disciplinary team in charge of the awareness should be built up.

6.5.3 A question of security environment

The security culture takes the place of the security environment. Being a part of a security culture means being aware of, following, and most importantly, understanding the procedures, instead of being part of a security environment, which only implies that you know these procedures. Culture is about employee behaviour. As such the security culture is a mature stage of the whole information security awareness program. To claim a security culture framework, a continuous security awareness program has to be built-up and implemented. Besides this, the concept of a "culture of cross-functional communication" is put forward by COSO.[19]

This concept considers the risk culture from another point of view, emphasizing the "how" rather than the "what." In fact the underlying idea is that the required "culture level" could be reached if communication took place on a broad level. This means that within an organization aiming to create a culture of security, the security issues should be communicated to all the organizational levels without holding "taboo subjects." This means that the

---

[19]   Committee Of Sponsoring Organizations; COSO, "Strengthening Enterprise Risk Management for Strategic Advantage," Committee of Sponsoring Organizations 2009. Available at http://www.coso.org/documents/COSO_09_board_position_final102309PRINTandWEBFINAL.pdf

different levels should not only be concerned by their local issues but should have a certain level of knowledge about the others' security issues.

Being an amalgam of the two previous phases, awareness and the training/education, two crucial constituent elements make up the culture of security:

- Knowledge (cooperation);
- Behaviour.

These two constituent elements respectively go through two maturity phases:

- Understanding;
- Adherence.

As we have seen above, the culture is about assumptions on how to solve a problem. For doing that, each employee of the organization has to respond positively to the same assumptions and, most importantly, have the same conception about what does constitute a problem within the organization. This is a key point to be considered when building an environment with an important security culture. From this point of view the variable of culture means possessing the same values and the same beliefs regarding a given subject.

6.5.4 A question of interrelated issues and levels

The information security culture is very closely related to the organizational culture that plays a directly important role in the implementation of the information security itself. Organizational culture could be defined as patterns of assumptions, or heuristics that individuals will use as guidance when responding to a situation in the organization that they have not faced previously. The security culture could be seen as the final result that an awareness program can provide and will be a function of the overall organizational culture and organizational practices, as well as a function of the way these components will be perceived by the employee.

The development of organizational culture is a collective activity with the requirement that a well-defined and integrative role of information security manager needs to be provided. Up to now this role was mainly performed exclusively by technical specialists, restricting thus the scope to those employees who possessed specific knowledge of technology. In fact the organizational culture will be the cornerstone and the source of a specific information security culture. A successful security awareness program exists when the process fits in with the culture of the organization. The necessary condition as well as the starting point to incorporate the information security into organizational culture is the information security policy.

The role of an information security policy is to create a platform of actions to be taken and procedures to be followed. Without aiming to analyse information security policies, which was the subject of another chapter, there are some minimum requirements making a policy useful in terms of security culture. In order to influence behaviour and thus have an impact on security culture, an information security policy should be conceptually conceived in a manner where there exist some more explicative and specific secondary policies, including explicative procedures for each sub-policy, in order to be accessible to all interested parties.

Three levels of organizational culture can generally be identified: espoused values; shared tacit basic assumptions and beliefs (Figure 6.1). These three levels of the organizational culture should be applied to three levels of behaviour:

- Formal organization;
- Group;
- Individual.

This way of categorizing the security culture and the related targets facilitates the comprehension of the information security issues and consequently the behaviour of each level of the interested parties with respect to information security. There is an evident link between the information security culture and the employee since the information security culture is created when a specific behaviour is adopted.

As we can see from Figure 6.1, the right-hand side that constitutes the security culture as a function of the different behaviours demonstrated by the three levels of the organization on the left hand side. By definition, as far as individuals and their basic and tacit assumptions are concerned, there is not much more that the organization could do in order to change them. Organizational actions could bring an added value starting from group level. This is because the behaviour from this point could be influenced by, and is directly related to, the organizational environment. The link between the behaviour and the security culture as a whole will be made according to what they call *the occupational culture*. The occupational culture is a number of distinctive clusters of ideologies, beliefs and cultural forms emerging among identifiable groups of people within the same organization.

Three main interrelated actors affecting security culture issues can be identified; namely end-users, IT professionals and managers. These groups of persons have their own occupational culture impacting the behaviour and thus the security culture of the other groups. It has been shown that the behaviour of the ICT professionals closely impacts the behaviour of the end-user in security terms. Positive or negative qualities, such as teaching and explaining capabilities, inaccessible jargon, and slowness of responses, will provoke the same behaviour in the end-user. Managers could impact also the end-users' behaviour and thus their security culture by the quality of their relationship with the ICT professionals. A good and trustworthy relationship between ICT professionals and managers will certainly legitimize the role of IT staff to the end-users, making the communication between them more efficient. Figure 6.2 proposes an example of an information security culture model.

The *organizational level* is the starting point of processes and structures that are very important in the security behaviour establishment. Processes such as risk assessment and incident response show how to behave, while policies dictate and define the employee's behaviour. The *entity level* will be mostly concerned by the management's behaviour in relation to information security. In fact, a clear management commitment and responsibility regarding

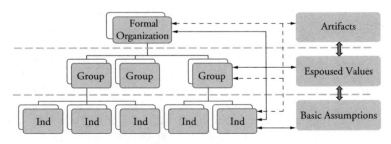

Fig. 6.1 Interaction between the organizational culture and behaviour.

the information security will motivate all personnel grades to adhere and respect the security instructions and guidelines. This adherence should also be enhanced if mutual trust exists between management levels and employees. Trust will be the second decisive element instilling the culture of security at a group level. At the same time, at an *individual level* the two most important elements enhancing the culture of security will be the awareness activities and the ethical code of conduct particular to each individual.

It has been shown that an enterprise adopting a governance approach is viewed as having a good level of security culture instilled among its personnel. Based on this, the organizational behaviour is expected to provide an organizational culture and consequently enhance the level of the security culture within the organization. There is a cause and effect relationship between organizational behaviour and organizational culture. Regarding the organizational behaviour, it is determined by the elements based on Figure 6.2 and discussed above. From such an organizational behaviour might derive a *healthy* organizational culture incorporating people through their knowledge, behaviour, experience, ethics, and commitment, allowing the organization to devise policies and procedures that will be people-centred and contributing to providing an ease-of-use technological framework.

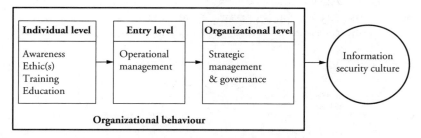

Fig. 6.2 An example of an information security culture model.

6.6 The human dimension evaluation process

6.6.1 Main steps and sub-dimensions

There are many ways of considering *awareness raising programs.*[20] The distinction between staffing, awareness, training and education activities is very important. The first category of staffing concerns the preliminary work to be done, in order to create favourable conditions in order to enable the three following stages. These preliminary conditions should include: job definition, the sensitivity of the position, applicant screening according to the job position requirements and the training and empowerment of the personnel involved in hiring. In providing such a preliminary effort the organization declares its own position with respect to the importance of information security, thus giving the very first signal to the future users about the way they should behave.

---

[20]   The term *awareness raising program* incorporates the three sub-dimensions of awareness, training/education and culture.

The different sub-dimensions and the different elements within them are independent and also relate to different goals. At the same time the means used within these elements have more or less the same nature, consequently providing different outputs according to the persons they are directed at. Another important element to clearly distinguish is the role and the responsibilities of the persons being the subject of the awareness, training and education.

The evaluation should firstly be focused on three main elements of each of the components of the awareness program, *the framework, the content and the process.* This structure of the awareness program components remains invariant but changes configuration from one element to another. For example, the framework concerning the awareness activities to enhance the accountability of all the employees relates to different objectives compared to the training that aims to enhance the information security knowledge of the different subjects within the organization.

As we can see from Figure 6.3 the whole program aiming to address the human related issues makes use of different practices based on the organizational behaviour that will depend on the rules the organization has imposed. Depending on the practice, a subject might be exposed to different levels of accountability that might be reached, going from the most basic regarding the *security attitude* to the more advanced ones where the security practices are automatically assimilated. All these activities should be bound into a close relationship with the roles and security concerns of the targeted group of persons. Based on that, the evaluation depth could not apply to two distinct categories of the end-users and security professionals in the same manner.

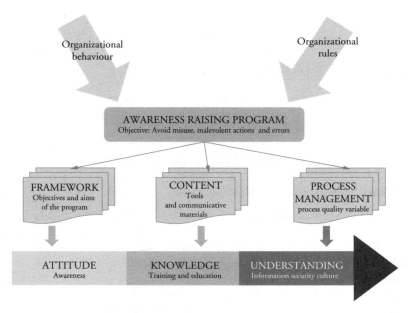

Fig. 6.3 Awareness raising program structure and outputs.

The objective of the awareness and training program is to increase the information security consciousness among the human resources. As such, each of the personnel grades should go through different stages as (see Figure 6.4):

- The recognition of the utility of the information security practices to decrease the risk exposure;
- The improvement of operational skills to increase the level of security;
- The understanding of the security issues and the adoption of a security culture.

The evaluation model identifies three sub-dimensions that are distinguished at the same time based on two attributes – the timeframe and the stages of maturity – as we focus on the same subject (employee). If the sub-dimension focuses on different subjects, they might be performed in parallel.

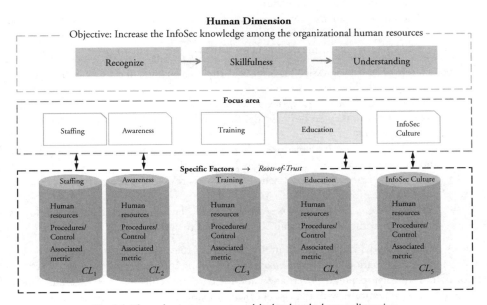

Fig. 6.4 The evaluation assurance model related to the human dimension.

6.6.2 Evaluating the sub-dimensions

The first sub-dimension, helping one to recognize the importance of the information security, is composed of two main focus areas, namely the staffing and awareness. As mentioned above, the framework is bordered by the meta-objective to get every employee of the organization acquainted with the security needs and the appropriate behaviour.

Regarding the *staffing* focus area the most important pieces of evidence are the structures previously built to accommodate new employees. This structure has to introduce to the future employee information security related obligations in order to enhance the employee's competence with respect to the security concerns. A potential metric aiming to express the effectiveness of the before-hiring practices could be the percentage of job description documents that include a section related to the information security duties that the candidate should accomplish.

In terms of awareness, evidence might be shown when the following elements are brought out by the security awareness program, providing thus evidence of the effectiveness of the program:

- Grouping of persons of similar level implying security needs and requirements precisely targeted to each one of them. For example, the operational levels will be mostly concerned by issues such as *appropriate use of electronic devices* while executive levels will be mostly concerned by issues such as information security needs regarding the critical resources of the organization.
- Written commitments, written reports, allowing the organization to give a particular importance to the responsibility charge among the employees. Possible performance indicators might also include:
  - The extent of the development of the security guidelines;
  - The extent of the dissemination;
  - The efficiency of the awareness process based on costs and (we will add) the number of the incidents being resolved;
  - The effectiveness of the deployment of the security guidelines.

Four levels of staff progression in respect of their savoir-faire and behaviour related to their job position, could be classified as:

- Level 1 – *Unconscious incompetence*: when employees are not aware of the task they have to perform, they do not have the skills and can not distinguish between what is right and wrong;
- Level 2 – *Conscious incompetence*: when employees know their task responsibilities and importance but they do not know how to perform;
- Level 3 – *Conscious competence*: when employees are able to perform the task by making a mental effort;
- Level 4 – *Unconscious competence*: when the tasks become so practiced by employees that they become "second nature" and a part of their culture.

A maturity model can be drawn up by preserving the same levels and adding the last one, which is information security *obedience*, and binding together three important fields – information security, corporate governance, and the corporate culture. User behaviour can be assessed by how it complies with the vision of senior management as defined in the corporate information security policy. As a consequence, to pass from level 1 to level 2 an information security awareness program has to be performed. In order to pass from level 2 to level 3 a security training program has to be performed. Passing from level 3 to level 4 a security education program has to be performed and finally in order to reach the *information security obedience stage* an experienced body of professionals is needed. Other evidence should be provided regarding the conceptual structure of the security awareness activities. A consistent documentation of the following elements should be possible to trace, including the awareness topics to be discussed, the way of achieving the awareness activities, the target public, the appropriateness of the communicated messages, and above all the means the organization is using to measure the result of the awareness activities.

From a measurement point of view multiple metrics could be constructed according to the specific context of the organization. We would propose, for example, the number of information security policy objectives that are categorized by a target group of employees, or even the information security policy objectives that have been the subject of a visible communication message. Based also on the importance of the repeated message, a metric might be constructed to measure the frequency of the appearance of the same message during a year, according to a predetermined order of importance of the subject.

The training/education sub-dimension will follow the same evaluation logic as the awareness process, except that the targeting should be more precise. In training/education the groups have a more specific need for the proposed knowledge to be acquired because this process is not only about the understanding of the importance but also about the implementation and the quality of the work. As such, the outline shapes will change very often, since the risk and security environments themselves change very often. Refresher training on policies needs to be performed and the acknowledgement form revalidated annually.

From a measurement point of view a potential metric could be the balance provided among the number of training courses taking into account the following stages: basic, intermediate and advanced training courses. Another metric could be the number of the ICT professionals having followed information security training courses or even possessing an information security certification. That would show the place that information security holds within the ICT department.

It has to be underlined that according to our model the education-focused processes fall in between the training and information security culture raising. This is because in our opinion the persons who have acquired different skills in the security field will be of great influence in disseminating internally the importance of security. As has been said before, the information security culture is a result of the preceeding processes. As such the evaluation of the information security culture will depend strongly on the outputs of their evaluations. Nevertheless it was argued that the information security culture will also depend on the organizational culture. To specifically evaluate the information security culture, alongside the awareness and training evaluation, the executive level involvement is of a great importance. Consequently evidence should be sought by looking for the existence in the financial statements of an amount allocated to awareness activities, or even for the information security policy commitment under the assumption that objectives in terms of awareness raising are specified.

From a measurement point of view metrics could be constructed by showing the number of persons coming from non-technical background directly involved within the security practices or teams. This would be a good indicator to justify the fact that cross-functional communication might be possible by arguing that capacities to make the information security concerns generally accessible do exist. In general, pragmatic metrics measuring the effectiveness of the information security awareness program might be envisaged, such as for example the evolution (an increased number) of reported incidents after an awareness campaign.

6.7 The maturity model related to the human dimension

To evaluate the level of maturity of the information security human dimension, we propose a five level maturity model as presented and explained in Figure 6.5.

6.8 Chapter summary

This chapter has focused on the human dimension of the information security, which is the dimension addressing issues and proposing measures related to the weakest link of the security chain. The expected output of this dimension is to increase information security knowledge among employees, as being the element in charge of the implementation of the security program. Three blocks of processes (sub-dimensions) corresponding to different stages of information security proficiency and to different levels of employees have been identified. The first is the

Level 1 Fortuitous	• *Existence of at least one dimension:* Generally situated within the awareness area characterized by some generic guidelines concerning the use of the infrastructure without any mention of individual responsibilities in terms of risks. • *No existing focus area structure:* Even the existing awareness and training practices are not structurally performed or instructions are not available on how to use the infrastructure. • *Isolated specific factors:* Generally situated at the procedure/controls level, as for example informative flyers on security topics. *No quality specification can be done.*
Level 2 Structured	• *A clear and formal existence of the dimensions:* Some efforts are made within the organization in terms of risk and security, according to the role of each organizational grade. • *Focus area structure mostly exists:* Awareness, training/education and staffing are carried out and the objectives to be attained are defined. • *Specific factors include two attributes:* For each identified focus area, the specific factors procedure/ controls and human resource can be assigned. *The quality level has reached the first level,* which means that which means that awareness, training/education and staffing activities are included within the information security policy or any other strategic document related to the information security field.
Level 3 Functional	• *The architecture is complete:* The three dimensions and the five focus areas exist, as described within the model, and the structural construction exists for each of them, including the framework, the content and the process concerns. • *Specific factors:* In general, the attributes for procedure/controls and human resources are identifiable for each related focus area. *The quality level* is characterized by an average weighting level of two, which means that awareness, training/education and staffing aspects are the responsibility of a specific person or several persons (organizational function, job function).
Level 4 Analyzable	• *The architecture is complete:* The three dimensions and the five focus areas exist, as described within the model. • *Specific factors:* The three general attributes are identifiable for each related focus area, which means that the level of metrics is reached for each focus area. *The quality level* is characterized by an average weighting level of three, which means that the that specific factors are minimally documented and/or monitored.
Level 5 Effective	• *The architecture is complete:* The three dimensions and the five focus areas exist, as described within the model. • *Specific factors:* The three general attributes are identifiable for each related focus area, which means that the level of metrics is reached for each specific factor. *The quality level* has an average weight that clearly equals four, signaling that a procedure for continual improvement is imputed to each focus area, where internal /external reviews and audits are regularly performed.

Fig. 6.5 The maturity model related to the human dimension.

awareness process aiming to enable employees to recognize the need to appropriately perform their information security tasks. The second stage of training and education concerned the activities allowing the employees that have identified such a need to increase their information security capabilities by acquiring a deeper knowledge of the security solutions. The third stage concerned what we called *the concluding stage of the security culture.* This stage assumes that through the two previous processes the security practices are understood and are thus inherently adopted by each employee of the organization. For each of these three focus areas, the key success factors and the elements for which evidence should be provided in order claim assurance have been defined. The most important one is to tailor to each hierarchical level its own security concerns with which staff should be acquainted. Based on that, a number of actions and procedures to undertake are recognized in order to build up a solid and effective enterprise-wide awareness raising program. A specific maturity model of the information security human dimension is proposed in order to allow the organization to state its specific security requirements.

Chapter 7

Evaluating the Compliance Dimension

The goal of this chapter is not to specifically analyze all the legal implications of laws or regulations on the organization's environment but rather to specify how to evaluate the capacity of the organization to create a suitable framework for the performance of information security compliance related activities.

7.1 Notions of trust and compliance in relation to information security

In spite of the high level of technical and managerial competencies that organizations have often attained, recent years have seen a number of significant financial scandals such as the Enron collapse in 2001. These scandals brought to prominence the role of information technology within enterprises in supporting various business functions and the trust that would necessarily be placed in it. Subsequently we have seen the generation of new legislation in order to prevent, detect and correct such aberrations, and attention has been increasingly focused on the way these competencies are used in order to ensure the most faithful representation of corporate realities in the financial statements.

Trust has become a very important component in the tripartite relationship of corporation-state-stakeholders. Trust requirements pointed out the need to focus attention on the control procedures, emphasizing thus the role of a non-technical field that can be subject to interpretation, and this has been expressed through a great number of regulations and laws focused on information security. Compliance and conformity lead to a situation where these regulations have become the most suitable way for organizations to inspire trust in their stakeholders or governmental agencies. The trust behind compliance comes from the fact that compliance is considered as a kind of public disclosure, and also from the fact that a given organization is certified to be in conformity with the legislation by reporting to the stakeholders that a required level is reached.

In the same way, regulatory compliance and conformity is likely to provide a kind of assurance, showing that organizational security functions are performed in a consistent way by incorporating the consensus those rules require. According to recently published security studies, regulatory compliance appears as one of the most important drivers in security spending, representing the biggest part of security operating costs. Just to take one example, the annual survey of the state of information security provided by PricewaterhouseCoopers in 2008[1] identifies compliance as one of the leading reasons to invest in security issues.

Best practices such as ISO/IEC 27002:2005 or the standard of good practices for information security (ISF)[2] emphasize the need for a process to be established in order to identify and interpret the information security implications of the relevant laws and regulations. This is the compliance process.

At the same time compliance can be defined as being the extent to which defined policies, standards and procedures are being followed. Compliance processes should be focused on security-specific legislation, security-related implications, and regulations having an impact on the topic of information security. Rasmussen[3] comments on the complexity of the compliance issues that: "No longer is it about meeting one compliance obligation, but a complex web of requirements that grows exponentially as organizations cross international boundaries." Indeed the number of legal and regulatory bills increases from one country to another and the globalization phenomenon obliges organizations to comply with a great number of national regulations and laws.

The multitude of laws coming from all over the world, and the great number of regulations and standards to which an organization has to conform, necessitate a real management approach in terms of due diligence and conformity to diminish the likelihood of non-compliance. The consequences of non-compliance may range from legal liability to financial penalties to criminal liability.

Generally, and from a more corporate perspective, compliance is designed as a system to detect and prevent violations of laws by agents, employees, and directors of a business. Two main currents of thought exist today. The first concerns a system for identifying laws or regulatory texts that might concern the organization and which arise essentially from a monitoring control system. The second is to enable as many resources as possible to be able to identify the impact of legislation on Information and Communication Technologies (ICT). This complex panorama requires not only specific legal proficiency but also obliges resources to possess information security know-how and, especially, a great knowledge of the organization's business environment. This means resources that can translate legal and regulatory requirements into procedures or actions to be taken in daily operational activities.

Regulatory compliance is very often mentioned as a driver for improved performance and accountability in security mechanisms and procedures. Through this mechanism it could be stated that compliance could improve the level of the information security itself. The compliance process has thus taken on an *incentivizing* role in providing security assurance because the objective of regulatory compliance itself is to allow businesses to operate and to show exactly what organizations need to do. The assurance argument within the compliance process and its quality stems from the fact that the result of the compliance process tends to

---

[1]	PricewaterhouseCoopers, "The Global State of Information Security" PricewaterhouseCoopers 2008. [Online] Available at http://www.pwc.com/Extweb/service.nsf/docid/B98693CB799AB1A5482575050031 15BD/$file/PwCsurvey2008_cio_reprint.pdf

[2]	ISO/IEC 27002:2005, Information technology – Security techniques – Code of practice for information security management, International Organization for Standardization (ISO), Switzerland, 2005.
	ISF-std. *The Standard of Good Practice for Information Security*, Information Security Forum, 2007.

[3]	M. Rasmussen, "Information Security Standards, Regulations and Legislation," Giga Information Group (2003). http://www.aitp.org/newsletter/2003marapr/article1.htm

be a certification or an assertion that the legislation requirements are met. This goal can be reached only by providing evidence, demonstrating that the reality meets the requirements.

7.2 The compliance program

7.2.1 Sustaining business objectives

Before building the conceptual model of compliance evaluation, it is necessary to understand the sources of the requirements and at the same time provide a conceptual classification of them. There is a wide range of legal subjects with which a given organization has to comply, going from internal policies and procedures to standards, guidelines, specifications and pieces of legislation.

Being compliant with and conforming to a law or a stipulation coming from a legislative body means, first of all, not breaking the law. This is an important mandatory target, not only for the information security teams (in charge of the conception and the implementation of the information security program or system), but also for managerial levels (for whom the continued existence of the organization remains the main assignment). Being compliant with and conforming to industry standards means consolidating its place within the competitive market. The result of these two objectives is transformed into practical and relevant internal policies and procedures.

Compliance means achieving organizational business objectives by meeting the security requirements raised by an organization's stakeholders. In this way, the concept of regulatory compliance is very close to the information security concept. By definition, all the regulatory texts, whether in reference to mandatory characteristics or not, incorporate the consensus, thus reinforcing the feeling of trust. The challenge for the organization is to state if the compliance process has to be considered as the final result or as a starting point. In our opinion, this decision will depend on the maturity level of the information security system and on the motivations of the organization for compliance. The answer will depend on multiple features, for example:

- The magnitude of the concern and penalties for being non-compliant for a given organization, considering the targets of compliance;
- The possible overlaps between different laws and regulations in order to save costs; and
- The priorities between different regulations related to the organizational needs.

In our opinion compliance should not exclusively be considered as a starting point. Compliance is usually a term referring to laws and governmental regulations, which are considered as mandatory by definition. In this case, compliance tasks have to be of the utmost importance and performed at the same time as the other security activities. Conformity is more often used in an optimization perspective, ensuring better IT security management and better risk control. It requires a well-defined framework of information risks and, thus, an existing basic level of IT security.

Nowadays there is a proliferation of regulatory challenges. According, for example, to the 2006 PricewaterhouseCoopers information security breach survey,[4] 75% of organizations

---

4   PricewaterhouseCoopers, "Information Security Breach Survey 2006," PricewaterhouseCoopers 2006. Available at http://www.enisa.europa.eu/doc/pdf/studies/dtiisbs2006.pdf

must comply with at least two regulations. If we take into account the multiple resources needed to be compliant, a compliance process can be shown to be a significant procedure often generating, as discussed later, considerable costs.

Compliance requirements serve a dual purpose:
- They help to reduce and manage risk exposure for the corporation itself;
- They help to reduce and manage risks for the economy and the wider environment.

7.2.2 Compliance and responsibilities

The compliance environment could be categorized into three main components:
- Legal compliance;
- Policy and industry standards compliance;
- Audit methodology compliance.

Generally Accepted Information Security Principles (GAISP)[5] clearly assign to top management the responsibility to be aware of and address all legal, regulatory and contractual compliance. It can be noticed that the top management is directly concerned, according to GAISP, only with legislation considered as mandatory. The requirement of being aware assigns preventive duties to the management level by forcing them to adapt themselves in both directions: legislative knowledge and knowledge of organizational information security issues. Another strong requirement of GAISP is the fact that top management is responsible for addressing compliance issues. Consequently this means that the board level is responsible for the effectiveness of systems ensuring the compliance. The risk perspective related to compliance has changed nowadays. More than the well-known and well-considered risks of financial penalties, the most harmful risk related to the non-compliance issues is associated with bad publicity. In our opinion this is one of the main reasons that the compliance efforts are more and more focused on control frameworks such as ISO, CobiT, and ITIL.

7.2.3 The notion of legal risk

By *legal risk* is meant any risk resulting from an infringement of a legal rule or any other agreement that obliges the organization to behave in a manner that has been defined as correct, or to produce a result seen as an objective to be reached. There are two constituent elements making up the legal risk, namely:
- A legal rule;
- An event.

In opposition to the other dimensions of information security, legal risk arises from rules enacted by a recognized body. This means that if the rule had not existed, the same event would not have provided a risk event. In fact, in other domains the risk could be the result of a single event, externally driven and inherently causing harm. This property makes the legal risk very special in management terms and attributes great importance to the identification and interpretation of legal rules. The risk will arise because of non-identification,

---

5   ISSA, "Generally Accepted Information Security Principles V3.0," Information Systems Security Association, USA 2003. Available at http://all.net/books/standards/GAISP-v30.pdf

misinterpretation or, more frequently, because of transgressive behaviour. There are three main consequences related to the occurrence of legal risk:

- *Penal consequences*, strictly related to the legal system;
- *Financial consequences*, resulting from both legal rules and contractual ones;
- *Reputational consequences*, which are very difficult to evaluate but are often considered as more disastrous than the penal and financial ones.

7.2.4 Legal compliance

Legal compliance is one of the sources of security requirements. This field includes legal, statutory, regulatory, and contractual requirements where each concerns a written or spoken agreement intended to be enforceable by law. By law (or legal rules) is meant a body of rules governing human conduct that is recognized as binding by the state and, if necessary, enforced, while by regulatory requirements is meant every rule or directive made and maintained by an authority. By *statutory requirements* is meant written laws passed by a legislative body or rules of an organization or institution. More specifically, by contractual is meant written or spoken agreements intended to be enforceable by law. To summarize, the legal compliance aspect of the information security compliance dimension could be divided into three main categories:

- General legislation with security implications;
- Regulations that are directly or indirectly related to information security;
- Specific information-security legislation.

7.2.5 Some legal categories

While requirements having a direct impact on information security are manifold and generally enacted on a national basis, there are still some issues that follow the same logic and that are treated analogously. These generally concern data protection issues, privacy issues, copyrights issues, and different cybercrime issues such as spam and scams, for example.

Figure 7.1 proposes a categorization of laws based on well-accepted principles or even on international rules that correspond to some invariable perceptions so that the main requirements and concerns rising from them are enacted similarly within the respective national legislations. In addition there exist some specific laws that concern particular aspects of information security; these are generally called legal requirements and concern issues such as encryption, e-mail, electronic signatures and electronic contracting. In contrast, in the field of administrative law the perception of the problem is rather similar from one legislative domain to another, but the legislation is not enacted in the same way everywhere. This means that the same topic is not perceived in the same way in different legislations.

Information technology legal requirements cover some inherent topics of cybercrime legislation. Despite the fact that considerable efforts have been and are being made to put cybercrime issues onto a common basis, there are still particular issues which are differently perceived and consequently differently enacted in each country's legislation. Here we refer to such phenomena as spamming, employee monitoring, mail bombing and virus distribution. In a more ubiquitous way, in order to give a common attribute to all these legislations in the scope of an evaluation, it could be claimed that laws, from a legal conception, demand an implementation in a literal manner with very little margin for interpretation regarding their

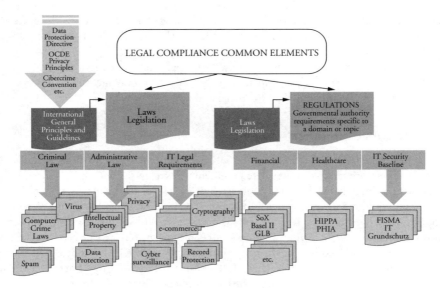

Fig. 7.1 Legal categories (a non-exhaustive list).

requirements or the way to satisfy them. Fundamentally, because of the fact that legal requirements are based on some solid and basic principles (laws, jurisdiction), legal compliance still
remains a moderate subject of change.

7.2.6 Regulations

In comparison with laws and legislation, compliance resulting from regulatory bills mostly
concerns specific domains and the way different systems are operated (e.g. control system,
risk management system, data retention system, and so on). This field of compliance aims to
regulate the way those systems are implemented, performed and managed (e.g. responsibility
issues). Regulatory bills force the creation of an environment (a system) where the general
and widely-accepted legal principles will be enforced. As far as the SoX[6] regulations are concerned, the requirement is largely for security professionals to do what they should have been
doing all along. There is often a tendency to present new regulatory bills as being a new concern for information security when in reality the regulatory bills do not introduce new items
or change the conceptual basis for activities. The requirements are designed with reference to
specific issues and concern issues that should already have been addressed.

As has often been mentioned during this chapter, regulatory requirements concern some
specific domains but show a clear tendency to be expanded. The main domains concerned
by those regulatory bills are:

- The financial management and reporting domain is mostly concerned by regulation
  such as the Sarbanes-Oxley Act (SoX), Basel II, the Gramm-Leach-Bliley (GLB) Act,
  or the EuroSox for the European countries, which has officially been in force since
  2008 but without any significant enforcement obligation;

---

6   "Sarbanes and Oxley Act 2002," Congress of the USA, 2002.

- The healthcare domain is mostly concerned by regulations such as the Health Insurance Portability and Accountability (HIPPA) Act for the USA, the Personal Health Information (PHIA) Act for Canada or the European equivalent EU Directive on Data Privacy;
- The security domain is mostly concerned by the burgeoning regulatory efforts after the 9/11 events, such as the Patriot Act in the USA, or the equivalents in the UK and other countries. Within these categories one has to distinguish between the first group of regulations, which correspond to strong political characteristics, and the second, which is the category of regulations that establish requirements on how the security systems should be operated in certain organizations such as governmental agencies. Inside this sub-group can be identified regulations such as the Federal Information Security Management Act (FISMA)[7] for the USA or the IT Baseline Protection Manual of the German Federal Agency for Security In Information Technology.[8]

Although these different regulatory texts concern different countries, there are some constant baseline aspects that have to be taken into account independently of the geographical influence of such regulations. Regulations covering the financial domain are mostly concerned with the pervasive influence of Information Technologies within organizational operational activities. This is the case of the control systems related to the financial statements and reporting.

Sarbanes-Oxley Act

SoX, for example, is mostly focused on the accuracy and reliability of the financial statements and establishes a standard to conduct activities according to due professional care. Without going into detail on SoX requirements, the main concerns are related to:

- The responsibilities of executives, who must attest to the adequacy and effectiveness of their internal control systems and are responsible for its quality;
- The transparency of their financial statements, which have to be audited annually and included in the final report;
- The role and the extent of the audit process.

In fact, SoX required nothing extraordinary regarding due care. The novelty was that all these necessities that previously existed were now put on a mandatory basis.

Basel II Regulation

The Basel II regulation[9] also concerns the control systems, but it is specifically on financial institutions such as banks. The intention of the accord is to implement an integrated risk-management approach governing the capital adequacy of internationally active banks.

---

7   "Federal Information Security Management Act of 2002 (FISMA)." vol. H.R.2458-48 Congress of the USA and House of Representatives 2002.

8   BSI, "IT Baseline Protection Manual," Bundesamt für Sicherheit in der Informationstechnik (BSI) 1996. http://www.iwar.org.uk/comsec/resources/standards/germany/itbpm.pdf

9   Basel Committee on Banking Supervision, "International Convergence of Capital Measurement and Capital Standards – A Revised Framework, Comprehensive Version," Bank for International Settlements (BIS) 2005. http://www.bis.org/publ/bcbs128.pdf?noframes=1

Basel II is based on three pillars:
- A minimum capital requirement;
- A supervisory review process that requires supervisors to ensure that each financial institution adopts effective internal processes in order to assess the adequacy of its capital based on a thorough evaluation of the risks;
- An effective use of market discipline that aims to improve market discipline through enhanced disclosure by financial houses.

The *integrated risk management approach* of Basel II consists of three components of risk, which are the credit risk, the market risk and the operational risk. The last concerns any loss that could have been prevented by the internal control system. Based on the same interpretation of the pervasive influence of information technologies, the internal control system of the IT infrastructure must itself be properly controlled. To do so the risk management approach should adopt a triple view assessment process that includes:
- People, by analyzing risks arising from employees;
- Processes and systems, by considering the fact that automation reduces the risk of human error and facilitates the segregation of duties, but increases dependency on ICT and increases the risk of loss of confidentiality, integrity, availability and repudiation of transactions;
- External events and other changes, by analyzing the risks of unexpected events.

Basel III is a new global regulatory standard on bank capital adequacy and liquidity that is due to come into force on 1 January 2013. This Accord was developed as a response to the deficiencies in financial regulation revealed by recent financial crises. Basel III strengthens bank capital requirements and introduces new regulatory requirements for bank liquidity and bank leverage. It has no immediate impact on the management and security of information systems.

Healthcare domain related regulations

Healthcare domain regulations such as HIPPA or the European Directive on Privacy[10] mainly focus on privacy issues regarding security and privacy requirements and their implementation.

The European Directive is mainly focused on the way that personal data are collected, stored, retained and used. A clear definition of personal data is provided by the EU directive where personal data means any information relating to an identified or identifiable natural person (…) by reference to an identification number or factors specific to his physical, physiological, mental, economic, cultural, or social identity. By way of contrast, HIPPA is focused on the access, disclosure, and use of health information, proposing both security and privacy rules. In security terms some baseline safeguards for compliance are proposed. These concern the following:
- The security management system;
- Information access management;

---

[10] "Health Insurance Portability and Accountability Act of 1996," Public Law 104-191: Congress of the USA and House of Representatives 1996.
"Directive 95/46/EC of the European Parliament and of the Council of 24 October 1995 on the protection of individuals with regard to the processing of personal data and on the free movement of such data." Vol. 31995L0046: European Parliament and the Council of the European Union, 1995.

- Security awareness and training;
- Security incident handling procedures;
- Contingency planning.

More generally speaking, in order to better protect this kind of privacy, a structural identification and classification has to be performed. A specific value related to their importance has to be assigned to the critical information in order to allow their protection according to their relative importance. But of course, as mentioned above, components should be subject to the baseline security controls that require a multidisciplinary team.

Security related regulations

The third category of regulations concerns the security posture itself, by providing requirements in terms of structures and characteristics of the information security controls. It requires the definition of the constitution of an information security management system, a baseline safeguard system and organizational structure, as well as the security process.

Just to take one example, in order to satisfy the requirements of the Federal Information Security Management Act of 2002 (FISMA),[11] the National Institute of Standards and Technology (NIST) issued a standard for information security programs, giving guidelines in order to provide an adequate information security program commensurate with risks.[12] Within NIST's standard, a list of minimum security controls and minimum security assurance requirements is presented in order to claim compliance with FISMA.[13]

7.2.7 Policies and standards

Being compliant with internal policies and regulations is another important aspect of the compliance system of a given organization. This stipulation comes from the necessity to transform high-level requirements introduced by laws, regulations or other mandatory texts into tangible objectives and procedures to be followed internally. As stipulated by the Generally Accepted Information Security Principle (GAISP),[14] as a part of compliance efforts, plans should also be in place to address legal issues through the organization's policies, processes or actions.

Policies can also be seen as a superset of legal and regulatory requirements specifically applied to an organization. In fact, policies set up organizational long-term objectives, and are a driver for the overall compliance process. The compliance with the internal requirements stemming from information security policies could be the first step of the compliance

---

11   "Federal Information Security Management Act of 2002 (FISMA)." Vol. H.R.2458-48 Congress of the USA and House of Representatives 2002.

12   NIST, "Recommended Security Controls for Federal Information Systems and Organizations (SP 800-53, Revision 3)," U.S. Department of Commerce, National Institute of Standards and Technology, Computer Security Division 2009. http://csrc.nist.gov/publications/nistpubs/800-53-Rev3/sp800-53-rev3-final.pdf

13   For a more detailed view of the minimum security controls see NIST's Information Security Baseline Controls. IST, "Recommended Security Controls for Federal Information Systems and Organizations (SP 800-53, Revision 3)," U.S. Departement of Commerce, National Institute of Standards and Technology, Computer Security Division 2009. http://csrc.nist.gov/publications/nistpubs/800-53-Rev3/sp800-53-rev3-final.pdf

14   ISSA, "Generally Accepted Information Security Principles V3.0," Information Systems Security Association USA 2003. http://all.net/books/standards/GAISP-v30.pdf

process. Then the definition of the standards that allow the organization to set up the rules of compliance could constitute a second step. There may be a gap between how designers and decision-makers think about the normal and effective use of technology and how employees actually use it. There could be two main types of regulatory actions:

- Methods that technically restrict the possibilities for use;
- Actions that facilitate or orient the appropriateness of the process and the development of employees' perceptions regarding ICT.

Both methods could be appropriate, but the evaluation scope should not be driven by the method itself but by the achievement of the requirements defined by the chosen method. The code constitutes an effective legal protection. But the research shows that even if the code allows for the evaluation of what organization deems acceptable or not, its influence on individual behaviour is limited and thus it is not a very effective deterrent. It should be mentioned that compliance with standards does not necessarily permit categorisation in terms of security evaluation. It merely provides some evidence that some conditions do exist inside the organization that allow conformity with some other specific requirements resulting from other regulatory standards. This is the case, for example, of ISO/IEC 27001:2005, of which the objective is to build up an IT control-related environment that satisfies the requirement of many other regulatory standards such as SoX.

It is important to underline the fact that the mere existence of a regulatory text within an enterprise is not sufficient for the pragmatic evaluation of benefits in security terms. These hypotheses are more a starting point to evaluate or test the fulfilment of regulatory requirements. In compliance terms, policies are of double importance. They include not only the requirements resulting from the legal compliance component, but also the requirements resulting from the managerial side in terms of risk management, security management, or other activities that the management level has formulated and expressed within policy terms.

7.2.8 Policy compliance context

As has been stated earlier, all the requirements resulting from different legislations and regulatory sources must be translated into actions to be taken, or activities to be undertaken that will appear within the different policies that the organization has written and adopted. This part of the information security policy will set up the objectives that have to be achieved by all the organizational levels. The achievement of the objectives will be the first element to be measured in compliance terms. The second element will concern the assigned responsibilities in terms of legal and regulatory compliance and also in terms of internal security requirements. In terms of responsibilities, policy-related compliance could be assessed at multiple levels, starting from the operational level (day to day compliance) to the audit level (high-level compliance). Wright *et al.* recommend in the "IT regulatory and standards compliance handbook" that the Human Resources department should be involved in policy compliance issues by insisting on the fact that the element making the difference is the understanding of the policy rather than simple compliance with it.[15]

---

15   C. Wright, B. Freedman, and D. Liu, *The IT Regulatory and Standards Compliance Handbook: How to Survive an Information Systems Audit and Assessment*, Syngress – Elsevier, 2008.

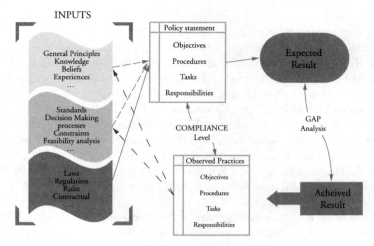

Fig. 7.2 Policy compliance framework.

The policy compliance activities are more complex than the legal and regulatory compliance. This is because in the case of legal compliance the requirements cannot be discussed in terms of pertinence, they simply have to be followed and applied. The requirements resulting from information security policies might be discussed and subsequently modified according to their coherence. As we can see in Figure 7.2, the policy requirements do not result only in authoritarian and rigid sources (e.g. laws) but also encompass some more flexible elements, which are a function of a logical analysis that is liable to be influenced by change over time.

In comparison with the legal part of compliance, the policy part is more dynamic. Security policies are a statement on how to protect but at the same time requirements are subject to small frequent daily changes, which is not the case for a legal and regulatory one. For that reason the compliance system focused on policies issues incorporates a review and analysis dimension to validate the coherence of the policy elements. This is the reason why in policy terms the organization should go beyond simple verification to address the understanding of such elements inside. Indeed, security policies have to be routinely reviewed for their effectiveness and validity. Nevertheless, as has been discussed above the policy conception process may be performed in two different ways: either by applying an analytical and decision-making approach, or by rigorously applying well-known standards or frameworks such as ISO/IEC security standards, ITIL, or CobiT. From this point of view, the policy compliance concern should be considered in two different ways:

- The first way will be the level of compliance with the policy itself, resulting in a policy enforcement level;
- The second way will be the level of compliance of the policy statements with the source standards, resulting in a level that meets the standard's requirements.

7.2.9 Controlling System

By *controlling system* we meant all those activities that will manage and oversee the operation of security activities with regard to internal and external compliance requirements. The controlling system as defined includes both the internal control (audit) function and the external audit one. The audit function, independently of its nature (external or internal), is the key contributor to the compliance program. The main output of this compliance element will be the reporting that will indicate the current compliance status and efforts in the context of external requirements. At the same time, part of the role of internal auditor is to provide assurance to the management that their approved internal controls are in place and are working effectively. In practice, controlling activities are often related to well-known frameworks such as the Committee of Sponsoring Organizations of the Treadway Commission (COSO) and Control Objectives for Information and related Technology (CobiT). While the object of those two frameworks remains the same – the evaluation of the control environment – their scope is different in terms of implementation. In fact, the COSO framework is more focused on the internal control issues than CobiT, which is actually a model of IT governance, and constitutes a solid basis for the external IT Audit.

Committee of Sponsoring Organizations of the Treadway Commission (COSO)

According to COSO[16] the Internal Control System will help the organization to achieve its performance targets, ensure reliable reporting, and ensure that enterprises comply with laws and regulations. COSO is based on a direct relationship between objectives (that the organization strives to achieve) and the components (what is needed to achieve those objectives). Compliance is one of the three objectives of the COSO framework. In order to reach a good level of compliance five components must be performed:
- Monitoring of internal processes focused on changing conditions – change management;
- Information and communication – the identification and the capture of pertinent information needed to manage the organization's control activities;
- Control activities – including policies and procedures allowing risks to be addressed;
- Risk assessment – including identification, analysis and management of relevant risks;
- Control environment – including human resources attributes such as ethical values, integrity and individual attributes.

Transformed into compliance terms COSO requires that:
- Continual identification and interpretation process of legal, regulatory requirements should be performed;
- A system capable of analyzing and automatically putting into the system new legal requirements should be put in place;
- A legal policy or something similar should be drawn up, capable of defining security objectives in legal terms;
- The legal risk should be managed at the same level as the other risks, by the same means;
- Efforts should be provided on awareness and training focused on legal matters, allowing awareness and training to be effectively implemented.

Generally speaking, an internal control (audit) system should:
- Measure the gap between what is required and what is supposed to be implemented;

16　　COSO, "Internal Control – Integrated Framework," Committee of Sponsoring Organizations of the Treadway Commission 1994. Available at http://www.snai.edu/cn/service/library/book/0-Framework-final.pdf

- Reduce the gap between what is supposed to be implemented and what has been effectively implemented;
- Review the pertinence of the implementation according to the internal objectives.

Control Objectives for Information and related Technology (CobiT)

One of the methodological frameworks commonly used to audit ICT Governance and its different aspects is Control Objectives for Information and related Technology (CobiT). CobiT constitutes a complete frame of reference making it possible to control the whole of the information systems related operations[17]. CobiT comprises 34 control objectives for systems grouped into four main fields:

- Plan and organize;
- Acquire and implement;
- Deliver and support;
- Monitor and evaluate.

Each one of these domains specifies the IT requirements and the controls that should be implemented to ensure a certain level of IT governance. CobiT considers an organization from a wide perspective by analysing the extent to which ICT governance is aligned with business objectives. It is important to underline that, based on this governance-related scope of CobiT, one of the identified business objectives is the compliance system.

7.3 Compliance versus security

7.3.1 Compliance and risk management relationship

ICT compliance is considered as a key element of the business risk management profile and a crucial aspect of good corporate governance. Legislation such as Basel II presumes a high level of ICT compliance to allow businesses to complete specific required assessments and reporting. As we have seen throughout this chapter, the compliance dimension of the information security program allows organizations to prevent risks related to the obligation of complying with different laws, legislation and internal policies and procedures. Having a good compliance function means that legislation with which an organization should comply is identified, requirements set out within this legislation are understood, and an active assessment is made in order to provide the evidence that they are implemented.

It has been shown that many surveys attest to the fact that compliance is one of the first incentives to invest in security functions. This fact shows the reality of the motivations for compliance and its added value to information security. In fact, if we wanted to interpret the position of compliance as a driver for security spending, it could be argued that there are two main elements providing a real added value, namely (i) responsibility and accountability, and (ii) the fulfilment of requirements. The first one will have a real and direct impact on the

---

[17]   ISACA & ITGI, *Control Objectives for Information and related Technology (COBIT)* Information Systems Audit and Control Association and IT Governance Institute, 2007. Available at http://www.isaca.org/Template. cfm?Section=COBIT6&Template=/TaggedPage/TaggedPageDisplay.cfm&TPLID=55&ContentID=7981

information security effectiveness, as responsibility and accountability are two elements that have a major incidence regarding the security quality.

Many of these legal texts hold the board level responsible for the quality of their internal control systems. This is the basis for a greater pressure from the top level downwards in security terms. The fact of having an identifiable person or function within the organization responsible in managerial terms for information security gives more confidence that the security activities will be performed in a favourable environment. Logically this means that in terms of resources the more optimal solutions will be selected. The fact that the high levels of the organization need to take responsibility for information security gives the assurance that the required processes and activities will be performed by all subordinate levels. This is in practical terms. In more strategic terms, because of the pressure of individual regulatory penalties for the high-level managers, the security and the internal control staff have more legitimacy in their daily work life and will be better able to perform their tasks.

The second element is to fulfil binding requirements that are mainly focused on legal requirements and regulatory legislation. Attention should be paid to this factor that arises directly from the mandatory profile of the law; this is the main reason that motivates spending efforts. Considering the added value from an information security point of view, it is less important than the first element, which was responsibility. There are multiple reasons for this. The first is that the binding character of compliance allows the organization to prioritize among a considerable number of legal and regulatory bills. The second is that to comply is a very expensive task. If these two reasons are combined, it can be expected that the largest "share of the pie" with respect to information security concerns goes to the compliance activities.

The general security level will be the one that is required by legislation. However, such legislation very often does not contain baseline requirements which would help to improve the general posture of computer security. Focusing one's attention on compliance activities and results might not take into account the security needs of the organization that arise from the risk assessment processes or the business needs that would really improve the security posture of their system.

7.3.2 The relationship between compliance and information security assurance

Does compliance equal security? Referring to the executive director of information security at Sony Pictures Entertainment in "Your Guide to Good Enough Compliance,"[18] the author states that compliance is more an interpretative than an empirical science. It is a matter of negotiation. In this way the most important issues are how to measure the degree of compliance and who is actually measuring. Regulations such as SoX still remain vague regarding the way the organizations have to comply with their requirements. In an auditor-board of directors relationship, the determinant point is to say whether or not the organization is complying with SoX. This shows that they have made a good faith effort to comply with the law, which does not necessarily mean that it is performed in the most beneficial way for the organization. This way of doing things presents two main risks:
- The risk of being non-compliant;

---

[18]   A. Holmes, "Your Guide to Good-Enough Compliance," (www.cio.com).

- The risk of being compliant, but with a negative return on investment and/or a low level of information security.

From an information security assurance point of view, compliance result in less than was hoped for, apart from a sense of accountability. But accountability does not equal assurance in security. Assurance is a more pragmatic concept, including the certitude of ensuring availability, integrity, authentication, confidentiality, and non-repudiation.

From an information security assurance point of view, what does it mean to be SoX compliant? On one hand, the notion of compliance linked to feelings of trust brings external pressures, compelling organizations to design, establish, document, test and monitor internal control processes. But at the same time, regulatory compliance makes it difficult to specifically understand what must be done to adequately protect data, putting forward arguments about *reasonable precautions*, in order to be compliant with these regulations. What does constitute reasonable precautions: encrypting data, providing some access controls, both, or other measures? Which is the most profitable combination? How far can one go into depth? How does this translate into actions to be taken to meet SOX requirements to have an adequate infrastructure in place? Putting in place a risk management framework can be presented to the regulator as a good faith effort to comply. But, it does not necessarily include the quality of the risk management framework in fulfilling the business and security objectives. What is needed is to:

- Base the information security program on a security framework such as ISO/IEC 27002:2005, ISO/IEC 27001:2005 or even CobiT, bearing in mind that a regulation typically only addresses one particular type of risk;
- Distinguish between security spending and compliance spending;
- Deal with changes in threats and regulations.

At the same time to be compliant is not an effortless task but a process able to consume a lot of resources. As stated above, compliance is a matter of interpretation and this is true even in the cost control case. To be compliant needs a lot of effort and money.[19] Often the amount of money spent is correlated with quality and used as an indicator of a good security level. In our opinion, it is not of great importance, although it could be a reasonable indicator showing that a good faith effort has been made to comply with the requirements. These variations are due principally to the lack of definable boundaries, organizational size and type. A relevant element when discussing compliance effectiveness is how far the organization has gone into depth to analyze regulatory requirements and the way compliance is measured. At the end of the day, from an information assurance point of view this is the most important thing to evaluate. Even if an organization is judged compliant with the regulatory requirement, it does not inevitably mean that it offers a good security level. Certainly it offers a better one than a non-compliant organization, but we cannot necessarily draw the same conclusion in respect of its overall security objectives.

---

[19] For example, some authors claim that 500,000 US dollars per year are needed to comply with SoX (J. E. Payne, "Regulation and Information Security: Can Y2K Lessons Help Us," *IEEE Security & Privacy*, vol. 2 (2), pp. 58-61, 2004.) whereas, an amount of 4.39 million US dollars are needed for the same objective (S. Blount, "white paper: The Role of Security Management in Achieving "Continuous Compliance," CA Security Management 2007. http://www.ca.com/Files/WhitePapers/role_security_mgmt_in_compliance_wp.pdf).

Another issue is that the mandatory regulatory texts such as SoX, the Gramm-Leach-Bliley Act or Basel II concern some specific domains such as fraud, financial risk and privacy data protection. Being compliant with these regulations certainly helps to address these problems but they have a small relative impact on the overall security level. This is a little bit contradictory with the leverage attempted by the organizations that maintain that the compliance brings a higher security level. If we consider the fact that these regulations are mandatory, this does not represent a higher security level but only a required security level. What can make the difference? We think that the organization must focus its attention onto more global solutions for information security such as the ISO/IEC standards, European or NIST standards – in brief, any solutions that address information security issues holistically.

7.4 Evaluating the compliance function

7.4.1 Information security compliance process

Just as in a risk assessment approach, a correctly performed information security compliance process needs to include the following elements:
- Performance of an impact assessment, in order to identify and prioritize the most important regulation with which the organization is concerned;
- Performance of due diligence, in order to perform the compliance process with an improvement scope and not only with a conformity scope;
- Analysis of the competing regulatory requirement in an optimization scope, in order to minimize cost and be more transparent vis-à-vis the shareholders and stakeholders.

Regulatory compliance is a very complex task for several reasons. The first is the multiple nature of regulations, governmental, industry or best practice. The second is that regulations texts cover wide geographical regions. An organization could be concerned by regional, national and international regulations. To take an example SoX does not only concern US corporations but every corporation registered on the US Stock Exchange. The third is that some regulations and laws are applicable to the whole organization while others apply only to some departments.

Moreover, just like the risk assessment process, the regulatory compliance process needs to be established in a perspective of optimization, in order to identify priorities and reduce costs. In order to do this, a formalized mechanism is required. We have to distinguish between legal compliance, regulatory compliance, and industry-specific and best practices compliance in order to prioritize the actions to be taken. Our proposition is to start by identifying mandatory or non-mandatory texts concerning the organization. In other words, a given organization must identify regulations with which they have to comply and frameworks or practices to which they have to conform.

There are two main groups:
- Complying with: Laws, Rules, and Regulations. Examples: National Data Protection Acts, Informatics and Liberty Law, Financial Security Law, SoX, EUROSoX, Basel II, HIPPA, etc.;
- Being in conformity with: Standards, Frameworks or Security Practices. Example: ISO 9000, ISO/IEC 13335, ISO/IEC 27002:2005, ISO/IEC 2700, COBIT, COSO etc.

In order to reduce the regulatory complexity, we can sub-classify regulations by application domain or finality, considering:
- Technical norms;
- Process outcome results;
- Managerial frameworks.

Once the organization has prioritized the regulations with which it must comply, the next action to be undertaken is to determine the scope driving the compliance efforts. This will depend on whether the scope is related to:
- Governance issues: transparency and accuracy of financial reports;
- Privacy issues: how user information is held;
- Information security issues: how critical infrastructures and assets are protected.

The final step that will determine the approach to be adopted will be the analysis of the relationship between different regulations based on the categorization we proposed above (Figure 7.3). Different regulations are interrelated. To take an example, in order to be SoX compliant two other frameworks are used in practice: COSO (industry best practices) and COBIT (control oriented framework). In the same way, for being in conformity with the Basel II regulation, ISO/IEC 27002:2005 is currently used to conduct a gap analysis. COBIT is also very often used to perform periodic IT system audits to evaluate the security level. As a result of SoX, the previously existing COSO and COBIT frameworks were emphasized. There is an intrinsic motivation concerning the regulatory compliance and conformity, which is to do the right thing, by obeying a set of values. In that sense regulatory compliance could be considered as a business issue driving information security.

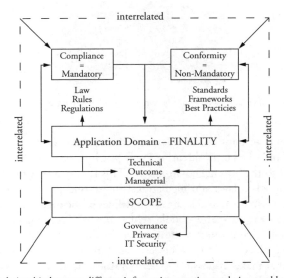

Fig. 7.3 Relationship between different information security regulations and best practices.

7.4.2　Compliance framework

For interested parties, external or internal, the objective of the evaluation of the compliance dimension will be the capacity of the organization to remain compliant with mandatory or desirable legislation. The specific goal is to evaluate the way organizations manage their compliance constraints by understanding how the compliance system in place is performed. The common objective of a compliance process within an organization, in an information security scope, is to ensure that appropriate preventative and detective controls are in place and are effectively utilized. Starting from the point that a compliance process carries costs, the organization has to consider the "desirable" notion. By desirable is meant any kind of compliance that is not in itself a mandatory requirement, but if chosen to be followed must be adhered to.

The compliance system follows a logical progression that is described in Figure 7.4. To begin from a risk management point of view, the organization should first conform to the mandatory external requirements driven by laws and regulations. In the case of the non-satisfaction of such requirements the primary objective, namely the continued existence of the organization, could be compromised.

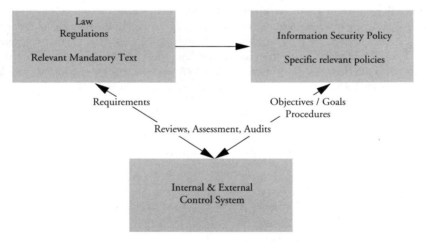

Fig. 7.4 Compliance system framework and relationship.

After taking into account the mandatory requirements, the internal objectives arising from them should then be clearly identified and put into the internal policies in order to adapt these policies to the internal environment. This is only a part of the internal require-ments that are imputed to laws and regulations; the second part will concern the require-ments arising from the strategic and business guidelines of the organization. Being compliant with internal policies means that a double goal is reached, compliance with relevant laws and regulation as well as conformity with the strategic direction of the organization. Finally, all these compliance objectives cannot be satisfied without a control system (internally or externally driven) that makes it possible to verify if the objectives and goals are reached and procedures are followed as envisaged.

7.4.3 Compliance evaluation structure and methodology

This logical and sequential description of the compliance process allows us to identify the compliance dimensions of the model, that is to say, the elements including the security objectives. The dimension of information security compliance has as its objective to adhere to specific laws, regulations, standards and all relevant rules enacted by the organization in order to mitigate the risk of being non-compliant which may cause penal, financial or reputation-related damages (Figure 7.5).

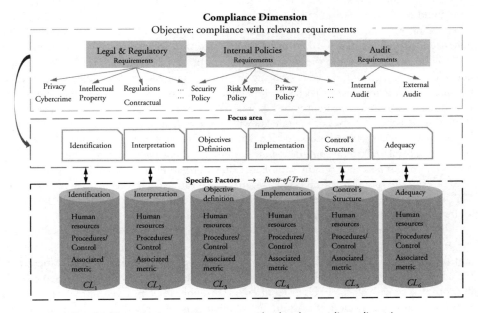

Fig. 7.5 The evaluation assurance structure related to the compliance dimension.

By financial penalties should be understood any kind of action providing direct losses that could be expressed in financial terms and that disturbs the ability of the company to operate. By reputation-related damages should be understood any kind of impact arising from a negative opinion that may disturb the ability of the company to operate in a longer-term perspective. Reputational damages are by their very nature very difficult to measure. Reputational damage is one of the most typical costs a given organization may suffer within the category of the so-called *hidden costs.*

As can be seen the high level objective (consequently the high level dimension, which is the compliance dimension) is divided into three more detailed dimensions, which constitute the basis of our analysis and which respond to three sub-objectives: to be compliant with and at the same time take into account each typical dimension's properties.

After having decided on the structure of the dimensions, the model determines the related focus area that represents the security issues according to the model. By security issue is meant every activity, action or attribute which has to be performed or managed, and of which the absence could impact the objectives. In this focus area structure related to the compliance dimension we follow the same logical progression as presented above. That is to say that based on the implicit relationships between dimensions, the retained security issues correspond to prevalent characteristics.

In respect of the legal and regulatory dimension two focus area are identified, namely *identification* and *interpretation*. The first concerns the identification of the relevant mandatory bills and of the requirements arising from them, while the second concerns the explanation and the meaning of such requirements with respect to the organizational profile. It is very important to put the requirements into a specific context, the organizational context, in order to ensure that a given requirement does not become a barrier. The identification and the interpretation focus areas could result in a non-compliance risk as a result of a lack of knowledge about the pieces of legislation with which the organization has to be compliant. All of these relevant and well-understood requirements have then to be transformed into security objectives to be attained that will be incorporated into the different policies in place. By objective is meant any selected tangible output regarding the state of being of an asset, tangible or intangible. The objective becomes thus a requirement that has to be fulfilled. For internal policies and the conformity with them, an important element to be taken into account is the issue of implementation. This is the way that the objectives of the policies will be reached, such as the resources that have to be allocated or the organizational structure that should be put in place to support objectives.

The risk related to the *objective definition* and *policy implementation* regarding the policy dimension might be a state of non-compliance due to the absence of clearly established objectives or even the total lack of objectives regarding a given legal and regulatory requirement. On the other hand, even if objectives are defined, a non-compliant situation could arise from an inappropriate and insufficient effort to satisfy such objectives.

Two focus areas, namely the control structure and the adequacy level, mainly concern the audit requirements sub-dimension. The objectives defined within the internal policies and the ways to proceed must be defined on the basis of effectiveness. The first focus area includes issues related to the internal capacity to build up a control system capable of providing compliance with all the levels of requirement through different levels of the organization on a daily basis. The notion of continuous compliance is performed through real-time, preventive controls that can drastically reduce the time spent on detective auditing, which is the subject of the second focus area. The adequacy focus area includes all the efforts that have to be made to create an auditable environment in order to create regular audit trails as well as to put in place the conditions that are needed to perform audit activities. The risk of non-compliance due to those two focus areas comes from an absence of control or a weak control system incapable of measuring the recurrent compliance, whereas a chaotic internal control system that does not correspond to clear objectives and strategies for accomplishment could reduce the capacity of audit projects to detect non-compliance. This structure of focus areas includes the philosophy of a classical risk management approach, which could be applicable even to compliance dimensions with a strong legal focus.

Once the dimensions (information security objectives) and focus areas (information security issues, source of risk) have been identified, the evaluation model is focused on the specific factors (information security measures) that will decrease the magnitude of risk. In order to ensure a continuum in the logical progression of the dimension, each focus area is related to a group of specific factors. Entering more into the details of the ISAAM evaluation model, we recommend categorizing compliance elements according to the target they should touch. For that purpose we propose:

- Objective focused requirements – aiming to identify requirements concerning factual objectives regarding the electronic data;
- Behavioural focused requirements – aiming to identify requirements concerning the targeted behaviour in order to satisfy the factual objectives;
- System focused requirements – aiming to identify the targeted proceedings that allow the attainment of objectives.

The aim is to identify the most relevant assurance elements that will provide the necessary evidence that the compliance system in place is able to manage the inherent complexity of the domain. As the compliance structure and compliance requirements change frequently, we have to introduce a generic model incorporating this characteristic of continual change. Our approach does not seek to specifically and exhaustively designate the assurance elements, but rather specifies the framework within which these assurance elements are positioned. To do that, in our model each specific factor corresponding to an assurance elements, considered as being "the root-of-trust", will be categorized in three main categories, namely:
- Procedural/operational measures;
- Dedicated human resources;
- Associated metrics.

This kind of categorization keeps the door open for any specific requirements related to the compliance issues of a given organization that operates in a specific domain, has a specific size or needs to respond to specific needs in terms of compliance.

The procedural/operational measure will concern the basic assurance element under question, showing that a minimal basic level of protection does exist. In that way, for each focus area such a measure must be performed as shown below:
- *Identification:* recurrent formal (empirical or automated) identification process concerning relevant laws and regulations;
- *Interpretation:* every identified law or regulation should lead to a conceptual explanatory schema describing the different impacts the regulation could have on the assets and business processes;
- *Objective definition:* the body in charge of the management of internal policies should obligatorily be informed of the conceptual and explanatory schema and use it as a basis for policy writing;
- *Policy implementation:* an explanatory schema mapping objectives to specific processes and resources stimulating thus a cost-benefit analysis that could be imputed to each objective. This mapping should be included in the policy itself in a further move towards aiding understanding. Automated tools could possibly be used to identify every change in the structure of objectives;
- *Control structure:* the structure of the internal control must be identifiable. This system must clearly impute to each hierarchic level its compliance related activities proportionate to their responsibility. Every hierarchical level has to be involved in the compliance activities;
- *Adequacy:* the performance of all these measures should allow the performance of constructive audit activities. A planning regarding the frequency of audits should be established.

The second level of the specific factors concerns human resources. Here the human resource will play a double role. The first is in respect of the resource's (asset's) role, which allows the compliance process to reach the compliance objective, based on its inherent capacities. In fact, the compliance success will strongly depend on the human performance. The second will be in terms of responsibility and the fact of being the backbone of the security activity. At least one responsible person should be specified for each specific factor and a multidisciplinary team should be created to carry out compliance challenges. Indeed a triple competency is required: for the first dimension some legal competencies would be preferable, for the second and the third dimension some managerial ones.

The final level of specific factors is the *associated metrics* that will provide the evidence that procedural/operational and human resources are effectively governed. The associated metrics should correspond to or measure the extent of the procedural/operational factors. In fact an obligation is accountable if a mechanism exists to verify that the obligation has been satisfied. For example some possible metrics might be:

- *Identification:* the percentage of identified legal and regulatory bills submitted to a re-evaluation procedure per year;
- *Interpretation:* the percentage of the identified legal and regulatory bills without a related explanatory schema;
- *Objective definition:* the percentage of identified legal and regulatory bills impacting on formal objectives within the internal policies;
- *Policy implementation:* the percentage of the objectives within the internal policies without a related cost-benefit analysis;
- *Control structure:* the percentage of the current internal control structure components compared with an hypothetical structure resulting from a referential framework;
- *Adequacy:* the percentage of items within the audit report including at least a recommendation for improvement.

7.4.4 The maturity model related to the compliance dimension

Based on these considerations and on the structure of the maturity model presented previously in this book, the following maturity model regarding the compliance dimension should be used as a basis for the evaluation of effectiveness from a requirements perspective (Figure 7.6).

7.5 Chapter summary

The compliance system of an organization should be focused on three sources, namely:
- Laws – an object subject to external requirements for behaviour;
- Regulations – responsibilities and managerial styles subject to external requirements on the way the observed activities (i.e. security activities) are performed;
- Policies – objects, responsibilities, and managerial styles subject to internal requirements for the achievement of objectives.

The overall expected rationale regarding the *compliance dimension* of the information security is the organization's ability to remain compliant as measured by the effectiveness

Level 1 Fortuitous	• *Existence of at least one dimension:* In general, the legal dimension is carried out without any formal reference to the internal policies. • *No existing focus area structure:* The security issues in compliance terms do not follow the model's reasoning, i.e. some internal objectives exist but there is no implementation effort. • *Isolated specific factors:* In general situated at the procedure/controls level. *No quality specification can be done.*
Level 2 Structured	• *A clear and formal existence of the dimensions:* The requirements of the three sub-dimensions (legal and regulatory; internal policies; and audit) are identifiable. • *Focus area structure mostly exists:* This means that it could be minimally verified, and that identification, objective definition and external audit are carried out. • *Specific factors include two attributes:* For each identified focus area, the specific factors procedure/controls and human resource can be assigned. *The quality level has reached the first level,* which means that legal and regulatory; internal policies; and audit activities are included within the information security policy or any other strategic document related to the information security field.
Level 3 Functional	• *The architecture is complete:* The three dimensions and the six focus areas exist, as described within the model, and the structural construction exists for each of them, including the framework, the content and the process concerns. • *Specific factors:* In general, the attributes for procedure/controls and human resources are identifiable for each related focus area. *The quality level* is characterized by an average weighting level of two, which means that legal and regulatory; internal policies; and audit aspects are the responsibility of a specific person (organizational function, job function).
Level 4 Analyzable	• *The architecture is complete:* The three dimensions and the six focus areas exist, as described within the model. • *Specific factors:* The three general attributes are identifiable for each related focus area, which means that the level of metrics is reached for each focus area. *The quality level* is characterized by an average weighting level of three, which means that the that specific factors are minimally documented and/or monitored.
Level 5 Effective	• *The architecture is complete:* The three dimensions and the six focus areas exist, as described within the model. • *Specific factors:* The three general attributes are identifiable for each related focus area, which means that the level of metrics is reached for each specific factor. *The quality level* has an average weight that clearly equals four, signaling that a procedure for continual improvement is imputed to each focus area, where internal /external reviews and audits are regularly planned and performed.

Fig. 7.6 The maturity model related to the compliance dimension.

assurance index of the compliance system. Based on the fact that compliance has become one of the main drivers of information security spending, this chapter presents the relationship between compliance and information security assurance and points out that a high level of compliance does not necessarily mean better security. After the identification of each dimension's focus areas, the key success factors and the elements for which evidence should be provided in order to claim assurance were identified. Some metrics related to the compliance dimension were proposed according to the structure of the focus areas. A specific maturity model of the *functional dimension* was proposed in order to allow the organization to define its specific security requirements.

Chapter 8

Concluding Remarks

8.1 Effectiveness and efficiency as a priority

A number of different evaluation methodologies, frameworks, and standards have been developed and numerous means of evaluation exist. The problem is that in general these means of evaluation are either focused on specific topics of information security or, even if they address all different facets of security, do so in a static manner and not globally. By static manner we mean that the evaluation would be performed according to methodological rules or advice, pushing the organization to follow the rules of the standards (or methodologies), rather than adapting those rules to meet its specific needs for protection. The *Information Security Assurance Assessment Model* (ISAAM) proposed within this book has as its primary objective to close this gap. It is a conceptual model based on a methodological approach to holistically evaluate the information security posture. It brings an approach that provides outputs from the evaluation process to inspire trust, not only in the evaluation results themselves, but also in the information security program or system that has been evaluated. It addresses *assurance requirements* based on the two following attributes:

- *Effectiveness*: the system/program under evaluation is doing the correct thing; and
- *Efficiency*: the system/program under evaluation is doing things correctly by achieving objectives with minimum wasted effort.

The main relevant literature resources including the methodologies, standards and published research papers related to this topic have been analysed. These literature resources range from those considering information security from a managerial point of view to those considering information security from a technological perspective, and these have been the raw material from which the model is designed through:

- Extracting from the literature sources recommendations addressing the different issues of information security and adapting these recommendations to the context of the evaluation model;
- Combining engineering security standards with non-engineering assessment models of information security in order to formalize the way information security is evaluated, taking advantage of the rigorous nature of the technical security standards;

- Putting all of these resources into a well-defined context that takes into account the specific business needs of the organization and the dynamic nature of those needs.

ISAAM is an integrative approach capable of providing an overall protection governance system rather than a piecemeal approach based on unstructured knowledge of the risks or safeguards to be implemented. It is a new way of evaluating information security based on a pragmatic assessment of the internal needs and internal roles of the organization being evaluated.

8.2 The value added by, and scope of application of, ISAAM

Very often methodologies and standards in this field require considerable external resources to be implemented. The ISAAM method has therefore been conceived in such a way that it could comfortably be performed internally and externally, because it needs no additional competencies or resources. In all cases, the internal contribution remains substantial because, by its nature, the model evaluates the information security posture based on internal security needs. The strength of the ISAAM evaluation model relies upon the fact that it reverses the tendency to adapt security practices to meet unchangeable requirements ensuing from standards, and leads instead to a context where internal business expectations become the reference points that drive information security activities. There is no globally optimal level of information security, but there is an optimal level of information security for each organization based on its requirements. In this context ISAAM prioritizes a transversal approach that requires a deep understanding of the organization through the knowledge of organizational requirements. The ISAAM evaluation platform integrates the knowledge provided through a large number of resources, resulting in a widely applicable but relatively simple model for evaluating Information Security. The ISAAM model enables organizations to better master their own information security issues from beginning to end, thus optimizing both the return on investment of the security efforts and their effectiveness.

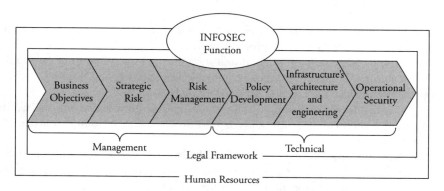

Fig. 8.1 Security vision as a result of interrelated processes.

The ISAAM model answers the challenge faced by most organizations, that is the integration of the notions of risk and of security in order to devise global risk and security policies for the organization based on the vision of security as a logical continuum of different efforts (Figure 8.1).

8.3 A new evaluation paradigm

The originality of ISAAM lies in the assurance structure that is based on the four principal dimensions of information security efforts, which are organizational, functional, human related and legal. The initial concept of splitting the whole information security system into four distinct domains was chosen in order to reduce the complexity of such a model that does encompass a great number of interrelated elements. Once the constituent elements were identified, issues and mitigating security-related elements were identified. This process allowed the creation of a holistic platform in order to identify foreseeable breaches of the information security system. In order to holistically evaluate the information security we proposed a way to structure the different and multidimensional security facets in order to identify the specific issues and the specific elements that contribute to address those issues. These elements are then put into a specific context and evaluated according to three distinct attributes, the assurance structure, the process quality and the effectiveness (Figure 8.2).

		Assurance Structure	Process Quality	Effectiveness
INFORMATION SECURITY DIMENSIONS-RELATED *Dependant variables*	**Organizational**	Organizational Security attribute value $X_{1\to ass}$	Organizational Security attribute value $X_{1\to qu}$	Organizational Security attribute value $X_{1\to eff}$
	Functional	Funcional Security attribute value $X_{2\to ass}$	Funcional Security attribute value $X_{2\to qu}$	Funcional Security attribute value $X_{2\to eff}$
	Human	Human Security attribute value $X_{3\to ass}$	Human Security attribute value $X_{3\to qu}$	Human Security attribute value $X_{3\to eff}$
	Legal	Legal Security attribute value $X_{4\to ass}$	Legal Security attribute value $X_{4\to qu}$	Legal Security attribute value $X_{4\to eff}$

TRUST-RELATED Information Security dependent variables

Fig. 8.2 A conceptual table representing the holistic information security evaluation according to the ISAAM model.

The aim of this evaluation is to generate trust first of all in information security itself rather than in the individual outputs of the evaluation results. As we can see in Figure 8.2, the evaluation outputs could be of a multiple nature allowing the interested parties to evaluate better either parts of the information security program or system or the information security program or system as a whole. One can for example determine a value according to the dimension being evaluated based on the information security attributes, for example in respect of the organizational dimension:

$$\text{Organizational dimension} = \sum_{i=1}^{3}\left\{X_{1\to\text{ass}} + X_{1\to\text{qu}} + X_{1\to\text{eff}}\right\}$$

Another possibility is to determine another value focused on a single security attribute throughout all the information security dimension, for example in respect of the quality attribute:

$$\text{Process quality attribute} = \sum_{i=1}^{4}\left\{X_{1\to\text{qu}} + X_{2\to\text{qu}} + X_{3\to\text{qu}} + X_{4\to\text{qu}}\right\}$$

The ISAAM model is designed to evaluate the information security posture of any organization based on a triple point of view: the structure, the quality and the capacity of the security program to achieve organizational requirements. The organization's security issues are addressed in a broad and global sense as opposed to a purely information security related one. This triple evaluation allows users to place the maximum possible confidence in the evaluation of the information security posture resulting from the model, which constitutes an innovation in the domain of security evaluation. In this way the objective of inspiring trust with respect to the expected result of the evaluation and, consequently, to the actual, current information security posture, might be attained.

The model and the methodological approach are independent of the size of the organization. This will not strongly influence the assurance level, except in the first stage that deals with the *information security assurance structure*. But even where the assurance structure is being defined, the model assumes that a certain security baseline should be provided. As such, and independent of the organization's size and its domains of activity, all four dimensions should be recognised and addressed at least in a minimal way for the existence of an information security program or system to be claimed.

The ISAAM evaluation model points to different elements involved in the evaluation of security, bringing an added value which could not be provided by the exclusive use of different current methods used to assess Information Security. This added value is inherent to the global, systematic, and holistic nature of our evaluation model, as has been explained throughout this document.

The proposed answer to the existing information security issues is a new evaluation-related paradigm, linked to a security evaluation model. Unlike the existing methods for evaluating the security posture, the ISAAM evaluation model takes into account different parameters for determining the global security posture of a given organization. Based on that, the first advantage of the model is that it is accessible to all levels of the organization's stakeholders, including persons who are not necessarily computer or security professionals. The ISAAM evaluation model is not a new audit methodology or a new security compliance related assessment tool. It is a conceptual and practical tool to measure the security level or posture according to different levels determined by the model itself.

By using the proposed maturity model that accompanies our evaluation structure, each organization could measure the evolution of its security effort with a view to optimization. It contributes to a self-education process with respect to the security issues and allows the organization to capitalize on the knowledge acquired in relation to the security culture. By doing that, the objective of reaching a good level of resilience is achieved. Based on the constitutive elements proposed within the ISAAM Maturity Model, each organization will be able to devise its own maturity model based on its specific business needs and its resultant security requirements.

In addition to interested internal parties, external evaluators such as insurers might also use the ISAAM model. It will contribute to answering one of the most frequently discussed issues in the realm of insurance, the idea of "moral hazard." That means that a party insulated from risk (as a result of an insurance policy, for example) may behave differently than it would behave if it were fully exposed to the risk. This makes insurers more interested in the future "security attitude" of their clients rather than the existing risk situation, which does nevertheless remain a good indicator for many other aspects. This attitude is taken into account by the ISAAM model because it evaluates the security state based on the needs and requirements that will be expressed in the definition of the security level to be reached according to these needs and requirements.

At the same time, insurers are also concerned by issues related to the *adverse selection problem* related to the asymmetric possession of information between *owners* and *evaluators*. The ISAAM model takes into account this aspect too, by presenting the current security state of a given organization in a more transparent way. The ISAAM evaluation is based on global efforts to build up a security program/system in order to achieve business needs and requirements. In that way, organizations that exclusively rely on technological solutions or focus their efforts exclusively on conformity issues could be detected and advised to provide efforts on the other security dimensions as well.

The fact of systemically, globally and holistically addressing security issues allows the ISAAM model to address the other concern of insurers, which is related to the interrelated risk. In fact our model aims to detect, and help organizations to identify, *the weakest link* based on a global view of the risks and vulnerabilities that might exist. The detection of such risks and vulnerabilities comes through constant efforts to understand and manage risks. The ISAAM model does not cease functioning at this stage, but instead goes further into discussing the continuing process from risk identification to the optimization of security measures. These two concepts are often dissociated within the different methods and norms. In this way ISAAM does not propose an *nth* method on how to evaluate specific security issues but rather puts forward a conceptual model based on a new evaluation paradigm. Because the ISAAM evaluation paradigm is based on the invariants regarding the organization's specific needs and relies upon a non-complex and stable paradigm, ISAAM is not affected by the continuous evolution of norms, standards, methods, or best practices typically used to perform security evaluation tasks.

Security is not a destination but an endless voyage, and the authors are firmly convinced that there cannot be a real conclusion when addressing issues related to security in general and, more specifically, to information security.

Bibliography

Main ISO related information security standards

ISO/IEC TR 13335-1:1996, Information technology – Guidelines for the management of IT security –Concepts and models for IT security, International Organization for Standardization (ISO), Switzerland, 1996 (withdrawn and replaced by the ISO/IEC 13335-1:2004).

ISO/IEC 13335-1:2004, Information technology – Security techniques – Management of information and communications technology security – Part 1: Concepts and models for information and communications technology security management, International Organization for Standardization (ISO), Switzerland, 2004.

ISO/IEC TR 13335-2:1996, Information technology – Guidelines for the management of IT security – Managing and planning IT security, International Organization for Standardization (ISO), Switzerland, 1996 (this part 2 was combined into the revised ISO/IEC 13335-1:2004).

ISO/IEC TR 13335-3:1996, Information technology – Guidelines for the management of IT security – Techniques for the management of IT security, International Organization for Standardization (ISO), Switzerland, 1996 (this part of the standard has been withdrawn and replaced by ISO/IEC 27005).

ISO/IEC TR 13335-4:1996, Information technology – Guidelines for the management of IT security – Selection of safeguards, International Organization for Standardization (ISO), Switzerland, 1996 (this part of the standard has been withdrawn and replaced by ISO/IEC 27005).

ISO/IEC 15408:2005, Information technology – Security techniques – Evaluation criteria for IT security – Part 2: Security functional components, International Organization for Standardization (ISO), Switzerland, 2006.

ISO/IEC 15408:2005, Information technology – Security techniques – Evaluation criteria for IT security – Part 3: Security assurance components, International Organization for Standardization (ISO), Switzerland, 2006.

ISO/IEC 15408:2005, Information technology – Security techniques – Evaluation criteria for IT security – Part 1: Introduction and general model, International Organization for Standardization (ISO), Switzerland, 2006.

ISO/IEC 27002:2005, Information technology – Security techniques – Code of practice for information security management, International Organization for Standardization (ISO), Switzerland, 2005.

ISO/IEC 27001:2005 (E), Information technology – Security techniques – Information security management systems – Requirements, International Organization for Standardization (ISO), Switzerland, 2005.

ISO/IEC 27005:2008, Information technology – Security techniques – Information security risk management, International Organization for Standardization (ISO), Switzerland, 2008.

ISO 31000:2009, Risk management – Principles and guidelines, International Organization for Standardization (ISO), Switzerland, 2008.

ISO 9000:2005, Quality management systems – Fundamentals and vocabulary, International Organization for Standardization (ISO), Switzerland, 2005.

ISO 9001:2000, Quality management systems – Requirements, International Organization for Standardization (ISO), Switzerland, 2000.

Other references

B. D. ADAMS, "Trust vs. Confidence," Department of National Defense, Toronto, Canada, 2005. Available at http://pubs.drdc.gc.ca/PDFS/unc48/p524541.pdf

J. ALLEN, *Governing for Enterprise Security*, The Software Engineering Institute, Carnegie Mellon University Pittsburgh, USA 2005. Available at http://www.cert.org/archive/pdf/05tn023.pdf

S. ANAND, "From IT Compliance to IT Governance "*IT Compliance Magazine*, Fall 2007, 7-9, 2007.

S. ANAND, "Information Security Implications of Sarbanes-Oxley," *Information Security Journal: A Global Perspective*, 17 (2), 75-79, 2008.

E. ANDERSON and J. CHOOBINEH, "Enterprise information security strategies," *Computers & Security*, 27 (1-2), 22-29, 2008.

S. ANGELO, "Security Architecture Model Component Overview," SANS Institute 2001. [Online] Available at http://www.sans.org/reading_room/whitepapers/basics/526.php

D. ASHENDEN, "Information Security Management: A Human Challenge," *Information Security Technical Report*, 113 (4), 195-201, 2008.

J. BABIAK, J. BUTTERS, and M. W. DOLL, *Defending the Digital Frontier: Practical Security for Management*, John Wiley & Sons, Inc., 2005.

W. BAKER and L. WALLACE, "Is Information Security Under Control? Investigating Quality in Information Security Management," *IEEE Security & Privacy*, 5 (1), 36-44, 2007.

I. BAZAVAN and I. LIM, *Information Security Cost Management*, Auerbach Publications, Boca Raton, FL, USA, 2007.

S. E. BARNETT, "Computer Security Training and Education: A Needs Analysis," in Proceedings of the *1996 IEEE Symposium on Security and Privacy*, 1996.

M. BIA and M. KALIKA, "Adopting an ICT code of conduct. An empirical study of organizational factors," *Journal of Enterprise Information Management*, 20 (4), 432-446, 2007.

M. BISHOP, "What Is Computer Security?," *IEEE Security & Privacy*, 1 (1), 67-69, 2003.

M. BISHOP, *Computer Security: art and science*, Addison-Wesley, Boston, USA, 2003.

J. BOTHA and R. v. SOLMS, "A cyclic approach to business continuity planning," *Information Management & Computer Security*, 12 (4), 328-337, 2004.

S. BUTLER, "Security attribute evaluation method: a cost-benefit approach," in Proceedings of the *24th International Conference on Software Engineering Orlando*, Florida: ACM, 2002.

S. E. CHANG and C. B. HO, "Organizational factors to the effectiveness of implementing information security management," *Industrial Management & Data Systems*, 106 (3), 345-361, 2006.

R. CUMMINGS, "The evolution of information assurance," *IEEE Computer Magazine*, 35 (12), 65-72, 2002.

S. CURKOVIC and M. PAGELL, "A Critical Examination of the Ability of ISO 9000 Certification to Lead to a Competitive Advantage," *Journal of Quality Management*, 4 (1), 51-67, 1999.

A. DA VEIGA and J.H.P. ELOFF, "An Information Security Governance Framework," *Information Systems Management*, 24 (4), 361-372, 2007.

C. C. DAVIS, M. SCHILLER, and K. WHEELER, *IT Auditing: Using Controls to Protect Information Assets*. McGraw Hill, New York, USA, 2007.

W. DELONE and E. MCLEAN, "Information systems success: the quest for the dependent variable," *Information Systems Research*, 3 (1), 60-95, 1992.

M. T. DLAMINI, J. H. P. ELOFF, and M. M. ELOFF, "Information security: The moving target," *Computers & Security*, (28) 3-4, 189-198, 2009.

N. F. DOHERTY and H. FULFORD, «Do Information Security Policies Reduce the Incidence of Security Breaches: An Exploratory Analysis,» *Information Resources Management Journal*, 18 (4), 21-39, 2005.

N. F. DOHERTY and H. FULFORD, "Aligning the information security policy with the strategic information system plans," Computers & Security, 25 (1), 55-63, 2006.

J. H. P. ELOFF and M. ELOFF, "Information Security Management – A New Paradigm," in Proceedings of the 2003 Annual Research Conference of the South African Institute of Computer Scientists and Information Technologists on Enablement through Technology (SAICSIT 2003), pp. 130-136, 2003.

J. H. P. ELOFF and M. M. ELOFF, "Information Security Architecture," *Computer Fraud & Security*, 2005 (11), pp. 10-16, 2005.

J.-N. EZINGEARD, E. MCFADZEAN, and D. BIRCHALL, "A Model of Information Assurance Benefits," *Information Systems Management Journal*, 22 (2), 20-29, 2006.

F. FARAHMAND, S. B. NAVATHE, G. P. SHARP, and P. H. ENSLOW, "A Management Perspective on Risk of Security Threats to Information Systems," *Information Technology and Management,* 6 (2-3), 203-225, 2005.

S. FELDMAN, "Quality assurance: much more than testing," *Queue,* 3 (1), 26-29, 2005.

K. J. FITZGERALD, "Information security baselines," *Information Management & Computer Security,* 3(2), 8-12, 1995.

T. FITZGERALD, "Clarifying the Roles of Information Security: 13 Questions the CEO, CIO, and CISO Must Ask Each Other," *Information Systems Security,* 16 (5), 257-263, 2007.

K. FORCHT and W. C. AYERS, "Developing a computer security policy for organizational use and implementation "*Journal of Computer Information Systems,* 41 (2), 2001.

E. H. FREEMAN, "Holistic Information Security: ISO 27001 and Due Care," *Information Systems Security,* 16 (5), 291-294, 2007.

E. H. FREEMAN, "Regulatory Compliance and the Chief Compliance Officer," *Information Security Journal: A Global Perspective,* 16 (6), 357-361, 2007.

M. GERBER and R. v. SOLMS, "From Risk Analysis to Security Requirements," *Computers & Security,* 20 (7), 577-584, 2001.

M. GERBER and R. v. SOLMS, "Information security requirements – Interpreting the legal aspects," *Computers & Security,* 27 (5-6), 124-135, 2008.

S. GHANAVATI, D. AMYOT, and L. PEYTON, "A Requirements Management Framework for Privacy Compliance," in Proceedings of the CAISE 06 Workshop on Regulations Modelling and their Validation and Verification (ReMo2V '06), Luxemburg, 2006.

S. GHERNAOUTI-HÉLIE and I. TASHI, "A Security Assurance Model to Holistically Assess the Information Security Posture," in *Complex Intelligent Systems and Their Applications,* Ed.: Springer, 2009.

S. GHERNAOUTI-HÉLIE, D. SIMMS, I. TASHI "Reasonable Security by Effective Risk Management Practices: From Theory to Practice," *12th International Conference on Network-Based Information Systems* (NBiS-2009); Indiana University, Purdue University, Indianapolis – Indianapolis, IN, USA, August 19-21, 2009

S. GHERNAOUTI-HÉLIE, I. TASHI "ISO Security Standards as Leverage on IT Security Management" *13th Americas Conference on Information Systems* (AMCIS 2007), Keystone, Colorado, USA, August, 2007.

I. GUZMAN, K. STAM, and J. STANTON, "The Occupational Culture of IS/IT Personnel within Organizations "*The Data Base for Advances in Information Systems,* 39 (1), 33-50, 2008.

J. M. HAGEN, E. ALBRECHTSEN, and J. HOVDEN, "Implementation and effectiveness of organisational information security measures," *Information Management & Computer Security,* 16 (4), 377-397, 2008.

J. T. HAMILL, R. F. DECKRO, and J. M. K. Jr., "Evaluating information assurance strategies," *Decision Support Systems,* 39 (2), 463-484, 2005.

S. HANSCHE, "Information System Security Training: Making it Happen, Part 2," *Information Security Journal: A Global Perspective,* 10 (3), 1-20, 2001.

S. G. HERRERO, M. A. M. SALDANA, M. A. M. d. CAMPO, and D. RITZEL, "From the traditional concept of safety management to safety integrated with quality," *Journal of Safety Research,* 33 (1), pp. 1-20, 2002.

D. S. HERRMANN, *Complete guide to security and privacy metrics: Measuring Regulatory Compliance, Operational Resilience, and ROI.* Auerbach Publications, Boca Raton, FL, USA, 2007.

L. J. HOFFMAN, K. LAWSON-JENKINS, and J. BLUM, "Trust beyond Security: an expanded trust model," *Communications of the ACM,* 49 (7), 95-101, 2006.

K.-S. HONG, Y.-P. CHI, L. CHAO, and J.-H. TANG, "An integrated system theory of information security management," *Information Management & Computer Security,* 11 (5), 243-248, 2003.

A. JAQUITH, *Security Metrics – Replacing Fear, Uncertainity, and Doubt,* Addison-Wesley, 2007.

G. F. JELEN and J. R. WILLIAMS, "A practical approach to measuring assurance," in Proceedings of *14th Annual Computer Security Applications Conference,* 333-343, 1998.

E. JOHNSON and E. GOETZ, "Embedding Information Security into the Organization," *IEEE Security and Privacy,* 5 (3), 16-24, 2007.

E. JOHNSON, E. GOETZ, and S. L. PFLEEGER, "Security through Information Risk Management "*IEEE Security & Privacy,* 7 (3), 45-52, 2009.

D. LANDOLL, *The Security Risk Assessment Handbook: A Complete Guide for Performing Security Risk Assessments,* Auerbach Publications, Boca Raton, FL, USA, 2006.

B. SCHNEIER, "Security and Compliance," *IEEE Security & Privacy,* 2 (3), 96-96, 2004.

A. SHOSTACK and A. STEWART, *The New School of Information Security* Addison -Wesley, Boston, USA, 2008.

F. O. SVEEN, J. M. TORRES, and J. M. SARRIEGI, "Blind information Security Strategy," *International Journal of Critical Infrastructure Protection,* 2 (3), 95-109, 2009.

M. SWANSON, J. HASH, and P. BOWEN, "Guide for Developing Security Plans for Federal Information Systems (SP 800-18, Revision 1)," U.S. Department of Commerce, National Institute of Standards and Technology, Computer Security Division 2006. [Online] Available at http://csrc.nist.gov/publications/nistpubs/800-18-Rev1/sp800-18-Rev1-final.pdf

F. TANEY and T. COSTELLO, "Securing the Whole Enterprise: Business and Legal Issues," IT Professional Magazine, 8 (1), 37-42, 2006.

I. TASHI "An assurance-based model to holistically assess the information security posture," Doctoral thesis under the direction of S. Ghernaouti-Hélie, University of Lausanne, 2010.

I. TASHI, S. GHERNAOUTI-HÉLIE "Information Security Management is not only Risk Management," The Fourth International Conference on Internet Monitoring and Protection (ICIMP 2009), 24-28 Venice/Mestre, Italy, May 2009 (IEEE proceedings available at www.acm.org).

I. TASHI, S. GHERNAOUTI-HÉLIE "An Holistic Model to Evaluate the Information Security Health State," European Telecommunications Standardization Institute (ETSI) 4th Security Workshop, 13-14 January 2009, Sophia-Antipolis, France.

I. TASHI, S. GHERNAOUTI-HÉLIE, "Efficient Security Measurements and Metrics for Risk Assessment," The Third International Conference on Internet Monitoring and Protection (ICIMP 2008), Bucharest, Romania, June-July 2008 (IEEE proceedings).

I. TASHI, S. GHERNAOUTI-HÉLIE: "A Security Assurance Model to Holistically Assess the Information Security Posture," Chap. 5 of book: "Complex Intelligent Systems and their applications" of the series "Springer Optimization and Its Applications," Vol. 41, 2010, ISBN: 978-1-4419-1635-8.

K.-L. THOMSON and R. v. SOLMS, "Towards an Information Security Competence Maturity Model," Computer Fraud & Security, 2006 (5), pp. 11-15, 2006.

K.-L. THOMSON, R. v. SOLMS, and L. LOUW, "Cultivating an organisational information security culture," Computer Fraud & Security, 2006 (10), 7-11, 2006.

H. TIPTON and M. KRAUSE, Information Security Management Handbook, 6th ed., Vol. 2 Auerbach Publications, New York, USA, 2008.

A. TSOHOU, M. KARYDA, S. KOKOLAKIS, and E. KIOUNTOUZIS, "Formulating information systems risk management strategies through cultural theory," Information Management & Computer Security 14 (3), 198 – 217, 2006.

D. M. UTIN, M. A. UTIN, and J. UTIN, "General Misconceptions about Information Security Lead to an Insecure World," Information Security Journal: A Global Perspective, 17 (4), 164-169, 2008.

R. WERLINGER, K. HAWKEY, and K. BEZNOSOV, "An integrated view of human, organizational, and technological challenge of IT security management," Information Management & Computer Security, 17 (1), 4-19, 2009.

C. WRIGHT, B. FREEDMAN, and D. LIU, The IT Regulatory and Standards Compliance Handbook: How to Survive an Information Systems Audit and Assessment, Syngress – Elsevier, 2008.

Index of Keywords and Concepts